WELLINGTON'S RIGHT HAND

WELLINGTON'S RIGHT HAND

ROWLAND, VISCOUNT HILL

JOANNA HILL

SPELLMOUNT

Writer and historian Joanna Hill is the great, great, great niece of Rowland Hill and as such has gained unique access to the Hill family archives. Her first book on the Hill family was *The Hills of Hawkstone and Attingham: The Rise, Shine and Decline of a Shropshire Family*. She lived for many years in south-west France, just a short distance north of St Pierre d'Irube at the foot of the Pyrenees, where her illustrious forebear won his own general action in the closing stages of the Peninsular War.

Front of jacket: Miniature of Rowland, Viscount Hill owned by the Author.

Back of jacket: 'The Last Stand of the Imperial Guards at Waterloo. General Hill Calling Upon the Enemy to Surrender' from the painting by Robert Alexander Hillingford. (National Army Museum)

Page 2: The Waterloo Medal, ordered by the Prince Regent in 1819; it shows Wellington and Blücher on horseback guided by Victory. Engraved by Benedetto Pistrucci over a period of 30 years, it was never struck. A half-size copy was finally produced in 1966 by Pinches. (From *Napoleon's Medals: Victory to the Arts* by Richard A. Todd; limited, numbered edition)

First published in 2011 by
Spellmount, an imprint of The History Press
The Mill, Brimscombe Port
Stroud, Gloucestershire, GL5 2QG
www.thehistorypress.co.uk

This paperback edition published 2012

British Library Cataloguing in Publication Data.
A catalogue record for this book is available from the British Library.

ISBN 978 0 7524 9013 7

Typesetting and origination by The History Press
Printed in India.
Manufacturing managed by Jellyfish Solutions Ltd

CONTENTS

ACKNOWLEDGEMENTS

I should like to mention the following who have been especially helpful to me over the research and production of this book: Mike Harkness of Durham University Library; C.J. Gibson, Assistant Archivist, the Gwent Records Office; Lieutenant Colonel Daniel Hughes, RHG/D, Commanding Officer Household Cavalry Mounted Regiment; Michael Ball, Head of Department of Printed Books, The National Army Museum; I. Brown, Chief Archivist, The National Library of Scotland; Mary Cockerill of the Wellington Archive, the Hartley Library, University of Southampton; many members of staff of the British Library; Major (Retired) Paul Stretton, (late RHG/D), Regimental Secretary the Household Cavalry, together with the volunteer staff of the archives at Combermere Barracks, Windsor, who did their best to dig out items of interest from a period which was not renowned for its record keeping. I should also like to thank Jean Francois Krause who responded so promptly to my requests for scans of the battlefield plans which he drew for the French magazine, *Napoleon 1*. Sincere thanks are also, of course, due to my editor, Shaun Barrington of Spellmount, who believed in the book, and to my agent, Duncan McAra, who has helped me to produce something which I hope will offer a 'good read' to the many who have an interest in this particular period of history. Finally, I must thank Lt-Gen White-Spunner for taking the time to write a foreword. As he points out himself, it is particularly appropriate because both he and General Hill are so closely connected to the Royal Horse Guards.

FOREWORD BY LT-GEN WHITE-SPUNNER

Barney White-Spunner CBE was commissioned into the Blues and Royals in 1979. By 2008 he was General Officer Commanding Multinational Division (South East) in Iraq and became Commander of the Field Army in the following year. He is the author of the definitive history *Horse Guards* (2006).

O f all Wellington's generals he probably felt most comfortable with Hill. He was from the same class, and one of the old English landed families, unlike Picton. He was also a professional soldier, who had come up through the officer ranks, or as much as anyone who purchased their commission had, and had seen service in France, Egypt and Ireland before he deployed to the Peninsula in 1808. He did not pose a military threat, in that he was happy to serve dutifully under the Duke, nor a political or social one, as Uxbridge did. Most of all he could be trusted to carry out his orders without trying to be clever, the one thing that Wellington abhorred, and it was Hill who was trusted with the more important independent missions. Perhaps the most significant was providing the flank guard against Soult during the advance into Spain in 1812. Starting with a successful action at Almaraz, his greatest achievement was in keeping Soult in Estremadura, thus enabling Wellington to defeat the main French army at Salamanca. He was also a corps commander at Waterloo, playing a most important if now rather unsung part in that great battle.

Military historians have rather neglected Hill because he served in Wellington's shadow. He was a safe general, who never commanded a campaign in his own right, but he was a most important soldier nonetheless, and it is important to remember that he was serving when this country's armies were led by one of our greatest operational commanders. He was also a most likeable man at a time when not all generals were, and his nickname of 'Daddy Hill' was well deserved. After Waterloo he would go on to be Commander in Chief from 1828 until 1842, and to hold the supreme military honour of being for twelve years Colonel of The Blues, my own regiment, in which three of his brothers had served, including Robert who commanded them at Waterloo. Arguably he stayed on a bit too long as Commander in Chief. It was a period when the British Army atrophied, living on the memory of Waterloo, and failing to learn the lessons from the campaigns in Europe and India, so that it was badly unprepared for its next major conflict in the Crimea. Hill saw the need to improve the conditions in which soldiers lived, but he thought major change was unnecessary, believing that the great army in which he had served so long had the fighting spirit that would ensure it was as successful in the future as it had been in Spain. Militarily flexible and resourceful when in command, socially he was conservative, as was Wellington, and it is social and financial pressures, rather than tactical ones, which shape peacetime armies.

It is a great pleasure therefore to be able to write this foreword to a biography of this great and attractive Englishman, and that is what he primarily was – an Englishman, rooted in the English countryside, determined to defend his country and its way of life against the extreme dangers of Bonapartism, and a man who appreciated his soldiers as much as they appreciated him. Today's British Army owes much to him, his legacy of loyal and reliable service, his patriotism and his care for those with whom he served.

Barney White-Spunner
Lieutenant General
Commander Field Army
30 September 2010

INTRODUCTION

The Peninsular Wars (1808–1814) came to an end with Napoleon's first abdication and with his armies from Spain and Portugal having been driven back into France, where they suffered one defeat after another until the final Battle of Toulouse. The principal reason that the Peninsula was of such interest to the Emperor was, of course, that the Portuguese steadfastly maintained their alliance with Britain, offering the British virtually the sole safe harbours on continental Europe now that Napoleon had overrun and crushed the rest. Britain had managed to 'steal' the small Danish fleet and Napoleon was determined to take Portugal and thereby close all of continental Europe from 'Cuxhaven to Trieste' to the hated British. The Emperor was at the height of his powers and was entirely confident in his abilities, his alone. He had placed his brothers on the thrones of Holland (Louis) Westphalia (Jerome) and Naples (Joseph). To him, the seizure of power in Spain and Portugal was something of a sideshow but one that would reinforce his iron grip on the entire continent.

On 13 October 1807, Manuel de Godoy, President of the Council of Spain, signed the Treaty of Fontainebleau by which Spain agreed to aid France in her battle to overthrow the Portuguese kingdom and then to divide the country between them. The Spanish, naively, had no idea that the seizure of their own country was also part of the plan, that their King was to be exiled and that Napoleon would install his elder brother, Joseph, in his place; for Joseph this would be a big step up from the Kingdom of Naples. Manuel de Godoy could have had no idea that his country would be invaded not just by one army – the French – but by two, the second being the Allied Army composed of the British and Portuguese fighting alongside the Spanish Army itself. For seven years these forces pursued each other from north to south, from east to west under the boiling sun of summer and the icy gales of winter. They crossed raging rivers, baking,

The Iberian Peninsula.

arid plains and steep, frozen mountains. It was bloody and merciless campaigning – not for the weak. General Junot[1] marched his army into Portugal in December 1807, just as the Royal Family, including John of Braganza, the Regent, carrying the treasury and accompanied by most of the country's nobility, fled to Brazil courtesy of Sir William Sidney Smith and the Royal Navy. Junot enjoyed grandiose dreams of making himself King of Portugal and immediately established himself as Governor General.

The Peninsula was to make a considerable contribution towards Napoleon's eventual downfall. To maintain war on a front thousands of miles away from either himself or his other armies and with concomitant huge logistical problems, was never practicable. One of the reasons on occasion that the French, despite their vast superiority in numbers, failed to gain the upper hand over the Allied armies was that they required so many troops to guard their supply bases from the predatory Spanish. The threat from *Guerrilleros* to supply lines prompted the formation early in the war of a corps of Gendarmes, 20 squadrons strong, roaming up and down from one manned strongpoint to the next as a deterrent. The French policy was to live off the land; not unnaturally, this made them extremely unpopular with both the Spanish and Portuguese. There was always, too, the Wellington factor. Convinced of his own superior skills as a commander, Napoleon never admitted, to the very end, that the 'Sepoy' General was at least his equal.

Two hundred years after the Peninsular War, or the Spanish War of Liberation, as one reads and re-reads the numerous accounts of the war with its reams of dispatches, orders, letters and other official papers, together with the hundreds of individual 'recollections', it is perhaps not surprising that errors have crept in and many of the 'received' accounts that are quoted in various volumes are quite often wildly inaccurate. However, the long years of warfare, the countless incidents of horror, of 'derring do' together with the moments of genuine entertainment, incredible bravery and glory, with celebrations of victories won apparently against the odds, can still stir the imagination today. The tales of fiercely fought battles, spying, guerrilla warfare and the breaking of codes can still rouse the blood.

'A Soft Answer Turneth Away Wrath', Proverbs (15.1) was written by Lord Hill at the head of one of his letter books; it would seem to sum up the man perfectly. There are many instances of those serving under his command describing his 'quietness of manner'; his comportment was the very opposite of bombastic commanders such as the foul-mouthed Sir Thomas Picton[3] and 'Black Bob' Craufurd[4] who kept their men in line by rigid discipline and did not hesitate to flog, or even hang, on the march. According to one of Hill's officers, as quoted by the Reverend Sidney in *Life of Lord Hill*, the foundation of Hill's popularity

> ... was his sterling personal worth and his heroic spirit; but his popularity was increased and strengthened as soon as he was seen. He was the very picture of the English country gentleman ... his fresh complexion, placid face, kind eyes, kind voice, and the total absence of all parade or noise in his habits delighted them ... his kind attention to all the wants and comforts of his men, his visits to the sick in hospital, his vigilant protection of the poor country people, his just severity to marauders, his generous and humane treatment of such prisoners and wounded as fell into his hands, made him a place in the hearts of his soldiers.

There are numerous mentions in the recollections of common soldiers, as well as officers, of small acts of kindness such as giving an exhausted soldier a drink from his own canteen and organising shelter for the night. Robert Blakeney, author of *A Boy in the Peninsular War*, was to write of Hill, late on in the campaign, 'he never forgot for an instance that he was a gentleman.'

Perhaps it was this very lack of hauteur that has led to Rowland Hill receiving relatively little attention from the Peninsular War historians. Of course, there are countless mentions of him in the books describing Wellington's armies, but he has only attracted two biographies, one of which, virtually contemporary with his life, is a tiresome and sycophantic volume only rendered of any interest thanks to the family letters it contains[5]. The author, Edwin Sidney, was domestic chaplain to the Hill family at Hawkstone in Shropshire. Sidney had already written, in much the same vein, books on Sir Richard Hill, Baronet, Rowland's evangelical uncle and also of another uncle, the Reverend Rowland Hill,[6] the famously eccentric Methodist preacher, brother to Sir Richard. Sidney also has the irritating habit of omitting names; this may have been because the people in question were still alive but it is infuriating for the historian.[7] He was, of course, fortunate in having free access to the General's correspondence up until he became Commander in Chief and perhaps we ought to be grateful to him for having possibly been responsible for collecting such a large archive of letters. The British Library acquired this portion of Rowland Hill's correspondence in the early twentieth century, probably during one of the all too numerous family bankruptcy sales, and has mounted them in eight albums.[8] The letters, sometimes domestic in content, make for fascinating reading and go some way towards rounding out this figure.

A second biography by an American academic, Gordon Teffeteller, offers much more information but contains a number of inaccuracies and gives the reader little feeling of the subject as a person. Teffeteller also sins by omission; there is, for example, almost nothing of interest when he writes of the General's fourteen years at Horse Guards; little about his problems with the Whigs, the bumpy passage of the Reform Bill, the commission on punishment in the Army, and there is only a short paragraph on his dealings with Lord Cardigan, the Mad Earl, when he was Senior General on the Staff, otherwise known as General Commanding in Chief. These exchanges were so extensive and so extraordinary that they deserve a more detailed investigation.

Rowland Hill is probably best known for his service during the long and frequently arduous years of the Peninsular War, although he had previously seen active service in Toulon, Egypt and Ireland. He was the most senior officer to reach Brussels in April 1815 on Napoleon's escape from Elba.[9] He also commanded what Wellington referred to as 'virtually an army' at Waterloo. He was subsequently second in command of the Allied Army of Occupation in France until the force was withdrawn in 1818. His career was crowned with his appointment as Senior General on the Staff, General Commanding in Chief of the British Army in 1828, until his resignation just a few months before his death in December 1842.

He knew and worked with Wellington for over thirty years. Of high intelligence, unquestionably brave and with a powerful military brain, he was equally able either to function under the Duke's instructions or, when in command of his own Detached Corps, capable of gaining his own victories. He seems to have lacked any of the self-importance of so many of his fellow generals and this made him as popular with his peers as it did with all the men; the latter appreciated that he never worked them pointlessly. When he was reviewing troops, if the temperature rose too high, he would put an end to proceedings. As a result, he got the best he possibly could out of them and acquired the nicknames 'Daddy' Hill and 'the soldiers' friend'. Though this paternal figure never married and thus had no direct heir, at his death, by special dispensation from the Queen, his nephew – also Rowland Hill – was permitted to succeed to his uncle's Viscountcy.

The most extensive part of the collection of Hill papers in the British Library[10] covers his years in the Peninsula and includes a large number of autograph letters/instructions to and from the Duke of Wellington, from the Quartermaster General, Sir George Murray, on the Duke's behalf, many letters to and from his eldest sister Maria[11] at Hawkstone and a number to other members of his family, such as his formidable sister Emma, and his father, Sir John Hill, Baronet. These letters give us a senior officer's view of the war through the long years of campaigning. Today, it seems almost incomprehensible that a soldier could serve for such a period and under such conditions without leave. Hill only went home once, when seriously sick of a virulent fever, probably a form of malaria, in February 1811, and hastened back to his division just as soon as he was recovered before the end of May. One can often detect the longing for home and Shropshire in particular, in some of the letters he writes to Maria, but his sense of duty was, to him, the natural way of things. If this tends to make him sound dull, nothing could be further from the truth. He was revered by the Army in general and his own Corps, especially the 2nd Division, in particular. Many of his peers apparently did not feel the same amount of commitment. Wellington had little time for requests for leave and responded brusquely to those who ventured to ask for it[12] but, in the case of Hill's illness at the end of 1810, Wellington could see that he was not recovering despite every effort of care in the Duke's own house in Lisbon, and personally ordered him home, adding the rider that he was to return as soon as his health permitted. This was something of a compliment in itself, because the Duke was always trying to get rid of the numerous unsuitable and inept generals sent to him by Horse Guards. During the course of the war in the Peninsula, London asked Wellington several times to release Hill to take command of other armies. Wellington always replied that he could not spare him. On one occasion in 1813, Horse Guards asked the Duke if he would release Hill to command the Army in Holland. 'Had you not better cut off my right hand?' was the Duke's reply.[13] Thomas Graham, Lord Lynedoch, went in his place and the affair was not a success; perhaps Hill was fortunate that Wellington would not release him on that occasion.

Hill writes descriptions of his commands, the battles in which he was engaged, and campaign life, together with more frivolous items of news such as plays, balls, shooting, and coursing, his bitch's puppies and visits from his brothers, three of whom were also serving in the Peninsula by the end of 1812.[14] The letters give a picture of his activities when he was leading his 'Detached Corps', often a long distance away from Wellington and the main body of the Army. One thing of which Rowland Hill can never be accused is harsh criticism of his fellow men; perhaps his report on Slade, a cavalry general of limited ability, after the Battle of

Maguilla on 13 June 1812 shows one of the few instances when he became furiously angry. The behaviour of Sir Nathaniel Peacocke at the crisis moment of the Battle of St Pierre d'Irube on 13 December 1813 provoked a similar reaction. The affair at St Pierre was a case of cowardice. Cowardice in battle was something Hill would simply not have understood.

Rowland Hill is often referred to as Wellington's second in command. This is not technically true. Wellington was loath to appoint anyone to such a position despite London repeatedly pressing him on the subject. The government feared the consequences should Wellington be killed in action with no named successor since there were a number of generals who would have squabbled over the succession. Sir Brent Spencer, by reason of his seniority, was known as Wellington's second for a short time but they did not see eye to eye and Wellington was infuriated by the pessimistic letters that Sir Brent[15] wrote to people in high places back in England. When Spencer remonstrated with Wellington that as next senior in line, he should know something of his leader's plans, Wellington is said to have snorted, 'I have no plans but to beat the French.' Wellington did not trust Spencer and was heard to refer to him as 'exceedingly puzzleheaded. He would talk of the Thames for the Tagus.' Spencer went home in 1811 to Wellington's relief, and was succeeded by Thomas Graham. Graham, an exceptional man, also served roughly in the capacity of second in command for a short time towards the end of the campaigns in Spain; but Hill was far too junior on the list of Lieutenant Generals[16] to be officially named as such, despite the fact that he was evidently trusted implicitly by Wellington and given what amounted to an independent command with his detached Corps. Wellington was happy to have such a reliable commander protecting the southern approaches and keeping the enemy, especially Soult and d'Erlon, in their place south of the Tagus. He also commanded, in Wellington's own words, 'what is virtually an army with many Lieutenant Generals serving under him' at Waterloo.

Thomas Graham held a special, perhaps unique, place in the ranks of senior officers. He had had no military experience prior to his arrival at the siege of Toulon, when he was already in his middle forties. At Toulon, he managed to obtain an appointment as an ADC to General Lord Mulgrave, as a volunteer. He not only distinguished himself but also made a life-long friend of Hill, who impressed the older man with his comportment and bravery. Graham was to raise the 90th Perthshire Volunteeers Regiment by mortgaging some of his property, and when he raised a second battalion he invited Hill to come, bringing with him a certain number of men, as Colonel. Graham spent in the region of £20,000 of his own money on equipping his regiment. He then applied to have his own rank made substantive. George III was opposed to this, having set out his stall against officers acquiring high permanent status when they had not risen through the junior ranks. Graham's request was especially annoying to the King since the Scot was known to hold liberal views; the request was refused. It was not just refused once but several times, to

Graham's great annoyance. However, he continued to serve as a volunteer and was, shortly after, entrusted with the blockade of Malta by Admiral Nelson. It was not until 1809 that the merit of his services finally received recognition: 'His Majesty has been pleased to direct that the established custom of the army may be departed from by your being promoted to the rank of Major General.'[17]

In his book *Great Generals of the Napoleonic Wars* Andrew Uffindell chose three generals from England, France, Russia, Prussia and Austria; the three he chose to represent Great Britain were Sir John Moore, the Duke of Wellington and the often neglected Rowland Hill. Wellington certainly recognised Hill's abilities and total reliability. He was no dullard, and his, by the age of 40, somewhat rotund form and open florid face, far from being that of a sedentary, stolid soldier, belied a very brave and, when occasion demanded, imaginative and intelligent leader, who frequently rallied his men from the front, exposing himself to great personal danger. He was to be wounded on several occasions and although many of his ADCs were killed alongside him, he survived serious injury. Several of his chargers were killed under him and at Waterloo his dying mount rolled right over him; he survived and took another horse from a dragoon. He was a bruising rider to hounds and loved coursing and other field sports. He did not seek laurels for himself but was staunchly patriotic, honest and exhibited throughout his career, as previously mentioned, a rare level of care for the comfort of his men.

He retained his ADCs for many years when they could have advanced to higher rank if they had returned to their regiments. Chief amongst these was one of his younger brothers, Clement, who was wounded on several occasions but never too seriously. Clement stuck with Rowland throughout the Peninsular War and was often chastised by the latter, like a schoolboy, for having failed to write letters home! Others who were with him through many campaigns were Edwin Currie, killed at Waterloo, Captain Fordyce, killed on the Cerro de Medellin at Talavera, Horatio Churchill, his Military Secretary towards the end of the wars, Digby Mackworth, made prisoner by the French but released when Hill asked the Duke as a special favour to try and secure his freedom by exchange, Orlando Bridgeman, Captain Squires and Colonel Richard Egerton. The latter, together with his wife, were to live with Hill in later years and looked after him until his death. Egerton served as Hill's private secretary and managed his financial affairs. In return, during his last illness in the autumn of 1842, Rowland asked Wellington to ensure that Egerton was looked after as a reward for his self sacrifice in giving up the possibility of senior rank by staying with 'his' General.

A brief note on extant sources: in the Dorset Records Office the correspondence of Hill's Military Secretary at the end of the Peninsular War, Captain (later Colonel) Horatio Charles Churchill, were deposited in what is known as the Dawlish Collection by some of his descendants, the Michel family. There are the Lynedoch Archives and George Brown papers in the National Library of Scotland, and there is also some limited material in the Shropshire County Records Office where the collections of the Reverend J.C. Hill, the Attingham Collection, and those of the Hill family solicitors, the Bygott Papers, all contain some relevant information. On his arrival at Horse Guards in 1828, Hill inherited, with gratitude, the services of Lord Fitzroy Somerset[18] from the Duke of Wellington, to serve as his Military Secretary when he became 'Senior General on the Staff, General Commanding in Chief'.[19] He obviously knew Somerset very well from the latter's long years of service with the Duke in the Peninsula, at Waterloo and with the Army of Occupation in France. Somerset's extensive collection of papers is in the Gwent Records Office. These also give one of the best pictures of Hill's life at Horse Guards, much of which was spent when, as a solid, true-blue Tory of the Shires, he was in opposition to the Whig Government. This, of course, made his life more difficult. Undoubtedly, one of the heaviest crosses he had to bear during these years as General Commanding in Chief, apart from the Opposition, was the interference of Lord Cardigan. The Raglan papers[20] are especially interesting because they include many of Lord Hill's own papers for this chapter of his life.

This period, the 1830s, whilst there was no major war in progress, was one of intense political activity and disturbing civil unrest. There were many affairs demanding the attention of both the House of Commons and the House of Lords. Chief amongst these were the Catholic Emancipation Act and the Reform Bill. Lord Hill either abstained or voted against both of these bills, despite the personal solicitation of William IV. In response to the King's entreaty, he replied that his appointment as Head of the Army was not a political one and that, therefore, he wished to abstain from voting for a bill of which he did not approve. From the perspective of some 200 years, this seems extraordinary, especially in a man who was such a committed Christian, but one has to place him in the context of the early nineteenth century. He came from the landowning ranks – a class that, at its best, looked after its people, its employees, its tenants; these were the men who created a great part of England's cultural heritage in the great houses and gardens of England.[21] That Hill was not against education and advancement can be demonstrated by the fact that he was responsible for the innovation of both regimental schools and the sergeants' mess while serving in the 90th Regiment. He simply felt that every man had his place in the hierarchy. His later years at Horse Guards were preoccupied with the Chartist Movement, slave revolts in the West Indies and also rebellion in Canada. One of the final events was to be the disastrous First Afghan War of 1841.

In the following pages, I have tried to show what made Rowland Hill such a highly successful and yet much loved and respected individual. *Who's Who in British History* describes him as 'A worthy contemporary of Moore and Wellington. In Rowland, religous feeling and a natural pugnacity went with a serene and unselfish temper.' This book does not pretend to be a history of the Peninsular War but rather focuses on Hill's place during that arduous campaign and then on his final role, the highest appointment for a soldier, Head of the Army. This post was probably more taxing than most of his years in the Peninsula.

I

PYRAMIDS AND FRENCH TREASURE

Surely, old Rowland²² and Sir Rowland Hill²³
Have done enough to gain the world's goodwill.
Each in his calling makes his foes retrench –
One thumps the cushion,
T'other thumps the French.

Rowland Hill was born in Shropshire in 1772. The Hills were a prominent Tory landowning family in the county where they had been acquiring property since the days of Henry VIII when the first Sir Rowland, Kt., bought the demesne of Hawkstone.²⁴ This man made his fortune as a mercer trading in the City of London and had risen to great prominence in the capital, eventually becoming Lord Mayor. The second Hill to add significantly to the family fortunes was the Honorable and Reverend Richard Hill, known in later life as the 'Great Hill'. Richard Hill was a loyal servant to both King William and then to Queen Anne; he served as a diplomat during the French wars of religion, and many of his years in service were spent in keeping the erratic and self-seeking Duke of Savoy in the Allied camp despite the blandishments of Louis XIV. Although a strong Tory, the 'Great Hill' had worked hard to ensure that the Protestant succession went to George Ludwig, King of Hanover, after Queen Anne's death without an heir. He was fiercely opposed to the possibility of a Roman Catholic Jacobite taking the throne. During his life, Richard Hill acquired a great deal more land around Hawkstone and began construction of the house itself. He died in 1727 with the house unfinished but he left to his eldest nephew, Rowland, the estate, the greater part of his fortune and the title, a baronetcy, which he had persuaded the Government to bestow on the younger man rather than on himself, since he was childless.²⁵ He left the nearby estate of Attingham Park to another nephew, Thomas Harwood Hill,[26] and his property of Shenstone in Staffordshire to a third, Samuel Barbour Hill.

Young Sir Rowland continued work on the house and gardens and is also remembered as the initial creator of the imaginative and beautiful landscape park for which Hawkstone remains famous today. In turn, his eldest son, Sir Richard, became the 2nd Baronet, and continued with extensive work on the grounds. He was MP for the county and a well known Evangelist and friend to Wilberforce. He died unmarried. Sir Richard's next brother was John Hill. Devoted to field sports, he served as an MP for the Borough of Shrewsbury.[27] John Hill lived at Prees Hall, which had been leased since 1764 from the Diocese of Lichfield. It was just three miles from Hawkstone and it was here that Rowland was born in 1772. In 1794 Hill's uncle, Sir Richard Hill, Baronet, arranged to exchange Prees with the Diocese for a piece of land he owned at Whitmore, Coventry. An Act of Parliament was required to carry this through.

Our Rowland was the second son and fourth child of sixteen, of whom thirteen lived to adulthood. He had six brothers and all but one, Francis, served in the Army. Francis was a diplomat. Rowland was by no means a strong child and was spared the hurly burly of a large school such as Rugby, Shrewsbury or Eton where most of his brothers and other Hill cousins had gone. He was sent to study in Chester under the Reverend Winfield. He was well behaved and avoided 'Supple Jack' but was apparently so gentle as to seem to have an almost feminine personality. He was very kind to younger boys, helping them with their studies and playing games with them.

As Rowland came towards the end of his education in Chester, his father proposed to him that he should study law with a view to going into it as his profession. His parents had no thought that their second son would wish to join the rough and tumble of the British Army. Rowland quickly wrote to his father saying that he had no feeling for the law and wished to pursue the military life. His father reluctantly acquiesced saying that he feared that he would not make such a success of the Army as he might have made as a lawyer. Although Hill's elder brother, John, was already serving in the Royal Horse Guards, Blue,[28] Sir John had little idea as to how one went about putting the first foot on the military ladder in earnest. Brother John, after all, was set to inherit Hawkstone eventually and was not, therefore, required to make another fortune for his family; with hindsight, perhaps he should have applied himself towards further enriching the great estate[29] that the family already had since it would be his eldest son's extravagance that was largely instrumental in bringing the family to its knees and eventual bankruptcy. However, Sir John took good advice and finally purchased an ensigncy in the 38th Regiment for his second son.

Rowland joined his regiment in July 1790. He then obtained permission to go to a military academy in Strasbourg[30] to study. This was his first taste of life abroad but he only remained there until the following January, when, having brought twelve recruits from Shropshire, he was promoted Lieutenant on 24 January 1791 in an independent company of foot commanded by Captain Broughton.[31] The regiment was then stationed at Wrotham, Kent. Two months later, on 16 March 1791, Hill transferred as a Lieutenant into the 53th (King's Own Shropshire Light Infantry). Rowland soon obtained permission from his new Commanding Officer, Major R. Mathews, who even after such a short time evidently rated him very highly, to return to the Military Academy in Strasbourg, there being no comparable institutions in England at that time. Later in life he was to discover that Marshal Beresford had also attended this institution. These two, at least, proved very worthy pupils at a time when few British officers undertook any formal military study; Wellington, Beresford and Hill were unusual in this. Thomas Graham was also unusual in having gone to Oxford.

Hill's second stay in Strasbourg was not destined to be much longer than his first. He had been there only a few weeks when two of his uncles, Sir Richard and the Reverend Brian Hill, came to Strasbourg and took him home with them, feeling that events in France, then in the turmoil of bloody revolution, were highly unpredictable and possibly dangerous for a foreigner. These two men had been on an extensive, somewhat dangerous and adventure-packed journey[32] that had taken them as far as Sicily, where they had fallen in with bandits and been reported as dead in Rome. Alive, they were now on their way home and trying to avoid the effects of the French Revolution. The three of them appear to have had a highly diverting journey down the Rhine and through Holland. Uncle Brian Hill evidently had a very sharp sense of humour.[33] (Brian Hill was a close friend of Reginald Heber, Bishop of Calcutta who wrote so many of the rousing hymns that are still sung today, such as 'From Greenland's Icy Mountains.' The Hebers lived next to Hawkstone at Hodnet.)

On 18 January 1792, Hill rejoined his regiment, which was jointly based in Edinburgh and Ayr and stayed in Scotland until the end of that year. He had command of a small unit in Ballantrae for some months during this period. Many years later Hill was to be Colonel of the 53rd[34] and his nephew, Colonel Richard Frederick Hill,[35] would command it in the 1830s. At the beginning of 1793, he was promoted Captain having raised an independent company of Salopians for the 86th Regiment, the Royal Irish Rifles; he was 21 years old.[36] He took his independent company to Ireland.

Rowland Hill's rapid move from his first regiment to his second and then to the third by the age of 21 demands a brief look at the structure of the British Army in the late eighteenth and early nineteenth centuries. Looking back, the system seems bizarre but, perhaps even more extraordinary, for the most part, it worked very well. Everyone understood it and apparently most accepted it, even if some very competent officers were forced to remain in a lowly rank because they lacked the funds necessary to purchase their promotion. These men were often of great assistance to their not infrequently incompetent superior officers, who did have the funds to buy their way up through the ranks.

A man had to have the money to purchase his original commission, an ensigncy in the infantry or a cornetcy in the cavalry, whereupon he would rise through the ranks, often moving to a regiment where there was a vacancy for the next step up, although he had to remain three years in each rank.[37] For these transfers, men used the services of regimental agents who specialised in the purchase and sale of commissions. There was a set price for purchase and anyone who paid over the odds was likely to be in great trouble and probably dismissed from the Service.[38] The sole initial requirement for a gentleman entering the Army was that he could read and write and have sufficient funds. It was rare to find any officer of the Peninsular Army[39] who had been to university and Hill was one of the very few who had undertaken any special military study. The highest rank open to purchase was Lieutenant Colonel. Seniority on the Army List was the way to advancement for Colonel and above. This is the reason why Hill became a full General only in 1824 when enough officers above him on the list had died. It was also possible to advance by brevet promotion. This was often given for service in action and gave advancement only in army and not regimental rank.[40] Very occasionally, a man might be commissioned from the ranks. In the main, other private soldiers did not take very kindly to one of their own being commissioned. They may have disliked and often even despised their officers but, as Rifleman Harris of the 95 (The Rifles) regiment, wrote,[41] 'we understood that "gentlemen" had more natural authority, to which we responded.' Most of the men who achieved commissioned rank were appointed Adjutant. There is an interesting note in the Raglan (Somerset) Papers[42] from Wellington to Somerset, when the latter was serving as Hill's Military Secretary, on this question. It concerned the commissioning of a Sergeant Major of the Rifle Brigade as Adjutant. He (the Duke) hopes his opinion will be remembered when the SM becomes 'a little familiar and at his ease with the officers' and 'a little wine will have been drunk; and there should be a black eye or two or a glass or bottle of wine thrown or a candlestick.' Although this was written in 1839, the Duke's or even Lord Hill's opinion would have been the same thirty years earlier.

Hill's first taste of action came in 1793. He had obtained consent from the Duke of York to accompany one Francis Drake,[43] appointed Minister Plenipotentiary to the republic of Genoa, as his Assistant Secretary. Following his arrival in Genoa, Hill obtained permission to go to Toulon where the forces of the British and Spanish were helping the Royalist French. He was anxious to see some action and the life of a junior secretary to an embassy had no appeal. Toulon, France's largest port on the south coast, was besieged from 18 September to 18 December and Admiral Sir Samuel Hood[44] could do little to assist the besieged English and French Royalist troops as he stood off the town with the British Fleet.

On his arrival in Toulon, Hill obtained an attachment to the Commanding General, Lord Mulgrave, as an ADC. Another of his lordship's aides was Thomas Graham,[45] with whom Hill was to form a lifelong friendship. In Hill's memoran-

The Siege of Toulon. (David Chandler's *Dictionary of the Napoleonic Wars*)

dum of events he wrote: 'On the 30th of September the enemy got possession of the port of Faron and on the 8th we destroyed the batteries in the Hauteur de Reiniere. On the 15th the enemy got possession of Cape le Brun.' This was the moment when General Charles O'Hara arrived to take command and Lord Mulgrave returned to England where, for some extraordinary reason, he made a favourable report to the War Office as to the state of affairs of the British forces then besieged in Toulon. O'Hara was furious, realising that his back was now against the wall and that there was little hope of retaining the city without a large number of reinforcements.

Charles O'Hara was an interesting man; the illegitimate son of General James O'Hara and his Portuguese mistress. Illegitimacy seems to have been no limitation in the upper level of society at the time. Beresford, for example, was the bastard son of an Irish peer, the first Marquis of Waterford. O'Hara was born in Lisbon but educated at Westminster and served with distinction in the American War of Independence. He became a close friend of General Charles Cornwallis and was his second in command. When Cornwallis refused to surrender in person at Yorktown on 19 October 1781, O'Hara did so in his place, first offering his sword to General Clinton, who deferred to General Washington, who in turn declined and deferred to Major General Benjamin Lincoln, serving as Washington's second in command! O'Hara had then spent some time in prison before being exchanged. On his return home, he was promoted to Lieutenant General and sent to Toulon in 1793. He was a very brave soldier but perhaps cut from the cloth of an earlier generation.

The French installed a battery above Port Malbourquet, which General O'Hara prepared to destroy on 30 November 1793, aided by Sir David Dundas,[46] who had just arrived bringing 2000 extra men. Unfortunately, although Sir David managed to obtain possession of the battery, the impetuosity of many of the troops led them to pursue the enemy or to plunder their camp and this

> … led us to relinquish the advantages we had gained. General O'Hara arrived at the redoubt as it was taken and perceiving the disorder of the troops was extremely displeased at their having left the hill. He used every exertion to form the troops and sent me to bring up the artillery men and order these to spike the guns and destroy them as effectually as possible. This was the last time I saw O'Hara[47] for before I returned to the battery he received a wound and was taken prisoner. During the time he was prisoner, General O'Hara, was treated very ill.[48] On our return to the town, which we did with great haste, Sir David Dundas assumed the command and I was appointed one of his aides de camp.[49]

Rowland had himself been slightly wounded in the hand at the moment that O'Hara was taken prisoner and had had a narrow escape from death just moments earlier, when it was between him and another young Captain, Captain Snow, as to who should climb a tree to observe the enemy. Snow went up and almost immediately received a mortal wound.[50] Needless to say, that this was by no means the only time that Rowland was fortunate to escape death.

Lord Mulgrave subsequently wrote to Francis Drake: 'For the particulars of the action of the 1st October, I must refer you to your relation and my friend and aide de camp, Captain Hill who was in the midst of it and whose intelligent activity, and courage rendered him of great service to me.'[51] This was Hill's 'blooding' and he had immediately gathered a commendation. However, things did not go well for the British and on 18 and 19 December they were forced to withdraw from Toulon. Captain Hill had the honour of carrying the dispatches following the encounter with the French and had already sailed from the port on 13 December, arriving in England a month later on 13 January 1794 where he delivered his dispatches to the Commander in Chief, HRH the Duke of York.

It was at Toulon that Napoleon Bonaparte[52] also first came to prominence. He was, at that time, a young artillery officer, just 24 years old, and it was in large part thanks to his intelligent deployment of the Republican artillery that the Royalist and British forces holed up in the town eventually realised that they had no chance of holding the place and withdrew. Bonaparte was subsequently promoted Brigadier General and it was said of him by his commanding officer, General Jacques Dugommier, 'I have no words to describe Buonaparte's merit: much technical skill, an equal degree of intelligence, and too much gallantry.'[53]

As the result of his actions at Toulon, young Hill had not only attracted the notice of his superior officers but also of his fellow ADC, Thomas Graham. Graham was much older and a widower. He had had no intention of joining the Army, his own political leanings being rather pro-republican at the time. Shortly following his departure from Oxford, his father died in 1767, which left Thomas with a sizeable property in Perthshire at Balgowan. He retired to Scotland and in 1774 he married Mary, second daughter of Earl Cathcart. Thomas Graham was described by his father in law as 'a peer among princes'. The couple had settled down to live a quiet country life but in 1792, Mary's health had deteriorated to such a degree that their doctor advised Thomas to take her to the south of France to a milder climate. She died just off Hyeres, on board the ship in which they were making the journey. Heartbroken, Thomas Graham had then hired a barge to take the body in its casket to Bordeaux for shipping to Scotland, but in the neighbourhood of Toulouse, the party was stopped by National Guardsmen supposedly pursuing Royalists. These men opened the coffin and 'molested' the body. Graham was so outraged by this behaviour that from that moment on, he detested the French and became a soldier himself, although already well into his forties, in order to take his revenge. Mary Graham was painted by Gainsborough, the portrait now hanging in the National Gallery of Scotland.

Early in 1794, Graham raised a regiment of infantry, the 90th Regiment known officially as the Perthshire Volunteers but also, unofficially, as Balgowan's Grey

Breeks.[54] He asked Hill and another officer named Moncrieffe who had both
been at Toulon to join him and to raise a certain quota of men. This Hill did,
although not without problems, by recruiting principally in Shropshire and the
Birmingham area, while Moncrieffe was in London. Hill became a Major and
then a Lieutenant Colonel 'without permanent rank or half pay' in the regiment.
By 6 May, Regimental HQ had 40 sergeants and 511 men on its books and by
June they numbered 1000 men; the 'Grey Breeks' had been born. It is estimated
that Graham had spent upwards of £20,000 to raise and equip the new regiment, which was an enormous sum at the time.[55] By September, the regiment
had raised a second battalion and was inspected by the King. Thus by the age of
only 22, Hill found himself already well on his way up the ladder.

He was certainly less pleased to be 'banished' with his regiment to the Vendée.
They evidently had a hazardous journey to the island of Noirmoutier, but then
found that it was occupied by French troops so they sailed on to the Ile d'Yeu[56]
off the west coast of France under the overall command of General Doyle. There
was precious little to do on this windswept island but drill the men and enjoy field
sports. Hill and Thomas Graham were kindred spirits where sport was concerned
and Graham asked Rowland to try and procure some greyhounds for coursing
and pointers and setters for shooting. A letter to his brother in Shropshire saw the
dogs swiftly dispatched. In December 1795, Rowland was delighted to receive
news that the 90th was ordered to Gibraltar; there was little scope for military
advancement on the island and during their stay the French had made no moves
to recover it, being far too occupied in other more important theatres of war.

It is interesting to note here that Graham was opposed to flogging and that as
early as this date he proposed a diet of bread and water 'which I am sure would
succeed if I could get my "patients" into separate dark compartments.'[57] This same
form of punishment was to be proposed during the Commission of Enquiry into
punishment (including flogging) in the British Army in the 1830s.

In the summer of 1796, the regiment was embarked for Gibraltar. The Governor
was Hill's old friend, General O'Hara. The General was known as 'Cock of the
Rock' both for his lavish entertainments and for the family he kept out of sight.
The two men were evidently delighted to see each other once again. 'I had not
seen him since the day he was taken prisoner.'[58] The General invited the younger
man to stay in his house, known as the Convent after its original purpose, and
generally made himself very agreeable. It seems that O'Hara had recognised in
Hill a young man of ability, of clarity of understanding and excellent judgement.
At the end of 1796, O'Hara entrusted Hill with a 'delicate duty'. This was to
convey a verbal communication to the British Ambassador in Lisbon. The message referred to the anticipated war with Spain. Hill managed to get to Lisbon
but by that time hostilities had already broken out and it was with difficulty that
he managed to return to Gibraltar. Once back on the Rock, he found life even
more circumscribed than it had been on the Ile d'Yeu, since the war between

Spain and Britain rendered any communications almost impossible. Of one thing the garrison was well aware and that was the increasing power and influence of Napoleon Bonaparte. They must surely have seen the French fleet sailing through the Straits of Gibraltar.

The year 1797 is best remembered in the armed services for the mutinies at Spithead and the Nore. They began with sailors in sixteen ships of the Channel Fleet demanding better pay and living conditions. A change was long overdue but it took a month before Admiral Lord Howe managed to broker a settlement at Spithead giving a pardon to all involved, a pay rise (it had not increased for 100 years) and better living conditions. The government really had little choice but to concede; it was another case where revolution, already so near across the Channel, could have erupted. It was also the year when Napoleon marched over the Alps and took control of northern Italy.

In 1798 Bonaparte took the small but strategically vital island of Malta and turned his eyes towards Egypt, which was the purpose of his expedition. He dreamed of continuing eastwards to India, seeing himself as a Charlemagne, conqueror of the world. When he captured Malta, he immediately banned all religious institutions including the Order of St John; when he sailed away, he carried with him all the treasures of the little island including the priceless library belonging to the Knights. In 1799 a number of Maltese rose in rebellion and killed many of the French occupiers. The island was blockaded by Captain Martin in HMS *Northumberland* until, eventually, the French Governor, Vaubois, was starved out and surrendered to British Forces under Major General Pigott on 5 September 1800.

In the meantime, Egypt was under the control of the Army of the Orient led by Bonaparte himself. The principal Mameluke force under Murad Bey, after one defeat, had retreated south to Upper Egypt. However, whilst the French leader ensconced himself in Cairo, Admiral Lord Nelson was approaching with the British fleet. The Battle of the Nile (The Battle of Aboukir Bay) was fought on 1 August 1798. Aboukir Bay lies off the mouth of the Rosetta branch of the Nile near Alexandria and the battle has been described as one of the most decisive in naval history. Napoleon's ships lacked a full complement of men and the seamen they carried were, for the most part, badly trained. Somehow, much to his chagrin, Napoleon was never as successful at sea as he was on land where he could – with the exception of most of the battles fought in the Iberian Peninsula – usually direct operations in person. The French Admiral, Francois Paul Brueys d'Aigalliers, was completely taken by surprise and fought much of the battle while still lying at anchor. Thanks to his having anchored too far off shore, his whole squadron became trapped between two lines of British ships when some of the British vessels sailed in between the French fleet and the shore. Most of the French ships were captured or sunk; the flagship, *L'Orient* exploded – some reported this was owing to the Admiral blowing up his own ship to avoid the ignominy of capture. Only two frigates, *Le Diane and Le Justice,* managed to escape.

Napoleon had lost most of his fleet but his army of academics had made discoveries of the utmost importance in Egypt; in July 1799, undoubtedly the greatest of all of these was the unearthing of the Rosetta stone. This block inscribed with the same decree in three different texts was to prove the key to unlocking the ancient language of hieroglyphics.

At the end of 1799, Bonaparte returned to France in great secrecy to avoid being taken by any of the British ships prowling the Mediterranean and to pre-empt any action by the squabbling members of the Directorate back in Paris. The General rightly surmised that it was time for him to make a move in order to establish himself as the leader of France. In the Coup of 19 Brumaire (10 November) the Constitution of Year III was abolished and the Consulate created. It took Napoleon less than six months to see himself appointed First Consul by dint of a 'public' referendum.

To combat Napoleon and liberate Egypt, a British fleet was assembled off Gibraltar. This had taken a great deal of effort on the part of both the Prime Minister, William Pitt, and Henry Dundas, Chief of the War Office; almost everyone was opposed to sending an army into the Mediterranean theatre and the King, George III, disapproved strongly. The man charged with command of this doubtful enterprise was Ralph Abercromby, who was 67. He well understood the risks of the campaign since the Army was, at the time, aptly described as a 'rabble'. The fleet of ships carrying the British Army assembled in the straits of Gibraltar but was soon scattered by a storm. Many of the future Duke of Wellington's finest officers were to sail in this force and to cut their teeth under Abercromby: John Hope, Hudson Lowe (eventually to be Napoleon's gaoler on St Helena), Dalhousie, Murray and Rowland Hill, amongst others. General Sir John Moore was one of the most senior officers.

 Fever broke out in the ships caused by the unsanitary, close-packed conditions on board; some had to be put ashore or even sent to Lisbon to recover. Eventually Hill caught up with the fleet in Minorca. He was soon laid low by a severe attack of fever and had to be taken back to Gibraltar, where he recovered in the Convent under the care of O'Hara. During this period, the old General was enraged by the sight and the news of the British Fleet sailing back and forth in the Mediterranean and he demanded to know the point of such activity. 'It is a diversion, General.' 'Diversion!' exclaimed O'Hara. ''Tis a diversion, for all Europe is laughing at you. Why, your Commander cannot see the end of his nose [Abercromby was notoriously short sighted] and, as for your fighting cock, Moore, he has trimmed his tail.' Sir John Moore had recently cut his *queue* and acquired a modern crop; he even paraded with his hair uncurled and unpowdered, which O'Hara thought very shocking.[59] The dreaded queues in which the men's hair was confined were formed by grabbing the long hair, dragging it back as tightly as possible and then coating it with a paste mixture of flour and grease, which then dried into a stiff 'tail'. In the night, rats would often come and nibble away at the flour-coated queues; they were unhygienic, hot, and uncomfortable.[60] Of course, it was only the rank and file who had to use flour, the officers used powder.

The fleet continued to sail to and fro off the North Africa coast suffering from poor food and bad weather. Finally, in November, the fleet sailed for Malta, now liberated from the French, and the men were relieved to be disembarked for a month. Rowland's diary and his letters make frequent and unaffected mention of his religious beliefs and here he refers to the shipwreck of St Paul. He was a committed and practising Christian throughout his life.

At the end of the year the fleet sailed again and January 1801 found the army safe in the well-protected harbour of Marmoris in southern Turkey where they met together with a Turkish fleet, the Turks now being allies. Entry to the bay of Marmoris is via a narrow, almost concealed passageway and the fleet sailed through, led by Lord Keith in his flagship, in single file under lowering skies and flashes of lightning. The men went ashore with joy and here they spent six weeks of relative relaxation. There was plentiful and good food and, what is much more important to the British solder, drink in abundance. The beautiful bay was large enough to hold the entire fleet. The town was small, not much more than a collection of hovels, and the moment the ships arrived all the women were locked up in the Castle.

One of the major problems for Abercromby was the Army's lack of horses for the cavalry. Some dragoons arrived in Marmoris on 12 January but their horses were in very poor condition following the voyage and the local beasts were unsuitable. It quickly became an urgent matter to find more mounts and this search led to long journeys inland to search for suitable horses. Eventually some very 'spirited' horses were purchased but they were very small and the dragoons were most unhappy. Meanwhile the infantry continued to drill; this had begun in Minorca and Malta and was just beginning to show results. On the whole the troops' stay was pleasant enough apart from the terrific storms that would blow up apparently out of nowhere and which are such a feature of the Mediterranean. Sergeant Robertson of the 92nd (Gordon) Highlanders, who were to serve alongside the 90th during the greater part of the Egyptian campaign, writes of the enormous hailstones and the lightning that struck and set fire to one of the gunboats.[61] The violent weather meant that the fleet could not sail for Egypt until the end of February and even then, they encountered some more fierce storms as they crossed and several of the smaller boats had to divert to Cyprus. Finally, on 1 March, after eight days at sea, they could make out the low-lying coast and the ruined village of Aboukir; they dropped anchor in Aboukir Bay on 2 March. Sergeant Robertson could not have been alone in wondering why he had become a soldier.

The 90th formed part of Major-General Cradock's brigade and was, together with the 92nd, to be the first to land; this was the doubtful honour awarded to the junior regiments.[62] General Sir John Moore led this first party ashore in landing craft only drawing 9 inches, while the bulk of the fleet had to remain well off the beach. The landing parties came under a hail of grapeshot from the French as they closed to the beach but once on land, they found that the enemy was not present in large numbers and they swiftly drove them away. On the 9th, the 90th under Hill moved forward together with the 92nd. On the 12th, they continued the advance and when the 22nd Chasseurs made an impetuous charge against them they were repulsed but Hill was wounded on the 13th. His own somewhat laconic notes record: '12th moved on towards Alexandria; 13th March attacked the French, defeated them and gained a glorious victory. Was wounded being struck in the temple and taken, unconscious, on board the "expedition".' What the word 'expedition' means here is not explained but he was certainly eventually taken on board the *Foudroyant*[63] which was Lord Keith's flagship. General Sir Robert Wilson subsequently described the conduct of the 90th Regiment in this affair 'to have been most praiseworthy and that nothing could have exceeded the intrepidity and firmness with which they charged the enemy.' The 92nd came under fierce fire from two French field pieces loaded with grape and the two leading regiments were slowed down by the difficulties of transporting their artillery, which had to be hauled by the men thanks to a lack of horses and the deep, soft sand. Hill may have been wounded and out of action for about three weeks, but he had the satisfaction of receiving high praise from Major General Cradock and, in addition, the 90th and the 92nd were the only regiments given the right to wear the battle honour of 'Mandora', site of their first scrap with the enemy, on their colours.

Hill had been rendered unconscious by the force of the musket ball that struck the binding of his helmet. He was slowly recovering when, on 21 March, his General, Abercromby, was brought on board and placed in the same cabin with a wound in his thigh. He was to die a week later. The brave 92nd (Gordon) Highlanders were so decimated by wounds and sickness that they were ordered to retire to Aboukir. The part played by these two Highland regiments, the 90th and the 92nd, is still celebrated in Scotland.

The British Army made good use of local camels for transport since horses were almost useless in the soft sandy soil. An officer was permitted a camel to carry his tent and other belongings and they also carried the ammunition. Strict orders were circulated that all camels were to be returned to the camel park each evening.[64] Another directive was that mutton rather than buffalo meat should be given to the sick and especially to those who had bowel complaints. The notebook with these orders is very small and the writing is certainly not that of Rowland; perhaps it was kept by the Adjutant or Quartermaster. It contains interesting local details of the operation in Egypt. The British Army was very strict about issuing receipts to the local village Sheiks as to the corn they had purchased and were told to be very careful to buy only 'clean' barley and threshed straw. The book also contains instructions on burying dead horses.

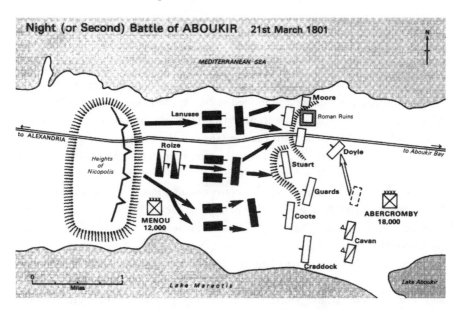

Hill served in Cradock's division at Aboukir. (David Chandler's *Dictionary of the Napoleonic Wars*)

General Cradock, as a senior general, now became second in command of the Army and General Hope took over his Brigade. While Hill was confined to the *Foudroyant*, he received a visit from Capitoun Pacha of the Turkish Forces who presented him with a sabre, a gold box and a handsome 'shawl' as testimony to the gallant manner in which he had led his regiment. He also invited him to pay a call on the Sultan Selim. The 'Capitoun' was a very splendid fellow with magnificently caparisoned horses and with his men dressed in 'Oriental magnificence'.

On 29 May, the Mamelukes, seeing that the British were now the victors, finally offered their support and the Grand Vizier, together with 'Copts and other Egyptians favourable to our cause such as Djazzar Pacha, have added 5,000 well disciplined troops.'[65]

Hill describes the troops plodding exhausted across the burning desert for two days, many dropping in their tracks suffering from heatstroke and dehydration. The temperature was in excess of 110 degrees for much of the day as they travelled towards the junction of the Delta with the Nile proper.[66] Once they reached the great river, there was greenery and water. The relief was unimaginable as they moved on through fields full of grain; but they were shocked by the miserable-looking houses built from mud brick and by the almost naked inhabitants. Somewhat revived, however, the army marched on and encamped outside the city of Cairo.[67] On the evening of the 21st, Hill was officer of the day. The following morning, a French officer came out of the city with a letter for the Commander in Chief who was now, following Abercromby's death, General John Hely Hutchinson.[68]

Hely Hutchinson, the senior Major General in Egypt whose appointment had been recommended by Abercromby, was not an attractive personality; brave and knowledgeable but virtually unknown to the troops.[69] He evidently suffered from bad health and extremely poor eyesight. He had a violent temper and the men did not respect him; there were indeed some on the brink of mutiny but John Moore would not agree to assist in depriving Hely Hutchinson of his command.

The result of this letter from French General Beliard was that a conference took place under a white flag and ended in the French agreeing to evacuate the citadel of Cairo in twelve days. Hill had a little time for sightseeing and visited the Pyramids and the Sphinx. A 'joke' going round concerning the Pyramids was 'were they wonderfully vast or vastly boring?' Senior officers were engaged in the ungentlemanly pursuit of hacking off bits of the Sphinx and of sarcophagi in the tombs to take home as souvenirs.

Meanwhile, Napoleon had issued a surprising document, a sort of *compte rendu* or explanation of the conduct of the French Government. He presented an historical sketch of the political world in every part where the French did not have troops and which had not been conquered. The First Consul of the 'Free Republic' made no mention of Egypt, Malta or the Baltic! These omissions are the most remarkable thing about it.[70]

On 15 July the march to Alexandria, where the French Army would embark, began. The Turks led the march, followed by the British and finally the French; it took fourteen days. As they approached the city of Alexandria, the French filed off to embark for France carrying with them a vast quantity of loot while the bulk of the British encamped among the date palms of Rosetta. Alexandria itself still held out under General (Abdullah) Jacques de Menou, who announced somewhat unconvincingly on 6 July that death was better than surrender. The cynical thought that the General, who was an apostate,[71] wanted to be allowed to have the best of both worlds. He finally surrendered on 30 August following an armistice that had lasted from the 17th to the 29th. The British cavalry had taken advantage of the fact that the French had to sell their horses before embarking and had acquired some prime and much-needed horse flesh.

On 30 August, General Menou was forced to sign his capitulation owing to food shortages inside the city. The question then arose as to who was going to have all the works of art and treasures that the *Institut de l'Egypt* had amassed during the past three years. When the British Commander in Chief, General Hely Hutchinson demanded the Rosetta Stone from Menou, the latter wrote to him:[7] 'It is true, Monsieur le General, that I have in my possession a stone which I dug up at Rosetta and which carries three different inscriptions. It was my property but I tell you that I intended to give it to the Republic on my arrival in France. You wish to have it, Sir, and you can take it because you are the stronger. I will not (hesitate) to make public in Europe that my property has been taken by the orders of an English General.' Hely Hutchinson remained unmoved, 'I have told you ten times and I repeat it to you again, I wish to have all the objects.' In fact, he did not press this point and the British took two sarcophagi, two obelisks and some statues, in addition to the Rosetta stone. These objects were to form the nucleus of the magnificent Egyptian collection in the British Museum. Most of the rest of the manuscripts, plants, minerals etc went to France and formed a basis for a similarly important collection in the Louvre. Rubbings of the stone had been taken by the French and it was using these that Jean Francois Champollion, the French scholar and philologist, became the first translator of the hieroglyphs.

The 90th was inspected by General Hope on 8 September and Colonel Hill was warmly commended: 'I tell you that the whole corps does you and the officers the greatest credit.' Hill also received his mail from England. One letter was from his uncle, Sir Richard, written in May. This letter was full of thanks to God for the safe deliverance of his soldier-nephew and told him that some newspapers had even listed him as dead. Letters from his sister Maria, who was to prove his most faithful correspondent from the Egyptian Campaign on throughout his entire military career, probably gave him more of the sort of news for which he longed – such as the state of his pheasants! A large number of the letters between the brother and sister are preserved in the British Library Mss[73] collection, most from the years of the Peninsular campaign.

On 23 September, Hill embarked his regiment for Malta where they anchored on 9 October. He had by now also received a letter from the Colonel of the Regiment, Thomas Graham: 'I rejoice to hear you are doing so well [probably with reference to his wound] and most sincerely congratulate you on the conduct of the regiment, which I never doubted would distinguish itself, though certainly the occasion was the most trying possible and its behaviour has established its reputation for ever.'

The Regiment stayed in Malta as the garrison until 28 February 1802 when it was embarked for Gibraltar. Rowland had anticipated a happy meeting with General O'Hara but, unfortunately, instead of being greeted by a friend interested in hearing all the details of the Egyptian Campaign, he learned of O'Hara's death.

At the beginning of April 1802, Hill found himself in quarantine off Spithead. On the 6th he went ashore at Portsmouth and a week later the regiment was landed at Chatham and marched to Chelmsford. After a few months, it was moved to Scotland and Rowland had every expectation of its being disbanded or reduced in size once it reached the regimental depot at Fort George. Mid-June found Hill finally at home in Shropshire, the county which he constantly describes in his letters as the best of all. Sir Richard gave a great fete in the Park at Hawkstone and erected the magnificent tent, formerly owned by Tippoo Sahib, which Hill had bought off an officer returning from service in India, for the company to dine in. It must have looked wonderfully exotic in the leafy green of rural Shropshire.

By the end of the year, any thoughts of reducing the size of the Army were banished by the unsettled affairs of Europe and, far from being reduced, the 90th had orders to make every exertion to recruit more men. In the spring of 1803, the regiment sailed for Ireland and was quartered in Belfast until August. Ireland was in a most 'disordered' state, to quote Hill's own words, and in August he received orders to march to Ballinasloe. Hill, having received his promotion to Brigadier General on the staff of Ireland, was to be stationed at Loughrea. As a result, he had to leave the regiment that he had had charge of almost since its birth and which he had commanded so effectively.

Now on the Staff, Rowland's duties were varied. Ireland was in a state of unrest and internal disaffection on the one hand and, on the other, great fears were entertained by the British that the French intended an invasion. His principal duties seem to have lain in Cork, Galway and Fermoy and his conduct was recognised by public addresses inserted in the Dublin papers. On leaving Cork, he was made a Freeman of the City.[74]

Frequent word of sightings of the French fleet were reported, without foundation. For example, there was an alert on 20 October when two Royal Navy frigates came in to take on fresh water and let their water casks float in to the shore – 'each was considered a boatload of French troops.' Soon, however, Hill was to be deployed on more interesting tasks than 'repelling incursions of water casks'. He was moved to Galway where he had considerable work to reorganise the yeomanry corps which were, for the most part, in a poor state. He acted with tact but firmness and by January 1804 he could report favourably on the state of the country under his control. He issued detailed instructions for the conduct of the yeomanry in the event of a French landing and also, with the help of Captain Edwin Currie,[75] his ADC, reconnoitred possible landing points. He encountered some trouble with local landowners but managed to win most of them over. He instructed them, where relevant, to destroy any bridges on their land should an invasion occur. One letter to a Richard Martin requests him to be vigilant and immediately to destroy the bridge of Tindella upon invasion and then to place a number of yeomanry on a hill at Oughterard, from which vantage point a small number would be capable of stopping the progress of the enemy advancing from Galway. The destruction of bridges, he pointed out, rendered the passage of enemy artillery impossible. Together with Currie and a Royal Navy man, Captain Trench, he established a signal communication between Loughrea and Galway. Captain Trench had prepared a dictionary of every useful word that they could think of. Hill's personal memorandum notes that he had great difficulty in recovering the expenses he had incurred over this and that it took a 'long and tiresome correspondence'.

By the end of February, the disloyal amongst the locals had firmly persuaded themselves that the French would come: 'The disaffected, particularly of the middling class, rather begin to show themselves, and look forward with much confidence to the invasion of this country, which they pretend to say will take place in the course of this month.' The yeomanry was now well trained and well disposed and the Athlone militia even went so far as to tender their services to

Rowland in Ireland or any other place in the United Kingdom. He slowly won the hearts and minds of most people with the exception of 'those who appear disposed to welcome the invaders.' In the months of May and June, he was able to report to the Lord Lieutenant that all was quiet. Hill was, however, still occupied in organising the construction of signal towers on the coast. This involved dealing with numerous landowners who objected to these being erected on their property. He was also deprived of the services of Captain Currie when the 90th received orders to embark for the West Indies and he was required to rejoin the regiment. Hill then had a succession of rather unsatisfactory ADCs until, in October 1805, he received new orders for himself. The West Indies was known to be a 'graveyard' station and Hill was fortunate to have Currie back with him a few years later.

The Commander in Chief requested that Hill should remove himself as quickly as possible to Cork where he was to superintend the embarkation of troops. In addition, should 'the Middleton transport' still be at Cork,[76] she should be diverted to England instead of sailing for Jamaica, her original destination.

On the Continent Bonaparte had crossed the Danube and forced the capitulation of Ulm. The troops from Ireland were to be sent to the Weser to assist Britain's allies to put an end to Bonaparte's advance. This, the ill-fated Weser Expedition, was the first occasion in which Rowland was to serve with Arthur Wellesley, (from now on, referred to as Wellington). The two men seem to have been well disposed to each other from the start. No amount of goodwill, however, was sufficient to save this expedition, under General Lord Cathcart, from catastrophe. The North Sea was no place for troop ships in the winter months but Pitt saw the situation as so desperate that he threw every spare soldier and transport at the enterprise. 'After a tremendous passage and serious losses, some of us had the good fortune to arrive in the Weser on Christmas Day 1805. When I reached that river, the headquarter ship of every regiment belonging to me was missing ... some [ships] were wrecked on the Dutch coast, and many souls perished on the Goodwin Sands.'[77] To rub salt in the wounds, Hill and his new ADC, Captain Peebles, received the unwelcome news delivered by a local, with a certain smugness one deduces, of the recent triumphs of Napoleon's armies. Following the Allies' defeat at the Battle of Austerlitz, the British troops were recalled to England and placed along the south coast for defence in the event of invasion and Rowland found himself stationed at Deal. It was January 1806. On his arrival back in England, the biggest piece of news had been that Pitt was dead, aged only 48. The other news that reached him was of the death of his mother, Mary Chambré Hill. Coming at a time, almost the only time in his long career, when he was to return frustrated from an expedition, it was undoubtedly a blow.[78]

In April, he moved to Brabant Lees, Kent, and established his HQ. He was under the overall command of General Lord Moira but he was also in touch again with Sir John Moore at Canterbury. His brigade underwent successive inspections by Lord Moira and the Commander in Chief, HRH Frederick Duke of York. He was now promoted Major General and one of his younger brothers, Captain Thomas Noel Hill,[79] became his ADC. At the end of December 1806, Hill was ordered back to Ireland where he was to remain for the whole of 1807, under the command of the Duke of Bedford.

In July 1807 the Treaty of Tilsit was signed. Napoleon was now supreme in Europe and many of the aims of the Treaty were directed at preventing Great Britain from trading anywhere on the Continent. Her only remaining allies were Sweden, Sicily and Portugal. As author Michael Glover pointed out, the leaders of both Sweden and Portugal were mad and the King of Sicily was 'feeble minded'.[80] These afflictions did not make for strong allies.

The fear of French invasion had now faded away and the great invasion camp that Napoleon had assembled at Boulogne had been broken up. Hill's work was mostly engaged in the suppression of local disturbances and the sifting of endless rumours, which were frequently inflated by his informants into insurrection and hostility towards the Government. The following year, 1808, was to change the lives of many soldiers and Rowland Hill was involved from the beginning together with Wellington. It was the start of the Peninsular War.

II

A PERSONAL VIEW OF EVENTS IN 1808

T he following was written by Rowland Hill some time between 1818 and 1820. It serves as a succinct resumé of the events, as he saw them, which led up to the long wars in Spain and Portugal.[81]

In this bigoted and degenerated state Spain and Portugal were found at the close of the 18th century, when France was visited by the most tremendous revolution that History has recorded, this Revolution threatened the civilised world. The Revolution in France gave the government absolute command of the [unreadable] of France and this prodigious power was at the disposal of an individual – Buonaparte – possessed of all the Qualities to form a perfect tyrant, his military genius of the highest order, his character and conduct in Egypt are well told.

Buonaparte thought he could obtain possession of Spain, Portugal and become Master of the Brazil and of the Spanish Indies.

Buonaparte's first step to accomplish his aim was to take the best Spanish troops from Spain – a force under La Romana of 16,000 men was marched to the north of Germany, another division to Tuscany under O'Farrill, at the same time French troops were introduced into Spain under the pretext of occupying Portugal.

It was well known that Charles IV of Spain was a weak ruler, the Court of Portugal virtually in a state of helplessness. Godoy 'Prince of Peace' was at this time Minister in Spain – he was almost universally detested. [Except by the odious Queen, his lover.]

Napoleon planned to remove the Royal Family and the flamboyant Junot[82] was to command the French troops of the Army of Observation of the Gironde.[83] Napoleon also made a secret Treaty between France and Spain to divide Portugal between the two countries, Spain was to help France to achieve this. The Spanish were initially, naively, unaware of Napoleon's true design.

The British were ordered to leave Lisbon, which was to be blockaded by the Russian fleet under Admiral Siniavin,[84] Junot advanced by forced marches and issued a proclamation in Portuguese abusing the British and promising the protection of the French. Junot reached Castello Branco on 19th November. Junot was at Abrantes before the Portuguese Government knew that the French had entered their country. The Princes and Royal family hearing of the approach of Junot were embarked (by a British fleet), and on the 27th, Junot arrived in sight of Lisbon to see the ships conveying the Family of Braganza beyond the power of his Mighty Master.

On 13th December, the French flag was hoisted at Lisbon – general dissatisfaction of the Portuguese with which was shown by violent tumult and riot.

A second Spanish Force of 2000 joined Junot and marched on Porto.

Violent language was employed in France against England, threatening 'to carry their victorious and avenging eagles into every part of her possessions' – Buonaparte at the time despised the military force of England. His projects for securing the whole Spanish Peninsula were now mature – January.

On the 1st (1807) it was proclaimed in Lisbon that Napoleon the Great had taken Portugal under his omnipotent protection – the flower of the Portuguese army under the Marquis d'Alorna were sent to France. The French executed nine men at Caldas – Loison,[85] who had only one arm, was detested by the Portuguese for his cruelty.

Junot's object was to be made King; he had, however, little leisure to enjoy his dreams of royalty – he was roused by the events of Spain in May.

Godoy narrowly escaped the vengeance of the mob in Madrid and Charles abdicated in favour of his eldest son, Ferdinand, the Prince of Asturias, amid great rejoicing and dancing in the street; such happiness did not last long.

Ferdinand's first act was to order that the French Army approaching Madrid be received as Friends and Allies – Godoy was sent as a prisoner to the Castle of Villa Victoria [Villaviciosa de Odon?] and his property confiscated (surely reason for celebration!). The King begged the French to reinstate him. The King considered the French as friends – the people of Spain thought very differently.

Murat came to take command of the invading Army.

The King begged Buonaparte to reinstate him. The vicious Queen's entreaties were only to reinstate her favourite, Godoy. She even declared that her son Ferdinand's character was 'bloody'. Ferdinand agreed to meet his 'ally' at Burgos. Ferdinand wished his father to congratulate the Emperor on his arrival in Spain. His father replied, 'Tell the messenger I have gone to bed.'

11th April. Ferdinand arrived in Burgos to find Napoleon was not there and Ferdinand was persuaded to go on to Victoria where he received a letter from Buonaparte. Ferdinand was urged to go on to Bayonne … 'I show no distrust of Buonaparte but to hasten forward to meet him as the only means to avert his displeasure and secure his friendship.'

The people of Victoria besought Ferdinand not to proceed ... urged it, and if refused was prepared to carry him off by force. The terrified Ferdinand accordingly renewed his journey tho' the People finding their entreaties of no avail cut the traces and led away the mules – Ferdinand arrived at Bayonne. Buonaparte embraced him, the kiss of Judas Iscariot was not more treacherous than the Imperial embrace.

Poor weak Ferdinand was required to renounce the crown of Spain – Napoleon was determined to force the Bourbon dynasty from Spain – that it was to be succeeded by the Buonapartes. Castanos[86] insisted on the rights of Ferdinand. Buonaparte replied 'I have a system of policy of my own. You must not sacrifice the prosperity of Spain to the interest of the Bourbon family.'

1,000 guards were set around Ferdinand to prevent his escape. He abstained from going out (this to avoid insults)[87] Godoy was taken to Bayonne under cover of night for his safety, to the fury of the people and Charles wrote a violent letter to his son, Ferdinand, accusing him of 'tearing the crown from his head.'

Charles and the Queen were now at Bayonne 'by order of the tyrant'. The Queen it is said told Ferdinand in the presence of the King that he was not the King's son.

Both Charles and Ferdinand abdicated all claims upon the Spanish Kingdom in favour of the Emperor Napoleon – the whole of this unhappy family, now that the mockery of negotiation was at an end, were sent into the interior of France.

May 2nd the People rose and many lives were lost as Murat[88] continued the work of death in 'cool' blood.

When Napoleon had dethroned the Spanish Bourbons, he had planned to install brother Lucien as King of Spain but he (sensibly) declined and the choice fell on Joseph. Addresses were presented from the Junta and Council in praise [of] this new King and [the] moderation!!! of Murat.

Buonaparte said 'I will place your glorious crown upon the head of one who is my other self[89] and it is my wish that your descendants shall preserve my memory and say of me "he was the regenerator of our country".'

The people were roused by the conduct of the French and agents were sent to England inviting her to unite against the common enemy and those thought to be favourable to the French were killed.

June. Castanas[90] prepared to resist the French when they arrived in Andalucia. Palafox[91] escaped from Bayonne to Zaragosa and declared that the Royal family had been entrapped and that 'the French committed cruelties that made Human Nature shudder.'

'To arms, to arms, the patriotism of the Spaniards was roused. The King has been "decoyed" from us, our religion is doomed to perdition, a foreign power has done this not by dint of arms but by deceit and treachery. To arms, to arms.'

Junot was now disturbed from his dreams of Royalty. He distributed his troops. Loison marched on Porto, he was a man after Buonaparte's own heart being 'equally devoid of honour and humanity, plundering without remorse.'

Baja was set on fire.

May/June/July various insurrections in Portugal and great cruelties committed.

Things were in this state when I arrived upon the coast of Portugal.

The above does not sound as if it was intended for others to read. Perhaps he was just recapitulating events in his own mind but it gives a succinct view of events as seen by a senior British officer.

III

WITH MOORE TO CORUNNA

An armament was preparing at Cork first under my orders, afterwards given to Sir Arthur Wellesley. We sailed from Cork on 12 July.[92]

I n volume 36064 of the Hill Papers[93] are Hill's General Orders dated 15 June, 1808: The 5th, 9th, 38th and 40th Regiments were to embark at Cork under Major General Hill. Also listed was the number of children and women permitted to embark, together with lists and stores for the sick and wounded. The men were to be divided into two divisions: one under Brigadier General Fane, while Major General Robert (Black Bob) Crauford would have the second. The instructions included the order that the men were to exercise and be kept on deck as much as possible to avoid the spread of sickness. The troops at this stage numbered 10,284 men and 444 officers.

Hill received a letter from Wellington on 23 June, saying how happy he was that they would be serving together again and that he hoped that they would have more to do on this occasion.[94] This refers, of course, to the disastrous expedition to the Weser where the two men had been together for the first time. He asks Hill to be sure that enough space will be kept on the transports for his horses. He also bemoans the lack of good cavalry horses.

Wellington, as senior general, assumed command on 8 July, with Major General Hill remaining as his second in command. On 30 July, a General Order was issued; lecturing the troops as to their behaviour once they landed in Portugal. They were, for example, to remember that Portugal was a country friendly to His Majesty and Wellington declared his determination to punish in the most exemplary manner all those convicted of acts of outrage or plunder. Hill was to give such orders as he thought fit on all subjects relating to troops, reporting to Wellington as necessary. Orders from Hill were to be considered as coming from the Lieutenant General himself.

'Landed in Mondego Bay 3, 4, 5 August.' This rather terse statement, together with the the following, comes from Hill's personal memorandum.

> The merchants of Coimbra, who warmly welcomed the British Army, sent gifts of oranges and lemons, other fruit, 12 calves, and fowl (500), 50 sheep, 100 turkeys, 50 pigs, 60 ducks, 2 cartloads of melons, 4 of cabbages, 3 of onions, 2 of French beans, peaches, pears, 4 cartloads of water melons, 24 boxes of preserved fruit, 50 sheep. These were sent to Lavos where the commissariat officers were to divide them.

Hill received instructions from Wellington on 8 August, concerning his march to Leira. He was to leave at 3am. Two captains had been detailed to show him the route.

When considering the movements, achievements and failures during the long years of fighting, one must take into account the difficulties of the terrain of the Iberian Peninsula. In the north, the chain of the Pyrenees forms a high and difficult natural barrier between Spain and France; not surprisingly, the only easy routes between the two countries lie at either end of the mountain range, one on the Atlantic and the other on the Mediterranean. For the rest, 'roads' were generally more like mule or goat tracks suitable for smugglers and guerrillas but not for an army of thousands of men, and wagon trains that sometimes stretched for as much as eight miles, hauling not just materiel such as tents, food, ammunition, but also the guns. Once the barrier of these mountains has been overcome, there is the high, barren plateau of central Spain which is swept by every wind and is not fit for much in the way of agriculture, most of which is carried out along the coastal plains and in some of the broader river valleys. Madrid sits in the centre of the high central plateau and one observer described it as having, 'the soil of the Sahara, the sun of Calcutta, the wind of Edinburgh and the cold of the North Pole.' The great historian of the Peninsular War, Sir Charles Oman, describes Spain as a land where the rivers count for little:

> In most countries great rivers are connecting cords of national life; their waters carry the internal traffic of the realm; the main roads lie along their banks. But in Spain the streams are useless. They mostly flow in deep-sunk beds far below the level of the surrounding country-side … in the rainy season they are dangerous torrents, in the summer all save the very largest dwindle down into miserable brooks … in short, they are of importance not as lines of transit but as obstacles. They form many fine positions for defence.[95]

So it was a difficult country in which to fight a war on traditional terms; in summer the days were burning hot and many men died of heatstroke; in winter snow lay thick on the uplands and in the mountain valleys and more men died of hypothermia. It was a cruel place to campaign. For the most complete analysis of the logistical challenge of the war, see Ian Robertson's magisterial *A Commanding Presence: Wellington in the Peninsula 1808–1814*.

Wellington had first landed at Corunna in the north on 20 July to be told by the Galicians that although they had no need of more troops, they needed money. The British, at this time, still maintained confidence, unfortunately to be proved greatly misplaced, in the Spanish Army. Wellington sailed on to meet the Spanish Junta and Don Antonio de Castro, Archbishop of Porto. This man was all-powerful and popular but he was not a politician; he was a self-serving churchman who led his own faction. He promised the British supplies and men once the British force landed. Having conferred with Admiral Sir Charles Cotton, in charge of co-ordinating the naval units lying off the coast, Wellington decided on Mondego Bay, near the fishing village of Figuera da Foz, as the landing point for his small force. Mondego was not ideal, being a wide bay open to great Atlantic rollers, but it appeared the most suitable of the few options available. The landing proved slow and very difficult. It was necessary to land the men in small boats, and despite the best efforts of the sailors, they were plucked like so much floss, thrown in the air and then flung into the boiling surf or crashed down onto the beach. A number of men, inevitably, were drowned; few could swim and all were encumbered by their packs. It was as difficult for the dragoons who were instructed to stand upright in the boats, holding their chargers' reins and to be prepared to mount at a moment's notice. This order was, however, a wise instruction because, even if thrown into the water, the horses could either swim or walk ashore. Other horses were simply lowered off the ships or pushed overboard, and left to make their own way to the beach. Once on dry land, the wretched animals charged up and down the shoreline in a mad frenzy, avoiding capture where possible. They had been cooped up in the transports for a long time, and many of them took days to recover their 'land legs'.

Wellington now had 13,000 British troops, 2000 regular Portuguese and not enough horses for his cavalry. His staff was new to him and consisted of totally inexperienced 'greenhorns', one of his chief annoyances. As the years in the Peninsula rolled by, his 'family', as he called his personal staff, became a great source of pleasure and often of pride to him; they formed his social circle, and almost without exception came from noble families.

With his customary foresight and attention to detail, Wellington had brought two small Irish wagon trains with him but it was necessary to hire wooden carts together with 500 mules and 300 bullocks with their drivers to transport the supplies under the control of the Commissariat Department. The shrieking of the wooden axles of these carts was noted in many contemporary accounts! Wellington was expecting Lieutenant General Sir Brent Spencer from Cadiz[96] with more men and he also hoped that the soldiers who had gone on the abortive Baltic expedition under General Sir John Moore[97] would now be diverted to Portugal. Once three days' rations had been distributed amongst the men,

Wellington marched south towards Leira. Here, he met up with Colonel Nicholas Trant[98] who brought a further 1600 Portuguese light troops. On 7 August, Lieutenant General Brent Spencer[99] arrived and took precedence over Hill by dint of his seniority on the Army List.

> Advanced guard marched 9th August, supported by Generals Hill and Ferguson. The first skirmish with the enemy was at Caldos on the 14th. The enemy took up a position at Roliça. Major General Ferguson was directed to turn the enemy's right and for Major General Hill to attack the left. Meanwhile Crawfurd, Nightingale and Fane are ordered to force the [?] centre. De Laborde[100] was forced to retire leaving his guns upon the field.

This was Hill's personal, rather cursory account of the Battle of Roliça. Wellington had sent the advance guard with General Hill along the beach to Caldos some 30 miles up ahead while he himself took the Leira road with the main body of the army and the commissariat.

De Laborde, considered at the time to be one of Junot's best generals, had withdrawn strategically on Roliça in the knowledge that he was about to be supported by Loison. Wellington also had information that Junot was on the road from Madrid and decided to attack de Laborde before he was reinforced. He had also received intelligence indicating that Loison, although still some miles to the east, was approaching across country to join with de Laborde. Wellington had his force under arms before the sun rose on 17 August. Roliça sat in a sort of horseshoe formed by steep ridges and with the road for Lisbon running down the centre of the valley. He divided the army into three columns and sent both General Ferguson's and Bowes' Brigades, together with six guns, to the east, and Colonel Trant with his 'ragamuffins' of three Portuguese regiments of infantry and one of cavalry (only 50-men strong), to the west to make an encircling movement behind the French Army. Hill was in the centre with Fane's Brigade, Caitlin Craufurd's[101] Brigade, Nightingale's Brigade and the Portuguese 6 Cacadores together with twelve guns and some light dragoons. They were to perform a diversionary role allowing the other two units to encircle the French.

De Laborde was too crafty a general to be caught like this and made a tactical withdrawal once he had drawn the British into the narrow gullies on the hillside. Here, his men inflicted heavy damage on the British and Colonel Lake of the 29th (Worcestershire) Regiment, who had advanced his men too impetuously and exceeded his orders, was killed. This had had the effect of forcing Hill to make a full attack, and he sent forward the 1/9 to support Lake's rash move and the battle was fairly joined as the men swarmed up the steep sides of the gullies.

It has been described, rather patronisingly, as an irrelevant and unnecessary little skirmish but it was the first battle of the Peninsular Wars and, although Wellington's tactics may not have been of the best, he had already learned a lesson.

In his despatch, he wrote that 'the 29th attacked with the utmost impetuosity' and 'deserve the highest praise.' He made no mention that Lake had disobeyed his orders; Lake had served under him in India and perhaps he did not wish to tarnish his name. Battle honours were given as 'Roleia'. It has been commented that the tactics employed by de Laborde were copied by Wellington in future engagements and these led him to be called a defensive general, which was not strictly accurate; it would be more correct to say that he took everything into consideration when planning his attacks and did not allow himself to be drawn onto the enemy unless he was as sure of success as any man could be. Since he was almost always heavily outnumbered by the French, it was a sensible tactic. If this approach was not to be successful in every single encounter, it achieved its aim on most occasions; he was to prove himself a superb tactician. In the case of Roliça, he had not been led to pursue the enemy when he knew that de Laborde's reinforcements had almost reached him.

'General Anstruther landed at Maceira near Vimiero on 19 August and on the 20th Sir Harry Burrard arrived.' News of the reinforcements together with news of the arrival of a senior officer having reached him, Wellington had the men march to the point of disembarkation to cover the landing and by the 18th they had installed themselves near the village of Vimeiro. Major General Hill was posted on the right, on the hillside at the rear of the village in reserve to the whole force. Anstruther and Acland had brought a further 4000 men to reinforce Wellington's army, which now numbered approximately 17,000 men. The newly arrived commanders had the same problems with their cavalry, the horses being very skittish and unsteady on their legs after the sea journey. Even with the addition of this cavalry, Wellington still had only 240 horses – the French had almost 2000. Wellington always considered the French cavalry to be superior to his own.

De Laborde had now been reinforced by Junot and Loison as anticipated. Unfortunately for Wellington, the arrival of Sir Harry Burrard would snatch the command from him but as the General did not choose to disembark immediately, Wellington took advantage of his absence that night and the following morning. A period of manoeuvring took place on both sides. Ferguson, Nightingale and Bowes were on the left of the line, then Acland and Anstruther, some cavalry and then Fane; Hill was behind Fane in reserve on the right of the line.[102] Junot sent two typical French columns into the centre. While the French held rigidly to their columns, the British almost always deployed in line. The enemy columns were 30 ranks deep by 40 wide; the French approached to within 100 yards before the British fired and delivered a crushing volley into the packed French column. This volley was followed at approximately 15-second intervals by a second and third that mowed down the French. The French General, Thomières, did his best to rally his men but it was a lost cause and they took to their heels pursued by General Fane's[103] riflemen.

Rifles, although not in general use, were the new 'secret' weapon of the British Army. They were much easier to fire and much more accurate than muskets even if they took longer to reload. They also needed to be kept very clean, which was not easy in the heat of battle.

The French abandoned several guns during their retreat. The British cavalry were not at their shining best in the Peninsula, with a few honourable exceptions, and on this occasion they showed their propensity for 'galloping at everything'. Colonel Charles Taylor was killed and they suffered many casualties, not for the last time. It would be fair to say that much of the Peninsula, especially Portugal and, obviously, the Pyrenees, was not cavalry country. Wellington was constantly bemoaning the lack of discipline in his cavalry.

It was at this moment that Sir Harry Burrard chose to make his belated appearance on the battlefield. He did not immediately take the command from Wellington but when the French began to retire soon after midday, having seen each of their attacks thrown back (although they did manage to recover some guns they had lost earlier) Burrard announced that the men should return to barracks and rest after their exertions. Wellington was apoplectic; he wished to pursue the enemy and take Torres Vedras, which would have placed the British Army between the enemy and Lisbon. However, he could not persuade the old, timid General, who had not been in an engagement for at least ten years, that it was essential and the latter chose to announce that he would await the arrival of General Sir John Moore with his army before resuming the offensive. Wellington is quoted as saying, 'Well, then, we have nothing to do but to go and shoot red legged partridges.' General Ferguson was especially taken aback by the order to halt. He had some of Solignac's brigade pinned into an angle of the hills from which it was difficult for them to escape.[104] Hill's brigade, together with those of Fane and Anstruther, was still untouched and had been in a position to cut the French off from their base of operations, when the cautious hand of Burrard put an end to a battle that should have been far more decisive. The entire British force was puzzled and angry; they had seen the possibility of driving the French out of the area of Lisbon and it had been snatched from them. As Wellington observed, 'I think if General Hill's brigade and the advanced guard had moved upon Torres Vedras, we had been in Lisbon before him; if indeed any French had remained in Portugal.'[105] Both sides appear to have claimed victory and Junot was described as the victor of Vimeiro.[106]

Sir Harry was not left in command for long, for the very next day an even more senior General, Sir Hew Dalrymple, arrived and the two elderly officers decided that no further action was necessary. The British Army had had three different commanding officers over 24 hours. General Francois Etienne Kellerman of the French Army arrived under a white flag and proposed an armistice, more in hope than expectation. Did the French really suppose the British would agree? Kellerman could not believe his good fortune when the British signed the so-called Convention of Cintra, by which it was agreed that the French Army would be repatriated, together with all their arms and any plunder they had accumulated, by courtesy of the Royal Navy.[107] It was the most bizarre set of terms. Wellington had not been party to the drafting of the Convention but had been forced by Dalrymple to put his signature to it. He was furious. Fortunately for him, there was enough proof that the cessation of hostilities and the drafting of the Convention had had nothing to do with him. The two old generals never served again.

The British public was shocked. What had appeared as a significant victory had been turned into a sort of draw with the French probably coming out on top. Byron wrote of the Convention: 'Here folly dashed to earth the victor's plume/ And policy regained what arms had lost.' Wordsworth even wrote an impassioned (book-length) pamphlet about the British officer class's betrayal of the Iberian patriots. Both the senior generals and Wellington were called to a Court of Inquiry in England. The British Government had finally come to realise that Napoleon was never going to be defeated by such timid and feeble soldiers as 'Betty' Burrard and Dalrymple, but they did mark Wellington down as an energetic and resourceful general. When you consider this 'Sepoy' General had already led large and successful forces in India and defeated huge Maratha armies in the Deccan of central India, one is puzzled that the British Government had not already taken proper notice of his abilities. Of course, he was still only a fairly junior Lieutenant General.

Wellington left for England for the Court of Inquiry and after discussions with his close ally in the Government, Castlereagh, returned to his old post in Dublin. He was not destined to stay there for very long. He was exonerated at the Inquiry.

In Hill's account,[108] he quotes Napoleon: 'I am determined, said he, to carry on the war with Spain with the utmost activity and to destroy the armies which England has disembarked in that country ... I have the hideous presence of the leopard (which) contaminates the continent of Spain and Portugal. Let your aspect terrify and drive him from thence.'

Negotiations for peace were commenced and terminated, the King of England declaring, 'he laments the [problems] by which the suffering of Europe were prolonged but neither his honour nor the generosity of the British nation would admit of his consenting to commence a negotiation by the abandonment of a brave and loyal people.' In Hill's own memoirs, he wrote in terse, diary form:

In October Buonaparte arrives in Spain to crown the King and place his eagles on the forts of Spain.

On 3rd November, he put himself at the head of his army – five days later at Victoria.

November: the battle of Espinon where General Blake (Spanish) was defeated, battle of Tudela in which the Spaniards under Castanas were defeated. The French took possession of Madrid on 5th December.

Bravado from Napoleon, 'for God has given me power and inclination to surmount all obstacles.'

The Spanish General, Carlos Galluzo, was appointed to defend Estramadura against the French but, being totally incapable, was soon recalled to answer charges of high treason. He was replaced by General Cuesta.[109]

Bonaparte dismissed the British, 'Oh that they may dye with their own blood which they have [illegible] with their intrigues. The day when we succeed in seeing these English will be a day of jubilation for the French Army.'

The Spanish armies were completely annihilated by the French (or fled) during this period and were of little or no help to the small British Army now commanded by Moore, which totalled only 26,000 men. Blake[110] was defeated at Medina del Sol Rio Seco and Espinosa. He was perhaps an unlucky general and he certainly had few successes in the field. He also had to contend with his senior officer, General Cuesta. This Spanish General, often totally inert, seems, for once, to have thrown any idea of caution to the winds and Torrens thinks that at Espinosa he had placed Blake where his men would bear the main force of a battle while Cuesta himself would bring up the main body of his army when his colleague had been 'humbled' and restore the fight.[111] Although Hill does talk of Cuesta in mild tones, he was more usually described as a 'lump of lard' or worse. He was so obese that he had to be lifted into his coach and on the rare occasions when he mounted a horse, he had six men to hold him upright in the saddle.

The difference in manpower between the opposing forces was immense; compare the tiny army led by Sir John, together with the defeated and often defeatist Spaniards, with the streaming horde of French soldiers coming through the Pyrenees; eight corps totalling approximately 330,000 men. It is hardly surprising that London had little faith in the success of this campaign.

With the recall of the two old 'fossils,' Burrard and Dalrymple, to face the Court of Inquiry, Sir John Moore was left in command of the Army. Moore was a highly respected soldier who had seen much action. He was also responsible for the innovative training regime that had led to the formation of the first light infantry regiments. Arthur Bryant wrote of him, 'Moore's contribution to the Army was not only [the] matchless light infantry ... but also the belief that the perfect soldier can only be made by invoking all that is finest in man "physical, mental and spiritual".'[112]

Moore boldly advanced his army consisting of only three brigades of infantry into Spain, ordering Baird and Hope to join him. He went as far as Salamanca, which he reached on 13 November and where he heard that the French were at Valladolid.[113] The Spanish armies were still proving poor allies in the field with even La Romana, the best of the Spanish generals at the start of the campaign, having poorly disciplined troops under him; Napoleon scattered them with ease, not to say contempt. Moore was forced to retreat. The behaviour of some of the

Spanish armies was certainly to improve over the following six years but at the time of Moore's retreat, they simply vanished 'like a cluster of wind-driven leaves before the tempest.'

The battle at Sahagun was to be the last before Moore began his retreat to Corunna. It took place on 21 December 1808. Moore had ordered Paget, who had General Slade under his command, to advance with the 10th Hussars hoping that the French were as yet unaware of his presence. However, Slade chose to delay his advance while 'haranguing' his men with a longwinded speech and had then spent an extraordinary length of time fiddling with his stirrup leathers. He lost valuable time, much to Paget's enormous irritation; it was Slade's first engagement. Paget lost patience and ordered Colonel Leigh to take command and the 10th advanced against the enemy under heavy fire. They charged bravely and routed the enemy, capturing a number of prisoners. It was one of the relatively rare successes for the cavalry, even if Slade could hardly be said to have made much of a contribution; this was another general with whom Hill was to be saddled to act as 'nursemaid' in the future. Slade has been criticised by everyone, including his peers and historians but somehow he remained in the Peninsula until the middle of 1813;[114] how delighted the Duke must have been when he finally went home – but not until after his disgraceful behaviour at Maguilla, which Fletcher calls the 'Unluckiest Cavalry Combat of the Peninsular War.'[115]

'I will sweep the English Armies from the Peninsula,' said Napoleon in his typically bombastic manner, and in the short term, he was correct. It is said that Napoleon's cavalry alone equalled Moore's whole army in numbers. The latter was to be reinforced with 10,000 men under Sir David Baird who now landed at Corunna, but these were still raw troops. Alarmed at events in Austria,[116] Napoleon left the Peninsula's affairs to his generals, principally Marechals Soult and Victor and returned north to lead his other armies. Hill was, at this time, in command of a brigade in General Sir John Hope's 1st Division.

Much has, of course, been written about the retreat to Corunna and also to the nearby port of Vigo,[117] where a smaller portion of the British Army was to board the transports. The route, about 250 miles, was similar to both ports. It was bitter winter weather, at the end of December, the way was mountainous, snow lay thick in the passes in Galicia and the icy winds made shelter impossible. Food was scarce, wine was only too easily available whenever they reached a village. These things all contributed to disaster; men just fell where they stood, bone weary and unable to put one foot before the other, and many froze where they fell. Those that were drunk were frequently left behind, unable to fall in when their company moved on. Some of these men were killed by the French and many others were captured. Rifleman Harris of the 95th Rifles has provided us with an excellent account of his own retreat to Vigo with all its appalling privations. The thing that he inveighs against, in the most forceful terms, is his pack. Harris was a small man and how he managed to carry his great 60-lb pack, one cannot imagine; he writes that more men were killed by their pack than by any of the other challenges. He recounts that the officers were in almost as bad a situation as the rank and file. Harris served in 'Black Bob' Craufurd's division and writes of his General's severity, an 'iron man', but it was this very trait that probably carried so many of his men safely to Vigo.[118]

The breakdown of discipline in the British Army was shameful on this retreat; it was Paget and his cavalry who maintained their proper order where many of the infantry divisions could not be held together. Thomas Graham said that it was on this final stretch that the troops, with the exception of the Reserve, became entirely disorganised and 'disorderly' with the officers also becoming negligent; everyone was simply desperately struggling to survive. Graham himself had only narrowly escaped falling into a ravine when his horse, inching along a narrow path, slipped and went over, leaving his rider hanging onto a bush. Colborne riding not far behind shouted to his sergeant to let down his sash tied to a pike and they managed to haul poor Graham up again.

Plundering was, of course, strictly forbidden but with the stragglers being numerous it was impossible to prevent it. Robert Blakeney described how the soldiers had their packs searched when they eventually caught up with their units and all the plunder in them was divided amongst those who had not descended to robbery. When some of their horses began to falter, Paget was forced to order his hussars to shoot them, to prevent them falling into French hands. This reduced many of his men to tears.

Hill with Sir John Hope's Division was bound for Corunna. When, on 13 January 1809, the exhausted men, with virtually no provisions left and many barefoot in the bitter conditions, finally arrived within sight of the sea in the expectation of seeing British transports in the harbour of Corunna, the port was empty. Contrary winds had detained the transports at Vigo and now the French Army was close on their heels.

Sir John Moore put his sick on board the few small ships that lay in the harbour and then tried his best to fortify the town; he intended to evacuate his army and blow the powder magazines before the French could take them. The transports finally arrived on 15 January. On the 16th, having put all stores and other 'encumbrances' on board ship, Sir John prepared to embark his army but at noon the enemy attacked. Suddenly, not a single face was turned towards the ships, all the men, who minutes before had been in the utmost state of dejection, were reinvigorated, becoming animated and cheerful at the prospect of action, of having something positive to do. This moment was to see Wellington's 'scum' at their best.

The British Army prepared to take on Soult despite some of Moore's officers trying to persuade him to negotiate his withdrawal without a battle. Rowland, forming part of Hope's division, had his brigade on the left on Monte Moro; Leith and Manningham were to his right. For most of the battle, Hill's troops were scarcely used; there were a few skirmishes when his old enemy from Roliça, de

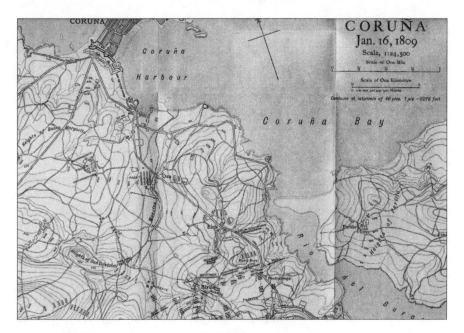

Corunna. (Sir John Fortescue's *History of the British Army*)

Laborde, pushed his *tirailleurs* out ahead, to, as Oman puts it, 'bicker with the skir-mishers of Hill, Leith and Manningham'. Meanwhile the 42nd (The Black Watch) and the 50th on the heights above Elvina, led by Colonel Sterling and Charles Napier, advanced, pressing forward and driving the enemy back into the village. The French, under Mermet, sent in support and drove out the 50th, capturing the wounded Charles Napier. Little of note had happened on the left wing bar General Hill having sent Colonel Nicholls and some companies of the 14th Regiment together with two companies of the 92nd Highlanders from the divisional reserves to clear out the village of Piedralonga at the bottom of the valley lying between the two enemy lines.[119] As dusk fell, both sides ceased to push forward and firing stopped. The French were beaten off and the British embarked for England.

On the death of Sir John Moore and the wounding of Sir David Baird, Sir John Hope had become Commander in Chief. General Hill's infantry brigade, together with that of Beresford, was involved in protecting the embarkation and was one of the last to board ship, rowing out to their transport as French shells fell around them. The British claimed a victory, as did the French. What is indisputable is that both sides had endured horrible suffering and it could logically be considered a sometimes more, sometimes less honourable 'draw'. Approximately 6000 men out of 33,000 had lost their lives in the course of the retreat.

It was on this voyage back to England and after disembarkation at Plymouth at the end of January that Hill was first to come to public notice for his care of the sick and wounded. Such an impression was made on the people of Plymouth that, later, he was to be given first the freedom of the city and later still, the governorship. The Mayor of Plymouth, George Bellamy, wrote to Rowland in 1812 to inform him of the Corporation's desire to offer him the Freedom of the City. 'When you were at Plymouth, I, in the midst of thousands, silently admired you, and had a greater opportunity than many of so doing, as I was employed in the Committee of Inhabitants to administer relief to the troops, their wives and children, when landed here from Coruna.'

The appearance of the roughly 26,000 troops who were landed on the south coast of England after enduring a very rough passage was so appalling that those civilians who saw them were shocked and distressed. There were some 3000 sick and injured, suffering in many cases from fever and dysentery. Oman wrote that it was seldom that a nation sees its soldiers returning from a battlefield with the grime and sweat of battle fresh upon them and the impression was a very unhappy one.

The retreat from Sahagun to Corunna had taken a terrible toll, and not only on the British Army; the French under Soult had not escaped the bitter weather and other privations during their pursuit and Old Salt's army was very relieved to reach Porto with all the stores and food the men could wish for.

IV

WAR WITHOUT END, A PIPE OF PORT

On his arrival back in England at the end of January, 1809, Rowland was first occupied with seeing to the welfare of his men after landing at Plymouth. He then had a very short stay, just five days, at home at Hawkstone. He had already received word that his uncle, Sir Richard Hill, 2nd Baronet, had died and that his father, John Hill, had succeeded his childless brother to the baronetcy and the estates of Hawkstone. One might say that John Hill more than made up for the fact that several of his brothers were childless, by producing sixteen children himself. Sir Richard had left Rowland the property of Hardwicke Grange a few miles distant from Hawkstone and also the sum of £2,000. Sir Richard had been enormously proud of his soldier nephew and must have been fully aware that living on one's pay as a Major General with no private income was very difficult.

Hill's arrival home was also greeted with the news that he had been awarded the Colonelcy of the 3rd Garrison Battalion; this was primarily an honorary role giving recognition to successful generals; such men often had a regimental connection. Hill is only recorded as holding this office for the year of 1809. In the same year, he was also made Colonel of the 94th, a position he held until 1815.

On 17 February, less than three weeks after he had returned, exhausted, from Corunna, Hill received orders from the Commander in Chief, HRH the Duke of York, directing him to take charge of regiments which were about to embark at Cork for the Peninsula. He realised that, after all, the British government had not given up hope of releasing the Portuguese – and perhaps eventually the Spanish – from Napoleon's grip. When one considers that many of the soldiers who had been on the retreat to Corunna were not considered fit enough to serve back in the Peninsula for many months,[120] it does seem extraordinary that Rowland was only home for three weeks.

Once at Cork, he received orders from Lord Castlereagh dated 23 March 1809 directing him to set sail for the Tagus just as soon as the troops under his orders had been embarked. On his arrival in Portugal, he was to be under the command of Lieutenant General Sir John Cradock, a most unadventurous soldier under whom he had already served in Egypt. 'Beau' Cradock was nervously awaiting Hill with the additional troops and had made no move against the French. Marshal Beresford, who was busy trying to put the Portuguese Army onto some sort of firm footing, was pleased to greet Rowland on his arrival. These two men were never close friends but each recognised qualities in the other. There was always considerable jealousy amongst Beresford's peers concerning his most elevated rank; in order to make him Commander of the Portuguese Army he had had to be created a Field Marshal but Wellington used to reassure those that were unhappy with this vast leap in rank by saying that it was only 'local' rank.

The Portuguese regiments had been in a disastrous state for years and many of the better officers had decamped to Brazil with the Court and the Royal Family. English officers, including Rowland Hill's brother, Thomas Noel Hill of the First Foot Guards, were now drafted in to command the Portuguese regiments and to act, 'like stiffeners in the jelly'. These officers were all promoted one grade. As soon as the Portuguese men had been drilled to a certain level, one Portuguese battalion was incorporated into each British brigade. On the whole, this worked very well and the Portuguese battalions became integral parts of the British divisions and more than proved their worth in combat. The British Army had been so decimated by the retreat to Corunna that without these Portuguese troops, Wellington would have been in poor shape for the new campaign. It was as well that they ultimately proved such good soldiers because their total upkeep was paid for by the British.

Hill received a letter from General Cradock dated 22 April 1809. For once, even Sidney[121] seems to have grasped the essence of this cautious missive:

Leyria, April 22, 1809

Dear Sir
In sending forward the corps under your command, I beg to explain to you that it is more to procure accommodation for the troops than for any other purpose. Were I to entertain any apprehension of the approach of the enemy beyond Coimbra, I should not think it prudent to station your corps at Pombal, twenty miles distant, and so far from the main body. But lest any unforeseen occurrence should arise, I conceive it proper to give you these instructions.

Situated as you will be, your chief object is to gain as much intelligence as your distant situation from the enemy will permit, and prevent any predatory incursion, either to annoy you, or give any alarm that would discredit the opinion of security from all insult which we imagine.

Should a small force of the enemy appear, I have no doubt but that you will make him repent his temerity; but if he approaches in superior numbers, or that you have reason to imagine his strength may be an increasing one, and such as would commit you in a general affair, I am to desire that you will fall back upon the main body, or towards them, giving me the most immediate notice.

Given the timidity demonstrated in this letter, it was fortunate that Wellington arrived in Lisbon the following day and the over-cautious Cradock went off to govern Gibraltar. Wellington's arrival to take charge was greeted with enthusiasm by the whole army including, one assumes, Rowland Hill.

Wellington had arrived in Portugal to find that his old enemy, Marechal Soult, had taken possession of Porto some three weeks earlier. Marechal Nicholas Jean de Dieu Soult had risen from the ranks, which was far more common in the French Army than in the British. He was one of Napoleon's most successful generals but, apparently, a most unpleasant man with delusions of grandeur. He was considered by many to be an excellent tactician – although Wellington would have disagreed. As far as the British Army was concerned, it was important to push the French out of the Douro valley with its abundance of freely available food together with fodder for the horses and baggage mules. So Wellington decided to take on Soult first before turning his attention to Marechal Victor, who was farther east guarding the road to Madrid and keeping an eye on the Spanish General Cuesta. At the same time, Ney was in Galicia trying to keep local uprisings under control.

Ever the imaginative tactician, Wellington weighed up his choices and decided to approach Porto between the rivers of the Douro and the smaller Vouga. He devised a cunning approach having discovered that Lake Ovar lay apparently unguarded behind the French lines. He decided to try and turn the enemy's right wing by carrying his troops, secretly, by water. General Hill was entrusted with the mission. The operation has been described many times but the story is never precisely the same. Here, I have drawn upon three principal sources, which seem to agree for the most part: the orders quoted in letters from Wellington himself, and in his orders conveyed by the Quartermaster General, George Murray, quoted in *The Life of Lord Hill*,[122] Oman's very full description and also that of Ian Robertson in *Wellington at War in the Peninsula*. Hill's division, the 3rd, consisted of 4,400 men. His brief was to take advantage of the presence of some small boats, *maceira,* used for the collection of seaweed, waiting at Aveiro. These craft, according to Oman, had been assembled by the local magistrates.

Wellington desired Hill to find boatmen willing to take the soldiers through the great lagoon, also known as Lake Ovar, at the mouth of the Vouga. This marshy, swampy stretch of water runs parallel to the sea separated only by a narrow sandbank and stretches for 15 miles. The town of Ovar lies at the northern end of the stretch of water and it was here that Hill was instructed to land his light infantry, just below the town in a place where the enemy was unlikely to discover him during the disembarkation. His first boatloads of men reached Ovar as the sun rose on the 10th and hearing from the locals that the French, under General Jean Baptiste Francheschi, were still at some distance, but that there was some French infantry encamped quite near, Rowland kept his men within the walls of Ovar and sent the boats back for Charles Stewart and the rest of his men. At noon General Mermet finally got word of the landing and drove in Hill's pickets with the 31st Leger. The afternoon was occupied in rather futile skirmishing but when Rowland heard that the Light Dragoons were approaching to his support, he pushed forward from Ovar and forced the French *voltigeurs* to fall back. On 11 May Hill was to advance as fast as possible on the Ovar/Porto road and complete the encirclement of the French by gaining their rear. Once Mermet and Francheschi realised that their flanking men were being driven in on either side and that Hill was marching on their rear to complete the Allied Army's encirclement, they ordered a retreat without delay.

What impressed Wellington most about this skirmish was that it was the first time the Portuguese had been sent into battle, and they had behaved excellently; it was a very great relief to him after the dealings he had had with the Spanish. Wellington had written to Hill in his orders that it was his intention to push the enemy right back into Porto if possible. In fact, they withdrew that evening to Villa Nova in the suburbs of Porto and by sunrise they had vanished into the city destroying the pontoon bridge behind them – the only bridge across the river. Once in the city, they joined together with Marechal Soult, who must have felt very comfortable, situated as he was with a broad river in full flood between him and the enemy. The layout of Porto makes it hard to attack. The streets are almost vertical as they descend from the heights rising behind the city on the north bank, which Soult thought impregnable, down to the river bank. The Marechal had given strict orders that all boats were to be either destroyed or brought to the northern side. By now, of course, Soult had heard of Hill's approach through the lagoons and his attention was totally focused in a westerly direction. He personally had an excellent view of the ground to the west from the villa he was occupying on the heights above the city. He did not apparently consider looking eastwards;[123] his view would in fact have been obstructed by the curve of the river where the cliff is surmounted by the convent of Our Sister da Serra do Pilar. He does not apparently seem to have given a thought to the possibility of an attack coming from this direction. He obviously felt that he could retire at his own pace, taking the road east for Spain. The following morning he sent off his wounded and all the baggage under the escort of General Mermet.

Wellington, on the south bank, hid most of his army, the columns of Hill, Sherbrooke and Paget, behind the reverse slope of the hill opposite a large building, where they were invisible to onlookers from the northern bank. This was to become one of his favourite tactics when the lie of the land was suitable and

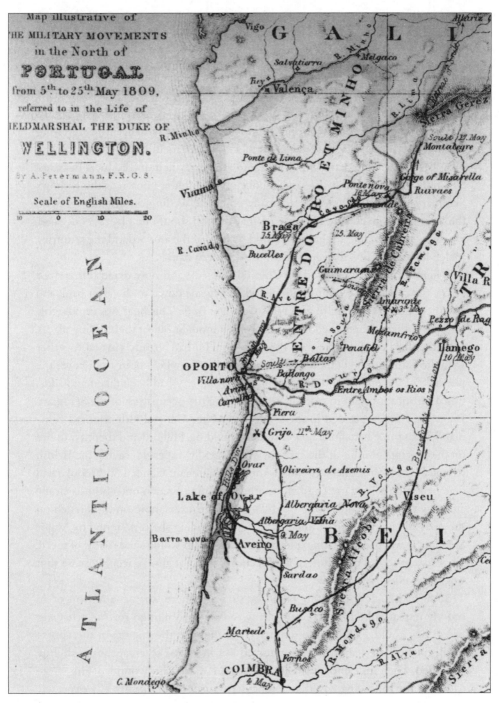

Northern Portugal showing Hill's crossing of Lake Ovar towards Oporto. (Sir John Fortescue's *History of the British Army*)

was to contribute to many of his victories. Wellington then gathered together a group of local Porto inhabitants who were familiar with the lanes of the city and the present disposition of the French troops and picked their brains for any useful information. As he stood on the cliff sweeping the river valley and the heights on the opposite side with his telescope, he could see no sign of the French upstream; in fact it looked extraordinarily quiet. He had sent out a number of scouts and now one of the best, Colonel John Waters, was to return with interesting intelligence. He had discovered a number of boats, including a ferry, that had been carelessly 'sunk', and which were now being bailed dry by local peasants. Secondly, he pointed out the large, unoccupied building known as the Bishop's Seminary, which Wellington had already observed. Wellington instantly grasped the importance of all this. He ordered that cannon should be placed, concealed, where he was standing so that they could be fired at the area around the seminary, which lay almost directly opposite on the northern bank.

When the boats discovered by Colonel Waters[124] and now dried out arrived below the convent, Wellington hurried Hill's brigade down to the river bank and saw them embarked. The first to cross were the Buffs. This boat was rapidly followed by others, which the local peasants now brought out of their hiding places, with the third carrying General Paget across. Hill had already crossed together with the 48th and the 66th. It had taken the French a whole hour to discover the presence of the enemy and by that time the Seminary had been taken and additional fortifications put in place. Early on during the occupation of the Seminary, Paget was badly wounded in the arm[125] and Major General Hill assumed command. With three battalions now inside the building, Hill ordered the men to fire on the passing columns of the French, which rapidly dispersed leaving the British five pieces of their artillery. In the meantime, Lieutenant General Sherbrooke had marched into the city itself and chased the remaining French out, enthusiastically aided by the local people. One of Hill's guns, a howitzer, bore on the French on the quayside below. It fired one of the new exploding shells designed by Major Shrapnel; it was packed with explosive powder which would send shards of metal, known as spherical case shot, in all directions.[126] If not always accurate, case shot was a very effective weapon.

Soult had been completely taken by surprise; there was no question of an orderly retreat as he instructed the army to take the Vallongo road in whatever order they could. Hill left the seminary and pursued the enemy. In the course of this pursuit, de Laborde was unhorsed but managed to escape, only slightly wounded, when his captor was killed; General Foy was also wounded. Hill wrote to Maria the following day that 'Events have turned out exactly as I expected. Marshal Soult's army got so completely beat and frightened on the 12th that their retreat became a perfect flight.'

ADC brother Clement had been struck by a spent ball and was listed amongst the wounded but made haste to assure his family that he was fine. He added in his

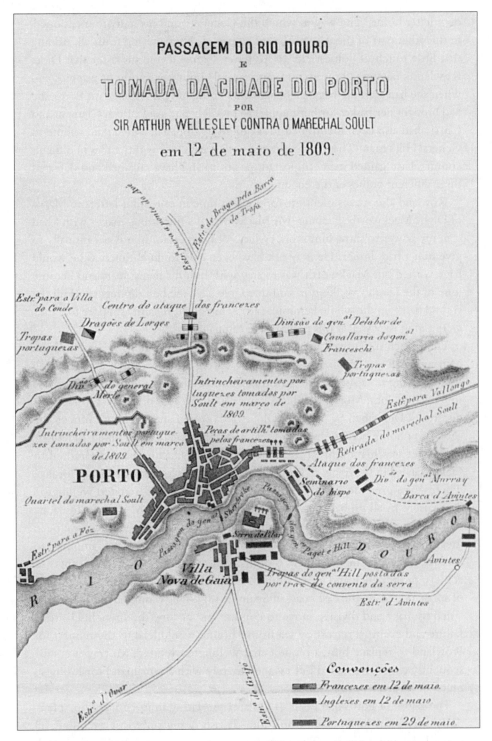

Porto, showing Hill's crossing point to the seminary on the north bank. (Sir John Fortescue's *History of the British Army*)

own letter home, 'The way in which the General[127] and his staff are mentioned, in the other part of the despatch, is, of course, highly flattering to us all.' Adding that little touch of domesticity to his letter, Clement told his sister that Dido, Rowland's favourite hound, was very careful about her family of puppies and when she had seen the baggage being taken off before the advance on Porto, she had brought her basket for her puppies to be safely put inside. Both Clement and Currie had also been mentioned in Wellington's dispatch, which paid tribute to General Hill's men: 'They have marched in four days over eighty miles of difficult country, have gained many important positions and have engaged and defeated three different bodies of the enemy's troops.'

Rowland also makes mention, for the first time in one of his letters to Maria, of Digby Mackworth,[128] saying, 'Mr Mackworth is a fine young man: I wish I had it in my power to show him more civility. All I can do for him is occasionally to give him a bad dinner.' He may not have been able to do as much as he would have wished but Mackworth was to stay with him for many years and became 'one of the family'. Wellington said that Cole gave the best dinners and Hill the second best[129] in the whole Peninsular Army but one can hardly suppose that they were eating very well at this point of the campaign.

The French might well have suffered much more damage if General Sir John Murray[130] had not remained a spectator, watching in safety from a neighbouring hilltop giving no assistance to his cavalry until Wellington sent Charles Stewart to fetch him. John Murray's military career, with the very briefest interludes, was disastrous. Described by Michael Glover as 'a stupid and irresolute officer', he soon went home because he feared that he might have to serve under Beresford. The latter was his junior in the British Army, but having been promoted to Field Marshal in the Army of Portugal, could be said to outrank Murray 'locally'. There was a great deal of this business of seniority and it irritated Wellington immensely. In all probability having already encountered Murray in India, he never wanted him in the first place. General Hill does not seem to have been greatly exercised by such squabbles and, although he must have had ambition to succeed (as indeed he did), there is no indication that he trampled on others to achieve prominence and glory. John Murray was put in command of an army of some 18,000 on the east coast of Spain in 1813. This was intended to serve as a diversionary and divisive move to confuse and occupy the French. His total failure and eventual retreat by sea from Alicante would lead to the request for Rowland to replace him; a request that Wellington refused. Murray was subsequently court-martialled but escaped merely with a reprimand for losing so much of his artillery.

The Battle of Porto had been, as Oman says, 'daring in its conception, splendidly successful in its execution'. The British Army only lost 23 killed, 98 wounded[131] and 2 missing. The French had lost at least 300 killed in the attack on the seminary. A story often quoted is that Wellington sat down that evening to eat Soult's splendid dinner. Wellington was to find the hospitals in the city full of wounded. The city was also overflowing with port wine[132] but there was not much else for the British Army, as usual the French had stripped everything like a swarm of locusts.

Soult was concerned because he had failed to receive a message from General Loison for several days and when he did get news it was disastrous. Wretched Soult had had a heavy fall from his horse during the retreat from Porto and now he learned that Loison had been thrown back by Marshal Beresford's encircling movement and was retreating to the north-west while Soult was going east. Soult was a brave and ingenious general, and he decided to make a drastic and rash movement. He turned off the road to go over the mountains. The nature of the terrain meant that he was forced to leave all his guns, supplies, prisoners and horses, and after a few days his men were in much the same state as they had been on the pursuit of the English to Corunna, half starving and ragged.

It was in June that Wellington applied to Horse Guards for permission to award the local rank of Lieutenant General to both Lowry Cole and Hill, in order that they could be advanced over their seniors on the list. This was granted officially in August. One of the reasons was that with the arrival of Major General Christopher Tilson, that officer would have been put in command of Hill's 2nd Division because he was Rowland's senior on the Army list. With this promotion, Hill retained Divisional Command as 'incumbent'.

Wellington was pretty satisfied with the past few weeks' work and on hearing that Marshal Victor had entered eastern Portugal, he withdrew to Abrantes to collect his forces. The Army was suffering from a serious lack of supplies, the soldiers were again too often barefoot, badly fed and unpaid. This all led to serious indiscipline, with men plundering the countryside – and who can really blame them? Wellington described his army as 'a rabble, who cannot bear success any more than Sir John Moore's army could bear failure, there is not an outrage of any description which they have not committed ... we are an excellent army on parade, an excellent one to fight but we are worse than an enemy in a country. Take my word for it, either defeat or success would dissolve us.' Thus Wellington wrote to Lord Castlereagh on 17 June 1809. On the credit side, fortunately, the money for which he had been waiting so long finally arrived.

In June, Wellington spent a great deal of time 'designing' the formation of his army. See Appendix 111, an article taken from Oman's *Wellington's Army*: 'Divisional and Brigade Organisation and Changes, 1809–1814'. This was compiled by C.T. Atkinson, Fellow and Tutor of Exeter College, Oxford and sets out with great clarity the composition and commanders of the various divisions and brigades and the changes during the period.

From now on, Hill had the 2nd Division. This Division was almost always on the right wing, the position of 'honour', because he became the senior divisional commander. The commander second in seniority took the extreme left wing with the Brigadier Generals in the centre.

From Placencia on 10 July, Rowland wrote to Maria:

> I trust we have entered the country [Spain] in more favourable circumstances than we did last year. Our immediate success is, I think, pretty certain but whether we shall ultimately succeed in driving the French from Spain depends more on what happens elsewhere than what we can do ... it is very evident that the people of this country are hostile to the French and take every opportunity of annoying them – no individual or small parties dare venture from their camp or quarters for fear of the people – a French general and his two ADCs were sent in here a few days ago by the peasants.[133]

He refers to General Blake's[134] action at Belchite, which had been an abject failure with his army of 15,000 men having been routed by a vastly inferior force. Wellington's brother Henry referred to Blake sarcastically as very popular because he had won one battle and lost seventeen!

The British Army advanced slowly via Guarda and Castel Branco to Abrantes, where it stayed encamped, many soldiers without shoes or any means of transport, for some days. Rowland wrote home on 17 June saying that they were awaiting events. He felt that should Napoleon beat the Austrians and therefore keep things quiet in the north, then the Emperor would turn his attention to Spain. 'At present, our immediate neighbour and opponent, Marshal Victor, is rather retiring but I dare say he will not go far, if he has reason to expect reinforcements.' Wellington's situation was made even more difficult thanks to the obstinacy and stupidity of Cuesta, when they were anticipating battle at Talavera.

On 24 July, when the enemy had surprised everyone by withdrawing without offering battle, Cuesta had suddenly, in what Wellington could only imagine was a fit of jealousy, rushed his Spaniards forward in pursuit of the French. He was soon driven back in total disorder, Marechal Victor having been reinforced by King Joseph and Jourdan with the Madrid garrison, together with units from General Sebastiani. Far more seriously, on the 27th, when Marechal Victor sent forward some skirmishers thinking to stir up 2000 of the unsettled Spanish, the latter panicked, fired a volley when there was nobody remotely near enough to have been hit, and then ran away. They were then, including some of their officers, found plundering the British baggage train in the rear. In the face of such devastating cowardice and disorder, Cuesta finally acted. He ordered the execution of 200[135] of the Spanish deserters following the battle. It took many an action and finally the enforced retirement of Cuesta after suffering a stroke for Wellington to put his trust in the Spanish; in fact, it was often their officers who were the problem and not the men.

Wellington, well aware that Victor was approaching, carefully disposed his forces placing his left wing, including Hill's 2nd Division, on the reverse slopes of the Cerro de Medellin,[136] a position of great advantage. Sherbrooke was in the centre with Campbell to his right and with Cuesta and the Spanish on the extreme right, just outside the town of Talavara itself, where Wellington evidently trusted that 'the blundering old blockhead' could do no harm. The battle itself was in three acts. The first was unexpected and could have been a disaster for the Allies. It was there, on the eve of the Battle of Talavera on the Cerro de Medellin, a long hill most strategically placed, that Hill nearly met his end. Perhaps he was just a lucky general, since despite leading his men from the front on numerous occasions and exhibiting the greatest bravery, his wounds were never too serious despite having a number of horses killed under him and being rolled on by his mount several times. The flight of the Spanish before Talavera and the result-ant upheaval and reorganisation of the Allied Army probably led Marechal Victor, always ready to seize an opportunity, to risk a night attack on the evening of the 27th. Night attacks were both rare and risky.

What exactly happened on the eve of the Battle of Talavera is hard to piece together. What does seem certain is that due to a staff blunder, Hill never received Wellington's precise orders with regard to his station, which would have put him on the front line on the Medellin on the Allied left. In fact, his Division was some way behind. Thus the French under General Ruffin almost succeeded in gain-ing the highly strategic Cerro de Medellin and also – what would have been a significant bonus – capturing General Hill. The General had been in the course of redeploying his Division, Brigadiers Richard Stewart and Christopher Tilson together with some of the KGL, which he had found to be out of correct station, and was passing behind the 3rd Division of Major General Alexander Mackenzie to reach his battle post on the left of Lieutenant General Sherbrooke, when he heard shots being fired up on the Cerro. Suddenly there were shouts of 'the hill, the hill'. Thinking it was one of his own regiments making a blunder (it is sug-gested that he thought it was the Buffs), he rashly rode up to put a stop to it. Far from being his own men, it was the French 9th Leger 'swarming up the shadowy slope with drums beating and cries of "Vie l'Empereur!".' They overwhelmed some KGL who were resting and having something to eat (how fortunate they were to have anything) before Hill and his few staff arrived to investigate. Hill was very nearly captured when a French dragoon caught hold of his arm and he only escaped by digging his spurs hard into the flanks of his wounded horse caus-ing it to leap out of range. He galloped into the ranks of the 29th Regiment. He instantly ordered these men up and they drove the French from the hill top and down into the gulley formed by the river Portina way below.[137]

It was crucial to Wellington's tactics that he held the Cerro and if the French had managed to gain hold of it, the battle might well have gone very differently. Although he described the event somewhat briefly to his sister in a letter after the second day of fighting, some years later he later wrote a fuller account in reply to an 'officer of high rank':[138]

I recollect on the 27th of July, I got some dinner in my quarters in the town of Talavera about four o'clock. Immediately after I rode out accompanied by Major Fordyce, towards the Alberche, in which direction we heard some fighting. I returned to the bivouac of my division, I suppose about sunset, when I found it had moved to take up a position. I instantly followed it and found it deploying in line and was shown by somebody where the right was to rest. I pointed out the hill on the line of direction we were to take up. I found, however, I had not sufficient troops to occupy the ground without leaving considerable intervals between the regiments. During this operation I recollect perfectly well that I was with the 48th Regiment, in conversation with Colonel Donellan, when it being nearly dark, I observed some men on the hill-top fire a few shots amongst us. Not having an idea that the enemy were so near, I said at the moment that I was sure it was the Old Buffs, as usual, making some blunder. I desired Donellan to get into line and I would ride up the hill and stop their firing. On reaching the hill top, I found the mistake I had made. I immediately turned round to ride off, when they fired and killed poor Fordyce and shot my mare through the body. She did not fall but carried me to the 29th Regiment, which corps, by my orders, instantly charged the French and drove them from the hill. I do not know what numbers the enemy had but I think they were not strong – perhaps some of their light troops.[139]

It was typical of the man that he did not magnify the opposing force as so many of his peers might well have done. He was lucky not to have been either killed or taken prisoner; a general was a valuable prize.

Act Two was played out the following morning after everyone had had an uneasy night's rest. The Allied Army – certainly the British part of it – was fighting on empty stomachs, the promised supplies had still not been provided by the Spanish. At 5am, just as the sun rose, the first guns were fired from the Casjacal ridge behind the French Army, announcing the start of the enemy's attack. Soon a huge force could be seen from the British lines, Hill's men on the Cerro could count at least 40,000 Frenchmen below on the plain. The French attacked with three columns moving slowly upwards. Hill's reaction was 'Damn their filing, let them come in anyhow,'[140] which certainly has a Wellingtonian ring to it. Thanks to Wellington employing the same tactic that had been so successful before, most of the men had remained lying down until the French columns were close enough to receive the full blast of the British rolling volleys at close range. Victor's attack was thrown back. There was now the *entre'acte,* when, under a truce, both sides collected their dead and wounded. The British buried their dead on the Medellin and the men drank from the Portina, the waters of which were probably sullied with blood and corpses.

There was still the third act to come because Victor was not prepared to give up and the reinforcements he had been waiting for were now almost on the ground. These were under the command of Generals Sebastiani and Lapisse. On seeing the vast, reinforced host opposed to him, Wellington asked Cuesta to give him support; the old general was so ashamed of his own men's perform-ance the day before that he agreed for once – but his idea of 'support' was to send Wellington two guns. The Allies were hopelessly outnumbered, as usual, but Rowland led the 48th down into the gulley and joined with Mackenzie's 3rd Division to fill the hole in the Allied centre while the Guards and the King's German Legion reformed behind them. These two regiments had taken a terrible beating. Somehow, out of defeat, the Allied Army conjured a victory; the French under Sebastiani retiring with General Lapisse killed.

Rowland wrote a more immediate description of the action for Maria from Talavera on 30 July:

God has protected Clement and myself in two of the severest battles I ever witnessed which took place on the 27th and 28th ... For the particulars I must refer you to the public dispatches but cannot help mentioning a few circum-stances which will show you the providential escapes we have had. About a week ago I told you that the French had retired from Talavera on our approach towards them. It now appears they did this, not with the intention of going off altogether, but for the purpose of meeting their reinforcements, which being done by the junction of Sebastiani's force of about 12,000 and King Joseph from Madrid with 6000[141]. Early on the 27th we heard of the returning of the French and as the day advanced they approached nearer. By four in the evening their whole force was in sight, and continued moving forward, driving in our outposts, till they came within reach of shot from our lines, when they halted; and as night was coming on we did not expect any serious attack till the next morning. It was however scarcely dusk when there was a heavy fire of mus-ketry on my post, and a severe struggle on the part of the enemy to carry it, in which they did not succeed and in about half an hour gave up the contest. On this occasion poor Fordyce[142] was killed, my horse was shot, and I myself had a fortunate escape from the hands of a French soldier who had got hold of my right arm, and would have secured me if my horse had not at that moment sprung forward. The Frenchman fired at me but did not touch me. Clement and Captain Currie were in the midst of the whole, but fortunately escaped ... In the morning when day broke, we observed the whole French army drawn up in order of battle; the greater part of their force immediately opposite my post which was evidently the point of attack and which, if they could have gained, would have given them the day ... the fire was tremendous on both sides, but the French could not force us. My horse was wounded early in the action. I got another from an officer. Shortly before the enemy gave up the conflict, I was struck by a musket-ball near my left ear and the back of my head. The blow was so violent that I was obliged to leave the field ... I continued unwell the whole of the next day and the next; I am, however, thank God, much better today. My hat saved my life; it has suffered as much as my helmet did on the 13 March.[143] Clement is safe; his horse was killed, and he had three musket-balls in him on the 28th. Currie is also safe, but had his horse killed under him ... In about four or five hours the enemy's fire slackened for a short time; they, however, afterwards began as serious [an] attack on General Campbell as they did on me, and meeting with the same reception from him, and the whole as they did in the morning, were fairly beat, and in the evening after dark, went off. The loss on both sides is very great. Indeed, ours probably 4000, the enemy's 7000. King Joseph was in the field though not in the fire. When it is considered that the French force was double ours, and solely employed against the British, we may count the battle of Talavera, amongst the most glorious that ever took place.

On 1 August he wrote her another letter from Talavera, saying that British losses were nearer 5000 men and 200 officers, and that it had been a 'dear bought' victory and not one that could be repeated as more such losses could spell outright defeat.[144] The battle on the 28th had lasted five hours. He reassured her that he was now feeling fine with just a little stiffness in his neck. He thought his horses would recover despite one of them having received two shots through the withers and one in the saddle! He tells her that her little mare is fine, as is Dido, his greyhound, who had a litter of puppies when they were at Abrantes.

Meanwhile the French had retreated to Toledo leaving behind wagons, fifteen cannon, a quantity of baggage, the wounded and prisoners, including a general. Wellington was especially gratified with the victory after the enemy had referred to him as 'incompetent'. 'If anything could add to the pleasure which we at present feel, it is that Sebastiani is among the wounded generals. We know this pert, bragging Italian-blooded Frenchman well and the contempt with which he habitually expresses himself of this Nation.'[145] Wellington was in no state to pursue the retreating French; he had no supplies and the men were receiving about one quarter of their allowances; the horses were also in a bad way. Hill even had one of his foraging parties fired upon by some Spanish who stole mule-loads of corn. The conduct of the Spanish was 'disgraceful beyond all conception. They would neither supply provisions, relieve the wounded, nor help bury the dead, refusing, as Sir Arthur [Wellington] observed, "assistance and necessaries which any other country in the world would have given even to its enemies".'[146]

Hill also refers to the action at Porto saying that he is rather surprised that Paget is given so much of the credit when he was wounded and put out of action, 'so very early in the affair'. This was careless of the Duke in not giving credit where it was due but he could frequently be accused of this; not necessarily deliberately but probably as the result of writing his dispatches under difficult circumstances. Rowland knew that brother Tom was safe and, although only some 30 miles away, was too busy with the training of his Portuguese regiment to pay them a visit.

Talavera had been the first major victory in the battle for the Peninsula for the British but it had no real strategic long term effect and the men remained half-starved thanks to the obduracy of the Spanish Junta who always made the classic promise of '*manana*' when it came to a question of supplies. Such in fact was the state of his army that Wellington was forced to withdraw back into Portugal, an action that the Junta put down to personal pique; but it did lead them to offer him the post of Captain General following Cuesta's stroke, which rendered him, fortunately, unfit for further service. He was succeeded by the equally inept General Areizaga but at least Wellington now had overall command. It was following his success at Talavera that Wellesley was to become 'Wellington'. Hill received the Colonelcy of the 94th Regiment and the thanks, announced in the House of Commons by the Prime Minister, Spencer Percival, of a grateful nation.

V

OFF THE LEASH

Rowland wrote to Maria on 10 November 1809 from his HQ at Montejo. He told her that a large number of the men were sick with 10,000 or more of them in hospital. He did not think that the Army could muster more than 13,000 in the field. Even Hill seems to think at this moment that the army would soon be evacuated to England and tells her not to send his man servant, Joseph, out from England. The sickness seems to have taken the form of a fever which could have been a type of malaria. Although Hill avoided it at that time, he was to be severely stricken a year later.

The two brothers, Clement and Rowland were now in quite a comfortable billet in the house of a prosperous farmer about 20 miles from the Army's HQ at Badajos. Clement describes the family as having 'a wife and two daughters not quite of the first class but dressing smart when they went to mass on a Sunday' and he added that in Badajos 'there was a great display of beauty and fashion.' He also comments on the quantity of wool which is sent from the region around Montejo to England. 'I cannot say much for the beauty of the sheep that produces it. Rowland has bought four from our landlord which are to accompany our milk goats, till we have an opportunity of sending or bringing them to England to improve the Shropshire breed. We lead quite a quiet country life going out a-coursing here several times a week though I should not wonder if Bonaparte gave us a chase of another sort some of these mornings.'

Rowland's division was inspected by Lord Wellington and Rowland was promoted to Lieutenant General, a rank that Wellington had been trying to obtain for him for some time. His previous appointment had only been 'local' rank. He was just 37 years old.

Hill wrote home, 'We have excellent coursing here and now and then a fox hunt and sometimes attack a wild boar and the deer.' By the end of November, he was writing in a more serious vein, saying that affairs in the country seemed to be drawing to a crisis and describing an unwise action undertaken by the Spanish, in the course of which they had lost 15,000 men as prisoners. He writes, too, that the army is still suffering acutely from sickness; his servant John Holding was almost recovered. He encloses a portrait that Clement has done of the Spanish huntsman with his horn being a sort of 'pipe lute or whistle' with which he plays tunes to collect the dogs and animate the sportsmen.

Wellington was no stickler for dress and unnecessary regulations and there was nothing to stop the officers, at any rate, from enjoying themselves. Grattan of the Connaught Rangers, who has left one of the best descriptions of life at this period, describes 'the Peer' as an indulgent commander who never harassed the men with needless reviews and the like, although the Portuguese and newly arrived troops did undergo plenty of drill. All that was required of them, Grattan wrote, was 'that we brought our men into the field well appointed, and with sixty rounds of good ammunition each, he never looked to see whether their trousers were black, blue or grey.' After the deprivations of Talavera, the men became more cheerful and found ingenious ways to amuse themselves. Hill, just a few miles from HQ at Portalegre, had the pack of hounds that had been sent out from Hawkstone by his brother John, which afforded much pleasure to the officers.

During October, Wellington had spent his time on horseback covering the countryside to the north of Lisbon; he was formulating perhaps his greatest plan of the whole campaign, a line of defence to protect Lisbon. This famous 'barrier,' the lines of Torres Vedras, was to render Lisbon virtually impregnable thus keeping open the Army's lines of supply and reinforcement and also reassuring the Portuguese that they were not being abandoned. To be sure, Napoleon's 'hideous leopard' was not going to be driven out easily. Colonel Sir Richard Fletcher, Wellington's chief engineer, was in charge of the project. He had an almost unlimited supply of manpower supplied by the Portuguese militia.

The works were started in the autumn of 1809 and consisted of a line of forts and redoubts placed on the summit of hills and on other natural and also man-made obstacles, with the first line stretching from the mouth of the river Zizandra on the Atlantic Ocean via Torres Vedras itself, to Pero Negro, Wellington's HQ, and on to the Tagus estuary, some 46km farther to the east at Alhandra. The western end of this first line was low-lying and by damming the Zizandra, a large area was flooded creating a vast bog, impassable to an army with guns. The second line lay about 13km to the south of the first, and reached from Ericeira on the Atlantic, passing just north of Mafra and south of Bucellas to the Tagus at Ribamar. The third line was 40km south of the second line and was much shorter. Its purpose was to protect the city of Lisbon itself and also a harbour on the coast, San Julian, where the army could be embarked if the necessity should arise. A fourth line was constructed on the southern side of the Tagus estuary to prevent attack from that direction. In addition to the forts themselves, which varied in size, there were deep ditches, 15 feet wide and 10 feet deep and some narrow valleys were

The Lines of Torres Vedras. (From Ian Robertson's *A Commanding Presence*)

filled with tangled olive trees which would have proved very difficult to shift. In addition to the construction of the fortifications, the Royal Navy helped to build semaphore stations, which permitted word to reach Wellington's HQ from any point in four minutes. The project took almost a year to complete and cost £100,000.

The most extraordinary thing about this whole undertaking, a mammoth task involving thousands of people under the direction of Colonel Fletcher, was that apparently no word of it reached the French.

In December, Rowland received the following letter from Wellington.

Badajoz, Dec 18, 1809

My dear Hill

In the arrangements for the defence of Portugal I shall form two principal corps, both consisting of British and Portuguese troops, the largest of which will be to the northwards and I shall command it myself and the latter will be for the present upon the Tagus and hereafter it may be moved forward into Alemtejo; and I will not make any arrangements either as to the troops that are to comprise it or as to the officer who is to command it, without offering the command of it to you.

At the same time, I will not separate you from the army, and from my own immediate command, without consulting your wishes; and I shall be glad to hear from you on this subject as soon as possible, as the arrangements for quartering and disposing of the troops depend upon your decision upon this point.

You will therefore send back either a messenger, if you can get one, or an officer, with your answer as soon as possible.

On 4 January 1810, Rowland wrote to Maria from Abrantes confirming that the entire British Army had at least temporarily left Spain and that they were now clear of the unhealthy plains of Estramadura. It seemed to him likely that the British would remain to defend Portugal and he tells her of his new role as commander of a detached corps that will remain on the Tagus. 'I am aware of the importance of the situation I am placed in, and trust, I shall be attended with the same good fortune I have hitherto experienced.' He is modest as ever in relaying this good news. It was another occasion for celebration at Hawkstone.

The early part of January 1810 was spent by Hill at Abrantes. The works of Torres Vedras were still under construction and Rowland lent several of his artificers to Captain Patton of the Engineers. On 6 January, he received a brief note from Wellington telling him that he was not forgotten but that the writer had been so busy that he had not had time to formulate Hill's orders. However, from 9 January onwards, correspondence flew between Wellington and Hill covering movements of troops, accommodation for cavalry, payments, commissariat, ammunition, magazines, bridges and all other relevant matters. Finally, on 12 February, Hill was instructed to move towards Portalegre from where he would keep an eye on the French who were thought to be approaching Badajos. He was also to be responsible for all convalescent and sick and to move them if necessary to the safety of Elvas. Rowland moved his corps forward and was soon once again billeted at Portalegre. Here he had the fortune to be quartered in the house of a most charming and attentive hostess, the Donna Francisca Rosa Barba. He and Clement reflected that their previous 'host' in Montejo would have been glad to exchange places with this Senora, since that poor farmer was now burdened by having the French billeted on him. A principal object of this present advance was to ensure the safety of the sick and wounded, most of whom were now removed to Lisbon.

Hill's corps consisted of his old 2nd Division, two brigades of Portuguese infantry amounting to 4000 and a brigade of British cavalry under Major General Slade, (which could not have imbued him with much confidence),[147] the 4th Regiment of Portuguese cavalry and one brigade of German and two of Portuguese artillery; a truly international army. The French having moved away from Badajos on receiving the news of his arrival at Portalegre, Hill was occupied in strengthening his position and making effective arrangements for communicating with Wellington. He was also in constant contact with the Marquis Romana,[148] one of the few reliable Spanish generals.

Around the second week in April, the French seemed to be making ready to attack Ciudad Rodrigo, one of the two toughest frontier fortresses, but the siege was not to commence until the beginning of June. Leading the siege was the grandly titled Prince d'Essling, Marechal Massena, a very able general, known as Napoleon's wily old fox, or rather more romantically, 'the favoured child of victory' and the first soldier to be created a Marechal by Napoleon. Massena was appointed to head the Army of Portugal, which would bring him into combat with his nemesis, Wellington. By now the French had approximately 320,000 troops in Spain but despite this enormous disparity in size between the Allied and French Armies, the latter still had to deal with the Spanish *guerrillas* who swooped down on French pickets and foragers, torturing and then killing their captives in terrible ways. These men operated in loose groups and were a good source of intelligence for the British Army who relied heavily on them, as well as on their own few 'observing' officers such as the well known figures of Colquhoun Grant, Rees Gronow, John Waters, Andrew Leith Hay and Charles Somers Cocks. The intelligence provided by these extremely brave men was of inestimable value. Meanwhile, Napoleon was still inveighing against the British: 'When I show myself beyond the Pyrenees the frightened leopard [Wellington] will fly to the ocean to avoid shame, defeat and death.' He had, however, probably wisely, decided not to take command of his armies in Spain but had turned his attention to acquiring his new bride, Marie Louise of Austria.

Hill was now in constant contact with Romana and, although he could not approve of or agree with all the Spaniard's requests, he was always most diplomatic in the language he employed when declining to assist him in any hazardous scheme, such as Romana's wish that Hill should move nearer to Merida, which Hill considered to be most imprudent at that time. Hill then returned to his old HQ at Portalegre. His instructions from Wellington included the recommendation that 'whatever you decide upon will be right. I recommend to you, however, to proceed with great caution in respect to intelligence transmitted to you by the Marquis de la Romana and all the Spanish officers.' Today, much of the information that these generals received would be considered 'spin' or disinformation.

The month of May passed quietly for Hill although he wrote home to Maria on the 30th saying that he heard the French had greatly increased the size of their army and at the request of General O'Donnell[149] he had himself moved forwards to Arronches. His move evidently scared off the French, who retired but were not, in his opinion, likely to go very far. Clement also wrote home saying that they were still inactive and in a state of uncertainty since they heard of possible action in the north but had no confirmation. He also tells her that he has heard from Tom and that Beresford says his regiment, the 1st Portguese Regiment, is in the highest order. Clement is more often found to be commenting on the weather and the scenery than Rowland in his letters home. Now, writing early in June, he tells Maria that the countryside at its most beautiful and that he wishes he could transplant some of the orange groves to Hawkstone. The rains have, however, been continuing unusually late in the summer and their long awaited plans for a wolf hunt have had to be postponed several times.

At such a distance from the main body of the Allied Army, news came slowly and was often inaccurate or indeed, misinformation and so Hill could not be certain that the great border fortress of Ciudad Rodrigo had fallen to the French until confirmation of its capitulation by the Spanish, who had been holding it, finally arrived on 11 July. Hill was following General Regnier's movements closely and on the 13th, the Frenchman showed signs that he was about to cross the Tagus. Hill immediately sent word to Wellington saying that he would, himself, cross at Villa Vellia if necessary. He informed Romana of his intentions and received an excellent, if ungrammatical reply from the good Spaniard:

Badajos 14th July, 1810
It is no doubt that the enemy is crossing the Tagus at the same points you have the goodness to inform me, and consquently I have other to say to you that if you deem convenient to make a movement for my part I am ready to support them. I have ordered to GL Odonell to move towards Alcantera.

I have the honour to subjoin a copy of a letter send me by Genl. Odonell,[150] wich I preay to you to forward His Excellency Lord Wellington.

On the side of Seville no was a movement of the enemy. Rumour was spread
yesterday that he began his retreat towards Sierra Morena, but that deserve
confirmation.

At least he got his point across! One doubts that Rowland would have managed
as well in Spanish.

Hill's Chief Engineer, Captain Patten, was kept busy maintaining bridges – he
had received an unusually tart letter from the habitually mild General at the end
of February saying that he had heard part of the bridge at Abrantes, a vital link,
had fallen in. Now, in mid July, he reminds Patten that the crossings at Villa Velha,
Puntrato and Abrantes must be kept in good condition and that he requires constant reports as to their state.

September found Hill with his Corps at Sazedas, near Castello Branco, and
from here on the 12th he wrote to Wellington informing him that Regnier had
marched northwards and that some of his force had already reached Guarda.
Hill placed Colonel Carlo Le Cor with his Portuguese Cacadores at Fondao
and General Fane's brigade of dragoons at Castello Branco. Thus situated, he
told Wellington, he felt he was in as good a situation to defend the passes from
Sabrera Formosa as from Sazedas. Apparently the Hill brothers were not alone
in regretting their departure from Sazedas; when they had arrived there it had
been deserted except for the priest who was also their landlord, but as soon as
the local people understood that they would be both paid and protected by the
British, they slowly returned and had transformed the town into a prosperous
little market. Hill was known as a great disciplinarian where looting and stealing
were concerned but he was thus able to offer Major General Lord Clinton a well-
stocked table when his Lordship arrived on a visit from HQ.

By now word had arrived that a large French force had entered the Mondego
river valley and Rowland collected his troops and held them at Espinahal before
moving on to Foz d'Aronce on 21 September. He had anticipated Wellington's
wishes; the C in C wrote, 'It appears to me that the disposition which you have
made of your corps will answer perfectly.' By now the whole of Comte Regnier's
army had crossed the Tagus and was attacking Hill's outposts. On the 8th, Hill
received another message referring to the exchange of a prisoner, an officer.
Regnier writes coolly *Je n'ai jamais été assez près de vous pour vous proposer son
échange.'* The name of the man concerned is not mentioned, which is frustrating
but he would surely have been an officer of some rank. The letter was date-lined
Zarza la Mayor. Regnier was shortly going to wish himself once more at a greater
distance from Hill, one from which no exchange of prisoners would be possible.
The British generals frequently put no place name on their messages in order to
confuse the enemy should the letters be intercepted. Many messages were indeed
taken – it has to be said more by the British than by the French, in part thanks
to the *guerrillas* acting as extra, (ill-disciplined), independent bands. Often several

copies of the same message, if of real importance, would be sent with different people to try to ensure that at least one would reach its destination.

Moyle Sherer describes this retreat from the Mondego towards 'the Lines'. He writes graphically of the abandoned villages; a 'scorched earth' policy had been adopted by Wellington to prevent the French supporting themselves. Sherer recounts the lines of miserable peasants carrying what they could, very few having mules or carts to help them. For example when they reached the town of Thomar, previously occupied by at least 4000 people, there were about 100, all engaged in collecting up what they could carry away with them. Sherer recounts that the General was established in a small roadside chapel while he himself was well housed in a large church where the men, finding their cloaks were still wet from the rain, used the church vestments to keep warm at night. These men were practical and resourceful after so many years of hardship. Sherer's 'Recollections' are interesting because they are those of an educated man with a perceptive eye[151] and with the ability to commit his thoughts to paper; and what is probably more important, he did so at the time.

Some people blamed Wellington both for letting the great border fortress of Ciudad Rodrigo fall and for fighting the Battle of Busaco. Napier wrote 'It was extraneous to his original plan and forced upon him by events.' A week after the battle, Wellington said 'notwithstanding that our loss was really trifling, but I should have been inexcusable if, knowing what I did, I had not endeavoured to stop the enemy there.' The greatest outcome of the Battle of Busaco, apart from the fact that it was a victory, was to be the enhanced standing of the Portuguese regiments. Their success gave them pride and confidence in their ability and naturally this gave added assurance to their British allies.

Hill had arrived for the Battle of Busaco from the Tagus by forced marches with exhausted and badly supplied men; but he crossed the Mondego and still managed to arrive on the Sierra de Busaco, which Wellington had selected for a defensive action, in time. Once again, Wellington had known that he could count on him. It would seem that the French went into battle on 27 September with every advantage; their numbers were vastly superior, their soldiers mostly seasoned veterans and at their head was the great Marechal Massena, probably Bonaparte's most able general. On this occasion, however, one of the Marechal's encumbrances was his mistress, Madame Leberton, in the unlikely and unconvincing disguise of a dragoon. Busaco was not to prove Massena's greatest moment: perhaps he was distracted! On 26 September, Wellington had his troops lined up in battle array along an eight-mile front, facing Ney on the left, Regnier[152] on the right, leaving Junot[153] apparently in reserve. Although some sources say he commanded the centre, which would appear to make more logical sense. Wellington's greatest strength was, as so often, his position; surely no general ever selected his field of battle with such astuteness. Busaco is in wild, rather dramatic country with 'gloomy tree-clad heights and cloven crests, round which the mists hung in sullen vapour, an ideal position for defence. In its front was a valley forming a natural ditch so deep that the eye could scarcely pierce its depths.'[154] Wellington liked to have safe, reliable, intelligent and brave General Hill ready to support any weakness that might appear in the line and thus Hill's 14,000 men were concealed from the enemy, on the extreme right of the British position. The French were shocked when they eventually became aware of such a great reserve force and did not risk pushing forward on Hill's flank. It was the final effort made by the French to regain a foothold in Portugal. They failed and Mareschal Massena now found himself virtually cut off from Spain and with little alternative but to march off to the northwest. Wellington, in his turn, had little choice but to retire on Lisbon, although far from being 'driven into the sea', he was going into the protection of the Lines, of which Massena still remained in total ignorance.

The residents of Lisbon had been in a state of abject terror for days, expecting the reappearance of the French at any moment. In Wellington's dispatch written from Coimbra on 30 September, he describes the action in detail. He also draws particular attention to the actions of the Portuguese: '... the 4th Portuguese Caqadores, and the 1st and 16th Regiments, directed by Brigadier General Pack and commanded by Lieutenant Colonel Thomas Noel Hill[155] ... showed great steadiness and gallantry.' Once again, the behaviour of the Portuguese was a great relief to everyone, even more notable in comparison with some of the debacles with the Spanish. It was in fact especially gratifying since an intercepted letter from Bonaparte to Mafiona, while giving him a tolerably accurate estimate of British numbers, barely bothered to mention the Portuguese except to indicate that he held them very cheap. Colborne wrote some years after the event, perhaps with some exaggeration, 'The Battle of Busaco was gained solely in consequence of Hill's precise attention to Wellington's orders, for which he was always remarkable.'[156]

However, even now, the French were not finished with Portugal and were marching to try and get around the British left. On 11 September, Clement wrote home from Alhandra with the news:

> You will probably before you get this have heard of the army having fallen back to near Lisbon, which no doubt people in England will be disappointed to find after the victory at Busaco. It certainly was always Lord W's intention to do so in the event of the enemy advancing in force, as of course the farther they are drawn on the more difficulty they will meet with when defeated, which most certainly they will be if they are mad enough to attack us in our strong position which extends from this place on the Tagus to Mafra on the sea, the whole country between which is fortified ... we are in every respect well off, get all the good things from Lisbon and live in a palace. We are both quite well. Tom is not far from us; but I have not seen him lately.

The strong position was of course, the lines of Torres Vedras. Hill's Corps was on the extreme east side on the edge of the Tagus. Once the Allied forces were tucked up in the 'safety' of the Lines, many generals began to ask for leave. This infuriated Wellington; he constantly complained about the poor quality of the general officers he was sent; although this was to improve as the long war wound on and for one reason or another, generals were sent home or even, in many cases, requested to return. He wrote a stiff note to Colonel Torrens at the War Office, 'I shall be very much obliged to you if you would tell any General officer who may come out in future to settle all his business before he comes out, for that he will get no leave to go home.'[157]

Rowland writing to Maria from Montejo on 10 October, tells her that he, Clement and Tom are all quite well, he had received a letter from Thomas only a few days previously and had even received one from diplomat brother, Francis, which had been written on 12 July. 'I ... intend to keep two pigs tho', I fear, I shall have as much trouble with mine as the old woman had with hers to get it over the stile!' Although some of the Spanish sheep that Clement and Rowland were keeping and some of whose progeny were to be sent to Hawkstone,[158] are referred to in subsequent letters, there is no further mention of the pigs; perhaps they proved to be just too much trouble and provided a good feast on some memorable occasion. He mentions in the same letter that she (Maria) will probably have seen his promotion in the *Gazette*.

Men of the two opposing forces had begun to fraternise during this quiet period and eventually Hill had to step in: 'I have been obliged to put a stop to the intimacy which was going on – it was by no means uncommon to see the soldiers of each army gathering grapes from the same vineyard, water from the same well and asking each other to drink wine ... by this intercourse we have however, procured more information. The French certainly seem tired and dissatisfied with the war. The men think that there are big reinforcements on the way and that they can hold their ground until these arrive.' Hill had only heard of 10,000 expected but the French could find it difficult to stay for lack of provisions: 'It is a difficult matter to starve a Frenchman.' It was also highly galling to the beleaguered, hungry French to see and hear that the Allied forces were enjoying an excellent time, well provisioned and amusing themselves with fox hunting and coursing within the security of the Lines.

Nevertheless, despite the victory at Busaco, what appeared to the men as a retreat lowered morale in the Allied Army. How, the men asked, can we continue to win our battles, and still retreat? It was certainly a problem and in addition to a lack of equipment, they had wretched weather to contend with. Many in England were to be disappointed over the following months by Wellington's retreat into Portugal but with no supplies, no reinforcements and scant assistance from the Spanish, there was little choice. On 10 November, another letter says that there is not much to report except that the Spanish have changed their form of government and established a Regency. Rowland does not see that this will make much difference. The following week, he writes home from Vila Nova saying that in the night of 15 November, the enemy had vanished. It is generally thought that this was owing to lack of supplies, sickness and the loss at Busaco. The British light troops pursued them and took a number of prisoners. Hill crossed the Tagus on the 18th and it was soon evident that the enemy had only gone as far as Santarem[159] where they were now gathered in considerable force. His opinion was that the enemy would await reinforcements but comments that this was not the general view.

VI

TRIUMPH AT ARROYO DOS MOLINOS

In the middle of December, Rowland was forced to retire to Lisbon. He had been struck by a violent fever which had been affecting many of the troops along the south bank of the Tagus. He wrote to Maria telling her of his indisposition but saying that he was sure the change of air would do him good. In fact, he says that he has been out riding and does not feel in the least tired. 'I have received your last kind letter. Nothing, I assure you would give me greater pleasure than to obtain permission to visit Shropshire, which, if I were to ask, I am sure I could procure; but under present circumstances in my mind, it would not be right to think of it, provided my health will admit of my returning to my post. Surely affairs in this country cannot long remain in a state of uncertainly.' He also tells her that it is his opinion that Massena is awaiting instructions from Bonaparte or reinforcements. It was known that General Foy[160] had been sent to Paris to speak with Napoleon personally and to receive the Emperor's instructions. So many of the messengers that had been sent to the Emperor for directions up to this date had never reached their destination, (thanks usually to the Spanish guerrillas or Portuguese peasants), that the able Foy, Massena's Adjutant General, was sent with an escort some 500-strong. His mission was to try and explain to Bonaparte why Massena had been unable to 'drive the leopard into the sea' thanks to the fortifications of Torres Vedras. It took Foy until February 1811 to return to Portugal. In the interim Massena was reinforced by the arrival of the 9th Corps.

Rowland continued to stay in the Duke of Wellington's house in Lisbon where he was well looked after but failed to regain any strength; in fact, he also developed a severe attack of jaundice, probably thanks to all the blood letting. He tells Maria that General Fane, who had been suffering from much the same complaint, was sailing for England, but that he himself hoped to be able to rejoin his corps in a couple of weeks. In this he was to be proved wrong and some subsequent events, especially the Battle of Albuera, might have turned out differently had it happened. While he was slowly recovering from the fever, probably a severe attack of malaria, we can see in his letters that his handwriting was especially shaky. The Chief Physician, Dr James Buchan, informed the Duke that Hill should be sent to England to recover. Wellington concurred but told Hill that he needed him back just as soon as he was better. Considering the fact that he had been thought rather fragile as a boy, and the long hard months, even years, of campaigning with food and other rations woefully inadequate even for an officer, Hill seems to have enjoyed remarkably good health in the Peninsula. His only problem seems to have been this fever, which was to recur occasionally for the remainder of his service.

Since he was the ranking Brigade Officer, Major General Sir William Stewart of Hill's division was put in temporary command. This was not a happy situation and he had to be replaced by William Beresford. Stewart was a brave man but not only lacking military skill – especially under pressure – but was also guilty of writing depressing letters concerning the state of the war to people in high places in England, a practice all too common in Wellington's experience and one that, naturally, enraged the Peer. Later on, in 1813, Stewart asked to be reassigned to serve under Hill's command since the Duke could not trust him on his own. 'It is likewise necessary that General [Stewart] should be under the particular charge of somebody … with the utmost zeal and good intentions and abilities, he cannot obey an order.'[161] Glover says of him, 'as a battalion commander Stewart was surpassed only by Moore; as a general he was a menace.'[162]

Marshal Beresford, who was making such a success of building the Portuguese Army, was not as effective when detached from the main army. On Hill's return in late May 1811, the Marshal (in the Portuguese Army) was sent back to his original job and never given a separate command again but always kept under Wellington's eye, this despite Wellington having once said that he thought Beresford was the man most capable of leading the British Army. The Duke was quite often guilty of these 'throwaway' remarks concerning his generals, which were subsequently to be proved inaccurate. In the beginning in his position as temporary Commander of Hill's detached Corps, Beresford had appeared to do quite well, he was a fine soldier in most respects but he took little account of the men's comforts and they grumbled and said how much they missed 'Daddy Hill'. The men appreciated that Rowland did not work them unnecessarily, was not a 'flogging' general except under the most extreme circumstances, and generally cared for their welfare; even more importantly, they also admired him as a skilful commander.

Rowland's return to England was in the company of Clement[163] and Captain Currie. Hill noted 'there is no climate for an Englishman equal to England.' He referred briefly to Edward, the youngest of the family, of whom nothing much is known beyond the fact that he served in the Royal Horse Guards, Blue, at least as a Lieutenant and he may have been a Captain in 1815. He is referred to in several of Rowland's letters but never in any detail although one does sense that he posed some kind of problem to his elder brothers, being usually referred to as 'poor Edward'. Household Cavalry records show that he left the Army in mid July 1815.

The party landed at Falmouth on 5 February 1811. It had been intended to land at Portsmouth but the weather was too rough. On the 9th they were in Exeter where they stayed with the Cornish family; Elizabeth Cornish was married to John, Rowland's elder brother. They also planned to spend a night in Wells with the Tudway family. The General's evangelical uncle, the Reverend Rowland Hill, was married to Mary Tudway and the two families were very close friends. He wrote to Maria that he anticipated being at Hawkstone in four or five days. He also comments on the news he had just received of the sudden death of his good friend, General Romana, the Spanish general who was almost the only admirable soldier amongst that crew.[164] Rowland was sad to learn that he had missed seeing his brother, Francis, by only about three hours when the latter had also passed through Exeter. The military brothers did not often have a chance to meet up with Francis, who served for some time in Brazil in the Foreign Service. Rowland also made a much needed stop in Bath to order himself some new clothes: 'I really have no coat except an uniform one, I believe I must halt there for the purpose of getting one made and to purchase a few necessary articles.' After more than two years in Portugal, he must certainly have needed some new clothes.

He was not to stay long at Hawkstone. He returned to the Peninsula in mid May just after the bloody Battle of Albuera, one of the worst of the campaign. Beresford had made some errors of judgement and although the British claimed victory thanks to the French having retired, it was an expensive one. Hill wrote a note home from Portsmouth on 12 May 1811, complaining that the Admiralty had not been very attentive in finding him passage to Lisbon, a small ship for him and General Campbell. They had had to await the arrival on board of a King's Messenger. He complained to Sir David Dundas that he should not allow his generals to be treated in such an off-hand manner! Rowland on his high horse, a rare sight.

Wellington sent him a short note, written from Elvas, to welcome him back:

My dear Hill
I am very glad you are returned in good health and I hope that we shall see you soon.
    You will have heard of events here, which I hope will enable us to obtain possession of Badajos, upon which we are busily employed.

Wellington was apparently not alone in welcoming the most popular General in the Allied Army back to his command. Napier wrote that it provoked 'the eager rejoicings of the army'.

He wrote home to Maria in mid June concerning the siege of Badajos. Was there ever a more stubbornly held fortress? Hill thought the siege was was badly conducted and was glad that he had had nothing to do with it. Accounts now came in that the different French armies with 60,000 men were converging on the area of Almendralejo where Hill's Corps was stationed. The enemy then managed to raise the siege of Badajos being far superior in cavalry and Wellington, having decided that it would be unwise to join in battle with an enemy on the open plains around the fortress, marched off to Beira leaving Hill in the south at Altemtejo. He now had 17,000 men and Tom, with his Portuguese battalion, was only 10 miles away. He has seen the Duke and had a long ride together with him. The horses had arrived in good shape (from England) and he had ridden the 'Colonel's' black', a valuable animal.[165] The Peninsula was hard on the chargers and obviously Rowland had taken the opportunity when he was in England to search out some replacements.

The French had written in official papers that none but madmen would stay in the plains during the heat of summer, a sentiment with which General Hill heartily concurred, and he surmised that Soult would go off to Seville and that Marmont would probably recross the Tagus. Dysentery, virulent in the heat, and known by the men as 'King Agrippa' was probably the army's worst enemy at this moment and Wellington was forced to withdraw once again.

It was now that the young, brave but impulsive Prince of Orange arrived at Wellington's HQ. He always got on well with the avuncular Hill who seems to have treated him rather as he did his numerous nephews. It was also now that poor Digby Mackworth, extra ADC to Hill, was captured by a French patrol. He was, however, well treated by the French, and the Duke himself eventually intervened at Hill's request and obtained his release. He would almost certainly have been exchanged.

On 20 August, Wellington marched part of his force to Ciudad Rodrigo, which Rowland thought would probably provoke the French into a reaction. At the end of August, Rowland was at Villa Vicosa. He describes the town as a handsome one and that the hunting palace and preserves, together with the picturesque rides and walks in the park which had, in former days, caused it to be a favourite country residence of the royal family, gave him a very fine HQ. He also comments on the abundant supplies available in the market and the excellent Borba wine, which he considered was the best in Portugal. Early in September they moved to Portalegre. Intercepted messages tell him that the French Army is weak and sickly but that Marmont has been assured of large reinforcements from France – perhaps 40,000. The French have also been able to boost their numbers against Wellington thanks to their recent success over Tarragona and Figueras and Soult's defeat of the luckless Blake and his Spanish army in Grenada. Intercepted information also gives the French's ideas as to the state of the Allied Army: Morillo, commander of the Spanish infantry and the Count de Penne, commanding the cavalry, with about '*3000 mauvaises troupes mal armés sont a Cácere. Hill, commandant d'une division Anglaise, est entre Villa Vicosa et St. Olia.*' The French managed to resupply the fortress of Ciudad Rodrigo and Hill thinks this will mean things will quieten down for the winter.

In a letter to brother John at Hawkstone dated 20 August, Rowland is very annoyed with Marshall Beresford about the promotion of junior officers. He has received a letter from the Marshall about Thomas Noel saying 'he deserves a Lt Col. far more than some who have got promotion but, unluckily for him, he is not an Irishman.' Beresford was, of course!

It was around this time that one Don Alonso sent Hill a present of Spanish merino sheep

> ... of the best sort, and on account of the high character he gives them and the appearance of their wool, I have made an attempt to get them to Shropshire but I think it doubtful whether they ever will reach Hawkstone. Colonel Abercromby has been good enough to take charge of them – he has directions to forward them from the place of landing with a letter – therefore, if you should see the ragged flock arrive one morning, I am sure you will not be tempted to have them killed for the table. Mr Dons [the steward] will have to take care they do not contaminate the Hawkstone flock. I have also sent a box of fir or pine seeds which grows to great perfection and is very handsome.

In the midst of a long campaign and with the imminent likelihood of a battle bringing the possibility of death, there is still time to organise the shipment of sheep.[166] It sounds as if it was considerably easier in the early nineteenth century than it would be two hundred years later! The sheep duly arrived at Hawkstone, and it must have been amazing to see the little flock trotting up the long drive. Some of them, or perhaps their progeny, went to John Hill who was Rowland's nephew[167] and who became a clergyman. He was a famous 'hunting' parson who also farmed the Citadel Farm at Hawkstone. When the whole estate was sold and all the farms and the stock went to auction, there were listed in the sale catalogue, the descendants of these Spanish sheep, nearly 90 years later.

In September, Hill, who was at Portalegre, writes to John saying he is feeling fine although sometimes a little 'bilious' but that he is sure that if he had not gone home, he would not be so well. Many brother officers who lingered in the Peninsula were eventually forced to go home. He asks his brother to please be kind enough to send him some local papers from Shrewsbury as he misses news of 'the county one likes best'. He tells John that Beresford has written a very nice letter to Tom, which was presumably concerning his promotion. He also sends news of the safe arrival of the long-awaited hounds.

The intercepted message of late September that described the state of the Spanish cavalry, 'mauvais ... mal armé' at Cáceres also referred to our General as a Commandant 'dur' which was probably gratifying to him. If the enemy thinks you are tough you are in a strong position psychologically.

Things did not, however, quieten down entirely and it was in October that Hill had one of his greatest successes and, in the words of Moyle Sherer, 'One all his own'. Over the past months little aggressive action had been undertaken by the British and Hill's brief had been principally to stay in the south and keep an eye on Soult who had gone to Seville. Hill finally managed to prise back some of the troops he had 'lent' to Wellington some time earlier. In the middle of October 1811, General Girard[168] crossed the Guardiana river at Merida under orders from General Jean de Dieu Soult and began to 'inflict the greatest annoyances on the northern district of Estremadura.' Hill set out to drive him from Cáceres. This was partially because there was excellent grazing there and the Spanish cavalry had urgent need of it for their baggage animals and chargers. Secondly, Hill wanted to drive Girard off before he could be reinforced.

It has been said that steady and reliable men do not usually make daring leaders[169] but Hill was certainly an exception to this and if he had not been especially prominent at several previous battles, it was generally because Wellington was covering his own back by keeping Hill in reserve, where he knew he could be counted on when required. This time, Rowland was to be on his own. He elicited the information that Girard had taken the road for Torremocha and he worked out, with the aid, no doubt, of his local guides who knew the ground, that there was another route and that he might be able to intercept Girard. It seemed that Girard had no idea that he was being pursued so closely and after a terrible march in wretched weather, Hill bivouacked on the evening of 27 October at Alcuesar only about four miles from the French. The light troops were sent into the neighbouring villages to ensure that no traitor could go off and warn Girard while the rest of the men spent the night in the fields with no fires or light permitted.

The men were exhausted after their long forced march, and when one of Hill's ADCs came to Robert Blakeney [170] and told him that he must take a message to General Hamilton who was in command of the Portuguese brigade, the young man objected, but he was told that General Hill had requested him especially and his orders were 'peremptory'. The message was read to Blakeney for him to memorise; there was to be no risk of his being taken with it on him in writing. Blakeney writes a colourful account with graphic descriptions of rain lashing down in sheets, and 'troops of wolves howling around us'. He got himself hopelessly lost as it transpired that the dragoons provided by Spanish General Giron, as guides, had no idea of the way! Blakeney eventually found himself, by complete chance, back in the middle of his own men. He also recounts the tale of a Spanish equestrian band they had with them who, when battle commenced the following morning, were determined to join in the fight against the French. They were, 'as intractable as swine, obstinate as mules and unmanageable as bullocks, they were cut up like rations and dispersed in all directions like a flock of scared sheep.'[171] Young Blakeney certainly had a way with words.

The soldiers evidently knew that they were close on the heels of their prey and made no fuss about the privations; anticipation of the action on the morrow seems to have raised their spirits. Everyone was under arms just as daylight broke and despite being hit by a violent hail storm, they arrived within a half mile of Arroyo dos Molinos undetected, remaining for a while hidden by a rise in the ground. Major General Howard had the left column, Lieutenant Colonel Stewart was ordered into the town while Colonel Wilson's brigade with two 6-pounders and a howitzer formed the right hand column and Sir William Erskine led the cavalry. The General suddenly turned from the calm, benign figure that was his usual self, drew his sword at the head of the first brigade, gave a loud hurrah and spurred his horse forward at the gallop, leading the charge towards the astonished ranks of the French. The Highland regiments played on the bagpipes 'Heigh Johnny Cope, are you waking yet?' General Howard moved swiftly around to the far side of the village to intercept the enemy troops as they were driven out. Soon the 71st and the 92nd were in the midst of Arroyo and fell upon the French just as they were filing out on the far side of the town. Despite their belated efforts to form squares, there was really nothing the French could do and they fled in utter confusion. A large number of prisoners were taken including General Brun and the Prince d'Aremberg. The latter was a valuable capture since he was related by marriage to the Empress Josephine. The Prince was seized from amongst a group of officers by Lieutenant Robert Blakeney of the 28th,[172] who leapt over a wall and seized hold of him. Girard, unfortunately, together with a handful of officers, did manage to escape, but amongst the booty taken were cannon, ammunition and, of course, a large quantity of baggage. The British, Portuguese and Spaniards serving under General Hill were thrilled with this success; some of them captured magnificent chargers that the escaping French had not been able to take in their unexpected retreat over the mountain. They took 1500 prisoners. The 34th (Cumberland) infantry took all the French drums. These items are in the regiment's museum and are used once a year on the anniversary of the battle. As Major Sherer wrote in his *Recollections,* 'one thing in our success at Arroyo dos Molinos gratified our division highly. It was a triumph for our General – a triumph all his own.' Hill gained great credit for this well-conducted enterprise, and he won what to one of his mild, kind and humane character was still more valuable, a solid and almost bloodless victory. Indeed there were very few men lost on the Allied side and the subsequent promotion of his ADC, Captain Currie, at his behest, was of great personal satisfaction to his General.

Wellington was highly satisfied by the success at Arroyo and wrote to Lord Liverpool, 'It would be particularly agreeable to me if some mark of the favour of High Royal Highness the Prince Regent were conferred upon General Hill; his services have been always meritorious and very distinguished in this country, and he is beloved by the whole army … in recommending him, as I do most

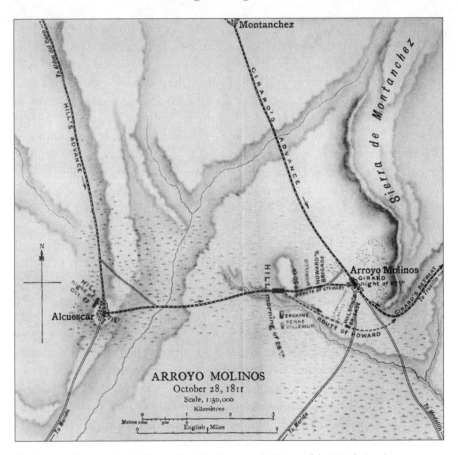

The Battle of Arroyo dos Molinos. (Sir John Fortescue's *History of the British Army*)

anxiously, I really feel that there is no officer to whom an act of grace and favour would be received by the Army with more satisfaction than on General Hill.'

On 5 November 1811, Rowland wrote home from Portalegre: 'I am sure my dear friends at Hawkstone will rejoice to hear of my good fortune – I feel under the Will of divine Providence – I thank God almost without cease.' Here again we have the brave soldier and the believer, sure that he fights on the side of Right. He thinks that Clement will carry the dispatch to London and he will thus be able to give the family a first-hand account of what happened. He added, 'Clement behaved very gallantly as indeed did all.'

The Prince and most of the French officers had dined with General Hill. Prince d'Aremberg was sent to England where he spent his imprisonment at Oswestry just a few miles from Hawkstone. A postscript adds that Clement has gone to Wellington with his report.

Following the victory, letters of congratulation were written to Rowland by his peers. General Murray wrote, 'I feel a peculiar pleasure in this fortunate affairs as it concerns yourself personally and assure you that I only repeat the sentiments which are in the mouth of every one whom I have heard speak upon the subject.' Wellington wrote him a note after receiving Clement with Rowland's dispatch:

Frenedia, Nov. 9, 1811

My dear Hill,

I have not written to you since the 22nd as I have had nothing new to interest you, and I would not interrupt your operations. Nothing could be more satisfactory to me than all you did, and I am happy that I had determined to send home your brother with the report of your transactions before I had heard that it was your wish that I should do so.

He and Churchill will tell you how we are going on here.

Rowland also received a kind note from his old friend General Graham:

Nov. 12th, 1811. Lagiosa

My dear Hill

I rejoice most truly on hearing of your success, but I delayed writing to congratulate you on it, till I should see your dispatch with the particulars. Lord Wellington sent me your letters two days ago at the same time expressing his high approbation of your conduct, a testimony more valuable than any.

He begs Hill to thank Captain Edwin Currie for the sketch of the ground and disposition of the troops

… which I prize much … I hear you have got hounds and have you a tolerable country and good sport? At headquarters I am told they have already done up all their horses.

Thomas Graham

What a remarkable mixture of war and peace, sudden death and sport was lived by these soldiers!

On his arrival in England, Clement had duly delivered the dispatch to Lord Liverpool who had sent him on to Oatlands to hand it to the Prince Regent in person but, the Prince being indisposed, was instead able to pass it over to the Commander in Chief, HRH The Duke of York who would, in any event, have understood the relevance of the details more precisely than his august elder brother.

Hill also received a polite letter from the imprisoned d'Aremberg. There was no chance of the Prince being exchanged; because of his connections,[173] he was too valuable a prize.

Although everyone had expected that the Army would now go into cantonments for the winter, there was to be one more manoeuvre. Hill wrote to Clement, who was at home on leave, telling him that he was instructed to move south to be in a position to help Ballesteros[174] who was being hard pressed by Hill's old friend Marechal Soult around the city of Tarifa and Gibralter. He planned to march on Almandralejo to divert Soult's attention and after being at Albuquerque on the following day he would move on to Merida. He told his brother Clement 'You cannot possibly be in time for the march, therefore you need not hurry.'

Rowland also told Clement, in confidence, that as soon as the Regency expired, it was intended that he was to be invested with the Order of the Bath, the KB, generally referred to in the Army as the 'red ribbon'. Apparently Wellington had also been informed that this mark of distinction was to be conferred and observed, 'It may fall to my lot to be the instrument of conveying to you the honour intended for you, as I have acted in a similar capacity in respect to others but I assure you that I shall perform this duty, if it should devolve upon me, with at least as much satisfaction as I have on any former occasion.'

The French decided not to give Hill the satisfaction of another encounter, and General Dombrowski[175] wisely withdrew from Merida in great haste under cover of night and leaving behind a magazine of bread and 160,000lbs of wheat, which was very welcome. Hill's push southwards as far as Almendralejo caused d'Erlon to retreat allowing a brigade of 3,000 Spanish troops to foray into Spain and stir up some trouble in the interior around the Guadiana river. Hill was pleased with Colonel Abercromby, son of Sir Ralph of Egyptian fame, who had 'had a small affair of great brilliancy' with a strong party of the French cavalry at Fuente del Maestra.' Hill's movement had apparently caused considerable consternation amongst the enemy and thus he had succeeded in his object.

VII

DESTRUCTION AT ALMARAZ

I t was now January, 1812 and the Allied Army had been in action for four years. They had crossed and recrossed much of Portugal and the western and central portion of Spain. They had marched thousands of miles as a rag-tag band clothed in whatever they could lay their hands on, often barefooted, while Wellington had struggled to maintain a force fit to fight the apparently endless flow of troops that France sent south. Both armies had a large number of sick but the British had finally been reinforced so that the Duke could now put about 45,000 in the field; this figure was, of course, as nothing compared with the combined French forces. The continuous campaign had honed the skills of even the poorest soldiers and, with more suitable ground, the cavalry was finally coming into its own. Despite Napoleon's preoccupation with Austria, Russia and Italy he was still determined to kick the British out of Spain and they feared that if he sewed up all his alliances in the north of Europe, he might himself descend on the Peninsula to direct operations. Would events have been different if the Emperor had been at the head of his forces in Spain during the campaign?

In spite of appalling winter weather, the siege of Ciudad Rodrigo was finally lifted on 19 January. The city had been in the hands of the enemy since July 1810. The 'forlorn hope,'[176] led by Ensign Mackie under General Mackinnon of the 3rd Division, was the first troop to storm the great walls; the men leapt into action at 7am with a horde of others in the storming party close behind. Hill was not involved with this bloodbath but brother Thomas Noel was in the thick of it and Rowland wrote home saying, 'I am happy to find that Tom and his regiment had an opportunity of distinguishing themselves.' One of Wellington's favourites, Robert 'Black Bob' Craufurd, of the Light division fell here under a hail of French canister. Wellington had taken the fortress in twelve days and with a loss of life less than one might have expected. He still had Badajos to deal with.

Hill was back again in Portalegre in February 1812. He received a letter from General Pack saying that Thomas Noel had been appointed Colonel of his own regiment, the 1st Portuguese. In a letter to Maria written on 5 February, he wrote, 'It seems that the Marshal[177] cannot do too much for our brother,' but he has not yet heard from Tom himself. He also comments on the fact that Currie's wife has had a baby. 'Mrs Currie's situation is really quite distressing, she has been in a constant alarm for the last two months in a country that affords no comforts … It is cruel, I may say to bring families, Currie is now convinced but should have known before.' When on foreign service, a proportion of soldiers' wives, four to six per company, were permitted to accompany their men folk. The 'lucky' ones were chosen by a lottery. Oman discusses this in *Wellington's Army* and paints a graphic picture of a rabble of women often mounted on donkeys, 'forming the most unmanageable portion of every regimental train'. They generally could not keep up with the pace of the march and tragic stories about their being left to die by the roadside in the snow or in childbirth were numerous.

Hill was quite right to condemn Currie for bringing his wife to the Peninsula but, on the other hand, the presence of the women was probably one of the reasons that there was little desertion in the British Army. The women would set up camp, cook, sew and do all other manner of jobs for the men. They did, however, prove a nightmare for the Provosts General and their staff! When one woman lost her husband, she would soon be snapped up by another. Apparently Mrs Currie, who was in a different category being the wife of an officer, was a most charming woman who gave endless entertainments, including tea parties, for the other officers whenever the occasion allowed. She also, circumstances permitting, dined with the officers and thus, apparently, added a welcome element of 'gentility'. The Frenchman Colonel Lejeune, who was a prisoner in Elvas, drew and described a family scene:

> The Captain rode first on a very fine horse, warding off the sun with a parasol; then came his wife very prettily dressed, with a small straw hat, riding on a mule and carrying not only a parasol but a little black and tan dog on her knee, while she led by a cord a she-goat to supply her with milk. Beside Madame walked her Irish nurse, carrying in a green silk wrapper a baby, the hope of the family. A grenadier, the Captain's servant, came behind and occasionally poked up the long-eared steed of his mistress with a staff. Last in the procession came a donkey loaded with much miscellaneous baggage, which included a tea kettle and a cage of canaries.[178]

The Currie *ménage* is a startling vision of an army at war.

On 23 January, Rowland wrote to Maria that he had been directed to return to Portugal and take up a position with his right at Portalegre, the centre at Niza and his left at Castello Branco. On the 28th, he was to receive a letter from Wellington concerning the Commander's plans to stop the various French armies from converging on Badajos and preventing the Allies from taking the stronghold. Wellington's thought was that the Army of Portugal would cross the Tagus at Almaraz and he directed Hill to go and try to destroy the bridge together with the forts that guarded it on either bank, and, in addition, to seize any boats that the French might have on the north side of the river.

Whilst Hill was laying his plans for the destruction of the bridge of Almaraz,[179] he was gratified to learn that the Prince Regent had alluded to his success at Arroyo dos Molino in his speech at the opening of Parliament. It was also pleasing to him to learn that Henry Wellesley (brother to the Duke) at Cadiz had referred to his actions in Estramadura as being the principal reason that the French had withdrawn from Tarifa leaving behind them all their ammunition and artillery.

The Duke was now himself at Portalegre and wrote to Hill on 10 March, sending him the insignia of the Order of the Bath. This must have been most gratifying to our General, the first tangible reward. Wellington asks Hill to meet him at Elvas on the following day so that he can invest him with the order formally. He begs him to bring his staff and says that they shall all dine with him following the ceremony. Hill was to receive the KB, Knights Companion of the Order of the Bath. This was an ancient order which George I had made into a Military Order. After 1815, the KB disappeared and was replaced by the Knight Grand Cross (GCB) and the Knight Commander (KCB), a more junior class of the order. Hill would eventually receive the more senior decoration. Thomas Graham was also to be invested at the same time and the ceremony took place in March.

Rowland's elevation to 'Sir' certainly did not bring a swelled head. 'When he was knighted,' says an officer on his personal staff, 'there was not one of us dared for nearly six months to call him *Sir Rowland*; he was quite distressed at being called anything but 'General,' and it was only very gradually that he could be driven to bear his honour.'

Correspondence towards the end of March now passed between Rowland and brother John concerning the design of his Arms, especially the supporters, which would be recorded in the College of Arms. He was opposed to the idea of having 'a jolly tar, a grenadier, a light infantry man or a heavy or light dragoon … such, I think are bad.' He had decided that animals would be best and what better than greyhounds given his interest in coursing. However he told John that the women of the family should be consulted as 'they have more taste than we have.' He was sure that 'Mrs Robert will give me her opinion.'[180] Rowland had evidently also been awarded the governorship of 'Blakeness' Castle[181] but how much this was worth is not recorded. As his stature in the Army grew, he would have more lucrative governorships such as Hull and Plymouth.

Badajos. A stronghold of immense importance thanks to its situation on the Portuguese/Spanish frontier and one of the great border fortresses that were to give Wellington such a headache. Two attempts in 1811 had failed thanks to the

Allied Army being almost completely lacking in battering train or other siege materials. A large part of what did exist was of considerable antiquity and there were some guns that were 200 years old, stamped with the arms of Philip III and IV of Spain. Many of the guns available, apart from their age, were of different calibration and the whole collection has been described as a sort of artillery museum.[182] However, by the end of 1811, better equipment had arrived and under the highly skilful and intelligent engineering officer, Alexander Dickson, things began to improve. The heavy weaponry had been hauled with the greatest difficulty overland from the Douro and its presence was unsuspected by the French. This had greatly assisted in the siege of Ciudad Rodrigo in January 1812. Hill wrote home from Elvas on 14 March that it was not his purpose to have anything to do with the duties of the siege but he was to form a covering army on the north of the Guadiana river in the direction of Merida. Graham with a similar force was to be on the south side. 'Tom is not yet arrived here, Clement is not yet arrived, there is also a Packet not yet come containing the letters of the beginning of last month.' Letters from home were of great importance to these men who served so long and so far from home.

This, the third attempt to invest Badajos, came in April 1812 as it had proved impossible to bring the guns from Ciudad Rodrigo thanks to the rough and mountainous terrain; to replace these, ships' guns were brought up from Lisbon. Despite a successful conclusion, the loss of life was appalling and drove Wellington to ask Lord Liverpool to have a corps of sappers and miners formed immediately. Rowland wrote a brief note to Maria from Almandralejo on 15 April saying that he knew Clement and Thomas had both just written to her describing the fall of Badajos, a dearly bought victory. He was himself approaching Badajos with 14,000 men to act as a safety screen while the great fortress was being repaired.

Now came Hill's second solo success, the taking of the forts and bridge at Almaraz approximately 100 miles north-east of Badajos. This bridge across the Tagus had been a route much frequented by Marmont with his Army of Portugal and Soult at the head of the Army of the South and its destruction would mean that the two French Marechals would have to go many miles round to communicate, or to cross the river. Wellington told Hill to take only the men he needed and to carry out his preparations in the greatest secrecy. In a letter to Wellington on 10 May, Hill writes that he expects that the essential repairs to the bridge he needs to cross at Merida will be finished either that evening or the following day and that he will then march with 'celerity and exertion'. He is certain that nobody has any idea as to his real destination and has instructed Colonel Dickson to let it be known that the equipment was for a bridge at Loban. On receipt of this letter, Wellington apparently said to Graham, 'I am very much afraid Hill will be late.' He should have known better. Hill's principal worry lay in leaving the rest of his Corps in the charge of Major General Sir

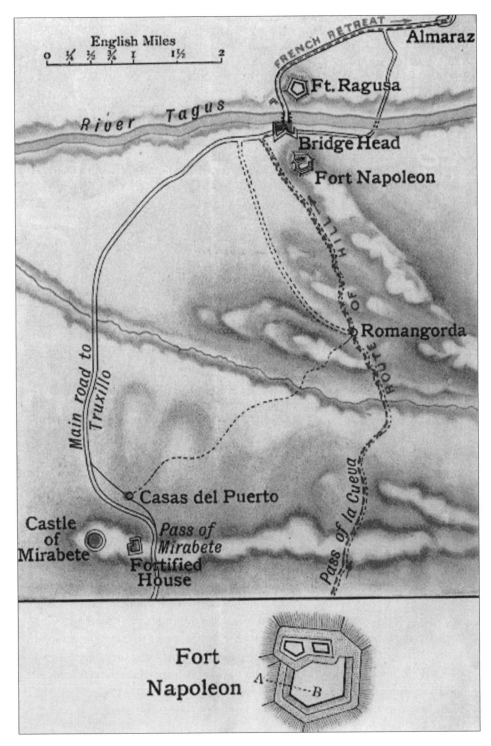

Hill's Raid on Almaraz. (Sir John Fortescue's *History of the British Army*)

William Erskine, a man already described as prone to rash and unpredictable movement.[183] He would have perhaps been reassured by the knowledge that Thomas Graham was not far away.

Before sunset on the 12th, all 6000[184] troops chosen to take part in the raid were across the bridge at Merida that had finally been repaired and by the 15th had reached Truxillo while, at the same time, Hill was making diversions with some of his men to confuse the enemy. French General Foy had recently returned from carrying the bad news of Massena and his army being encamped in front of the formidable barrier of Torres Vedras with nothing to eat, to Napoleon in Paris. He was apparently totally deceived. The march was a forced one and by the 16th, Sir Rowland was at Jaraicejo. It was wild, rugged but beautiful country plunging steeply down to the narrow green valley of the Tagus. Hill is not much given to flights of fancy over beautiful scenery in his letters home, but Clement's letters are often full of such descriptions. Local guides had been employed to lead the men down what were really nothing more than goat paths. The soldiers were divided into three columns to make three assaults; one on the bridge itself, one on the two forts guarding the river, one on either bank, and a third on the great fortress of Mirabete together with a fortified house sited in the pass a short distance from the river. Lieutenant General Christopher Tilson Chowne[185] was in charge of the first column which was to 'attack' the castle and act as a diversion, the second was under Major General Robert Long[186] and Hill took overall command of the third, Howard's brigade. They feared that the element of surprise had been lost when, first, the Spanish guide leading Tilson Chowne's column seems to have lost his way and then an unexpected sentry was found in front of Mirabete. This man immediately fired his musket thus alerting the garrison. However, the British troops being invisible from the forts in the dim light, the Commandant thought that the sentry had merely seen a goat or at worst, a scout.

The General decided to bivouack, concealed, on the hillside and the next two days were spent in reconnoitring the area to see if a different approach could be made. Things did not look promising. However, late in the evening of the 19th, Hill led Howard's brigade down a path that was hazardous even by goats' standards, muskets wrapped to avoid the metal glinting in the moonlight. Their passage was rendered even more difficult by the 30-foot scaling ladders that they were carrying and which soon had to be sawed in half in order to carry them round rocky outcrops and other obstacles. Their pace was so slow that they only covered one mile in five hours; but by first light, they lay concealed on the left bank of the river approximately 800 yards from one of the two forts, Fort Napoleon. The rear of the party soon followed and was in place by 8am. The contour of the hill concealed them from the forts.

A feint made on the tower of Mirabete by Tilson Chowne's men served as an effective diversion and caused the enemy manning the two riverside forts to turn their attention in that direction. Immediately, Hill led his men in an assault on Fort Napoleon, which covered the near side of the bridge. The sight of the scaling ladders must have come as a great shock to the French; they were caught entirely unawares and very rapidly the English men were up the ladders – despite the fact that these were found to be too short after having been sawn in half on the march – and had overcome any resistance which was, in any case, minimal. The French were incredulous and, indeed, the Commandant of the garrison of Fort Napoleon, a brave Piedmontese named Audun, refused to surrender and stood with his back against the wall, sword in hand. He was eventually taken prisoner. Some of the boats forming the pontoon bridge were loosed by the French on the far bank and several Frenchmen were drowned as the boats forming the bridge swung out into the stream.

Now that Hill was in possession of Fort Napoleon, he turned that fort's own guns on the second fort, a much weaker target, across the Tagus, Fort Ragusa, which was also rapidly reduced with the Commandant fleeing 'panic stricken' to Navalmorale, where he was court-martialled and shot. When the French, on the far side, had cut loose the pontoon bridge, it had swung out into the current with some desperate Frenchmen hanging on for their lives. Two resourceful British grenadiers of the 92nd Highlanders, James Gould and Walter Somerville,[187] swam across to bring back the boats that had been cut loose. These two men were rewarded by Hill with a gold coin apiece. The men then set about destroying the forts, the stores, the ammunition and the last of the boats that had formed the pontoon bridge. Unfortunately, none of the stores could be carried away due to the steep and rugged route by which the British had to return. They were forced to destroy eighteen cannon, which they did by firing one into another, 120,000 cartridges, shells, grape, muskets and quantities of food and brandy. They set fire to twenty of the pontoon barges that had spanned the river. Virtually all that they carried home was the colours of the 4 *Etrangers*.[188] Hill did not, however, forget to let his men enjoy their triumph and a pause was made to allow them to eat some of the food and drink they had recovered. He must have been feeling euphoric at his success but he was anxious, as always, to let his men share something of his pleasure.

Hill also had to take the rational decision that, unfortunately, he did not have the tools to destroy Mirabete itself. The castle stood on high ground a little distance from the bridgehead. He had studied the solid mass of Mirabete and had quickly realised that he had no chance of taking it with his inadequate equipment and that he could not remain cut off from the main body of his Corps, which was some four days' march away. Hill lost 15 officers and 162 private soldiers killed or wounded in the action; 250 prisoners were taken together with the enemy's colours.[189] It was a daring assault that succeeded brilliantly by sheer nerve but if one can say that one makes one's own luck, then Hill certainly made his on this occasion.

As Hill was standing on the remains of the boat bridge looking across at the fortress of Mirabete, a courier had arrived with an alarming message from Sir

William Erskine. This subsequently turned out to be occasioned by a cunning diversionary move made by Drouet but Hill had no way of knowing whether Erskine's report was accurate. He was disappointed not to be able to fulfil the final part of his mission and he knew that Wellington would not be best pleased but, cut off as it now was, Mirabete was not of much further use to the French and was to be abandoned shortly afterwards. In his letter to Wellington from Merida written on 26 May, he explained, 'Indeed I do not think there was a single thing left that could be of any service to the enemy ... I, at one time had an idea of blockading Mirabete, but [on] ascertaining they had provisions in the place for six weeks I did not think it was right for me to delay my return, particularly as Foy and Drouet both appeared to be in motion.' Wellington was extremely annoyed at Erskine's false intelligence as it had also caused Graham to go to Badajos, just when the Duke had planned to bring him back to join the main army. It was strange that Wellington did not get rid of Erskine but 'influence at home' was said to be at work. From the very start of the war, Wellington grumbled loud and often as to the quality of many of his general officers, saying that they were either too old or had never seen action. When he had been informed by Horse Guards that Erskine was being sent out to Portugal, he had 'remonstrated saying that he had generally understood him to be a madman.'[190] The reply was, 'No doubt he is sometimes a little mad, but in his lucid intervals he is an uncommonly clever fellow; and I trust he will have no fit during the campaign, though he looked a little wild as he embarked.'[191] This extraordinary observation was hardly likely to set the Duke's mind at rest, who promptly put him under Hill's auspices!

Hill's ADC, Edwin Currie, now a Major, was sent to London with the dispatch. On the way, he wrote to Sir Rowland from Wellington's HQ. 'Lord Wellington expressed the greatest joy and satisfaction at what had been done; in a word he seems fully to appreciate the merits of the troops and everybody connected with the expedition. Foy, he says, has been prettily humbugged and must now go round by Toledo ... "Yes, Hill has done it well and ably".' Currie also pointed out to Wellington that despite Hill's inability to destroy the fortress of Mirabete itself, there were numerous Spanish guerrillas in the area and that they would probably soon manage to dislodge the French; they did. These wild fellows were a constant source of frustration to the French. On 25 May, Foy sent a captain to Sir Rowland with money and letters for the prisoners that he had taken – all very civilised. He was, however, incensed at the size of the escort he had been forced to provide for this messenger, Captain Guingret. It had been thought necessary to send an escort of 50 cavalry just to protect the messenger from the guerrillas!

Not the least of the pleasures felt by Hill at the successful conclusion of this action was the knowledge that King Joseph was furious. This was not solely because the vital bridge, an essential link between two of his armies, had been destroyed but also because it had been achieved without detection by Drouet. You can hardly help but feel sorry for Joseph. Placed, as he was, in so many lofty roles, he simply could not live up to his brother's expectations; his final humiliation at Vittoria was yet to come.

The success at Almaraz, although not a full-scale battle, was, on the other hand, greeted with great enthusiasm in London. After years of disappointments and many retreats, people sensed that the British were now finally gaining the upper hand and news of the victory almost overshadowed the assassination of the Prime Minister, Spencer Perceval. The *London Gazette* for 19 June 1812, reported Major Currie's arrival at Lord Bathurst's office and referred to Wellington's comment that Hill's had been a 'brilliant exploit', describing the difficulties encountered. Hill had now proved again that he could not only command a detached corps bent on keeping French armies at a distance but that, when required, he could personally execute difficult manoeuvres with imagination, skill and bravery. He was not merely serving as an 'eyes and ears' corps – sometimes referred to as a Corps of Observation, keeping a watch on the likes of Soult – but taking proactive measures and with great success. In addition to these two major independent successes that he had in 1812, a portion of his cavalry under Sir William Erskine routed three regiments of enemy cavalry at Villa Alba. Hill described this to Wellington 'as a very handsome affair'. The Portuguese authorities awarded Sir Rowland the Grand Cross of the Order of the Tower and Thistle.

While Hill was advancing against d'Erlon, he sent the inept Major General Sir John Slade, commanding a brigade of cavalry, on reconnaissance, with orders 'not to commit himself to any serious engagement'.[192] Historian Ian Fletcher in his *Galloping at Everything,* has done a very good job in trying to put the pieces of the puzzle together since there are several different accounts. The essence of the matter seems to have been that Slade went far too far and suddenly found himself face to face with the enemy. Unlike his opposing French general, Lallemand, he had kept no troops in reserve, and although his first attack was successful, he did not know when to stop, as so often occurred with the Allied cavalry at the time, and led his brigade at a furious gallop in pursuit. Suddenly, there came a loud warning cry, 'Look to your right.' Lallemand had kept a squadron in reserve and this now came thundering down scattering Slade's force in a 'disgraceful' manner until they were finally collected together miles from the start of their frenzied gallop at Maguilla. Precise details of this affair are not clear but it is possible that Slade pursued the French for about eight miles, 'a wild and reckless pursuit' according to both Oman and Fortescue. Evidently Slade was then in a panic and galloped hither and thither even offering the princely sum of £50 to any man who would stand with him – not that any did![193] The men were totally demoralised and were now more anxious to save themselves than to save their General's already tattered reputation. Slade's report to Hill was full of praise for the bravery exhibited by his men but, of course, both his behaviour and his account of the action were considered a joke by the entire Army. Hill was furious, as was Wellington. Wellington commented in a well documented letter to Sir Rowland,[194] 'I have never been more annoyed than by Slade's affair.'

Hill was so enraged that he was moved to hold an enquiry. The results of this enquiry were then passed on to the Duke. There is no doubt that in the early years of the war, British cavalry regiments frequently threw their ground away by charging in a sort of blind fury. Wellington's tirade is well known:

> ... our officers of cavalry have acquired a trick of galloping at everything. They never consider the situation, never think of manoeuvring before an enemy, and never keep back or provide for a reserve. All cavalry should charge in two lines and at least one-third should be ordered beforehand to pull up and reform, as soon as the charge has been delivered and the enemy been broken.[195]

The phrase 'galloping at everything' has often been repeated! It was surprising that Slade kept command of his brigade until May 1813. It was yet another indication that Wellington still did not have control over appointments to his general staff. Wellington issued a fierce threat to the Dragoons to the effect that should they ever behave like this again, he would take away their horses.[196] Robert Ballard Long, who had had a somewhat similar experience to Slade at Campo Mayor the year before, wrote to his brother, describing the Slade Affair. 'I know from experience how difficult it is to contain a British victorious cavalry in sight of a fugitive enemy, and I know equally well how much better the enemy has his men under his hands than we.'[197]

Hill and Soult played cat and mouse with each other over almost the entire central and western part of the Peninsula. Two months later, in August, Hill crossed the Tagus again at Almaraz, which had been evacuated by the enemy. He now had more leisure to look at the fortifications in detail and was pleased to discover that it would have been impossible to have escaladed the castle of Mirabete. Apart from the outworks, it consisted of an enormous circular tower, the door of which was halfway up, which would have been entirely beyond the reach of his scaling ladders. Any lingering doubt he may have held that he should have tried to take the fortress and destroy it on his first raid was thus erased.

Hill only heard of Wellington's victory at Salamanca, fought on 22 July, on the 29th when he was at Villa Franca. A passing Spaniard on a mule first brought the news but this was discounted as unreliable and it was not until the evening of the same day that confirmation reached Hill's HQ. Rowland wrote to his sister, Maria, on 4 August from Zafra, 40 miles south-east of Badajos. He reports the victory of Salamanca where Wellington defeated Marmont. Wellington had begun his march on Salamanca on 13 June. As it was his first great offensive since Talavara three years before; it is hardly surprising that he was known for his defensive tactics. Back in London, the Government was in need of a clear-cut victory in Spain to boost their popularity and smooth the voting of funds for Army supply. Rowland told her how the Duke tricked Marmont into thinking he had only a small force with him and then let loose Sir Edward Pakenham with the 3rd Division and caught the French unawares. The French General Clausel[198] had managed to pull his forces together and inflicted a great deal of damage on the Allied Army. The Allies eventually counterattacked and drove the French from the field. Both sides suffered heavy losses. When the news of the defeat at Salamanca reached Napoleon in Russia, he was in a furious rage with Marmont.

Hill and his 2nd Division, together with Hamilton's Portuguese and Power's new Portuguese brigade, remained in Estremadura. At that moment, Hill had more infantry under his command than ever before. He also had three brigades: Slade's, Long's and John Campbell's Portuguese of Erskine's cavalry division. These totalled 18,000 men.

Rowland was in much the same position as he was so often; keeping an eye on various French armies and always ready to move if occasion – or the Duke – demanded. At this moment, he had the Comte d'Erlon in his front and Marshal Soult at Seville, with around 4000 troops, ready to follow him should he choose to go after Drouet. When he next wrote to Maria on the 31st he told her that d'Erlon had left Estremadura and was marching on Cordoba presumably to join together with the Army of the South. It would be impossible to draw an easily comprehensible map of Hill's marches through the two countries of Portugal and Spain during the long campaign. They crisscrossed and doubled back so frequently that any plotting would resemble a cat's cradle. One must also take into account the fact that the huge Peninsula contains a number of large rivers. The central spine of Spain forms a watershed with the Ebro running from west to east. The other main rivers were the Zezere, which joined the mighty Tagus south of Tomar, the Tagus itself, flowing into the sea at Lisbon, the Douro, which flowed across the north of Portugal and through Porto to the sea and the Mondego passes through Coimbra from the northeast. All of these, together with those which would be encountered in southern France, almost always proved severe obstacles and were often impassable in the spring due to the runoff from melting snow in the mountains, or, indeed, at any time after heavy rain. Whilst Wellington was engaged in defeating Marmont, Hill had joined with the erratic, ambitious General Ballesteros and his Spanish regular troops to keep Soult occupied in the south. Rowland had moved against the Comte d'Erlon to give assistance to a hard-pressed Ballesteros, who was well beaten on 1 June at Bornos.

The victory of Salamanca led the British Government to raise Wellington to the rank of Marquis and Spain awarded him the Order of the Golden Fleece. With Goya ready to paint his celebrated portrait and a royal palace to lodge in, Wellington must have felt he had ascended to the throne!

It is an interesting fact that Napoleon managed to maintain such large armies in an almost entirely hostile Spain whilst he was also taking troops for Russia. The French numbers in the Peninsula still outnumbered the British, Spanish and Portuguese combined by about 2:1. Wellington was always conscious of this vast superiority in numbers and it was certainly one of the reasons why he was always reluctant to engage the enemy until he was reasonably certain of success; he simply could not afford to lose men and he knew that should he suffer a defeat, he could well be recalled, making all his efforts in the Peninsula over the past years wasted.

Wellington marched into Madrid on 12 August, 1812. His entry was triumphal: people pressed around his horse kissing any part of either the Marquis or his horse that they could reach, church bells pealed and the Spanish people of the city expressed their joy at their 'liberation'; it would not last long. Somers Cocks wrote in his memoirs, 'The Earl made his way into this place on the 12th ... Our arrival produced a joy far beyond description ... I was never kissed by so many pretty girls in a day in all my life or ever expect to be again.'[199] Somers Cocks was was right about that. One of Wellington's brightest young stars, he was to be killed shortly after.

Rowland wrote home saying that if people in England thought that with the fall of Madrid to Wellington, the Spanish would provide more troops, they were much mistaken. For one thing, the people soon seemed to be of the opinion that the great events of the campaign were all thanks to the bravery and exertions of the Spanish themselves; Wellington was in despair. The Regency had little or no power. The people had next to nothing to eat and while there was no sign of a Spanish Army, the *guerrillas* in Charles Esdaile's words[200] 'deprived of the cloak of patriotism ... were revealed as the brigands which they had always been, whilst there were few signs of willingness either to pursue the French to fresh hunting grounds or to enlist in the regular army.' When Wellington left Madrid on 31 August, he seems to have been almost obsessed with the notion of taking Burgos, the thorn in his flesh.

On 31 August, Rowland wrote to Hawkstone saying that the Comte d'Erlon had quit Estramadura and was marching to Cordoba. On an entirely different subject he encloses a letter from the first aide de camp to Comte d'Erlon, Colonel Salaignac, whose brother is a prisoner at Whitchurch, Shropshire. If Salaignac wishes to send a reply, Hill will ensure that it reaches Comte d'Erlon's HQ. He adds to Maria,

Colonel Salaignac is reckoned a very good sort of man and liked by the Spaniards much better than Frenchmen in general are. He has shown great attention to some of our prisoners and I should have no objection to show some little attention to his brother, if circumstances would admit of it. I have had a letter from Monsieur Salaignac by which I see he writes and understands English perfectly well.

Maria is also to let him know that her brother has every expectation of being able to arrange an exchange for him. It was an extraordinary coincidence that two such high-profile French prisoners, Salaignac and the Prince d'Aremburg, should both be held prisoner less than an hour's ride from Hawkstone, home of their captor.

Soult left the city of Grenada on 15 September and the city was occupied by Ballesteros on the 17th. Evidently, the French had destroyed all the guns and fortifications in Jaen and Grenada before they left. Soult was said to be heading for Guadin and Caravaca with the notion that he would join Joseph and Suchet at Almanza. Hill had planned to take the strategically placed castle of Consuegra, but found that it had aready surrendered to the Spanish General Elio.

On 20 September, Hill was at Carpio, Joseph was still at Valencia and Soult was heading towards Hellin. Rowland wrote home saying that Clement had not been well – a bilious fever had some ten days previously confined him to bed. 'The Doctor recommends that he should go to Madrid for a change of air. Clement won't hear of going home.' Hill's detached corps was now to the south of Madrid and his brief was to guard Wellington's southern flank while the Duke had another attempt at Burgos. Brother Tom was to be involved in this siege at the head of his regiment of 1st Portuguese.

The Duke had definitely underestimated the strength of several of the great Spanish fortifications. Tom was there at Burgos and involved in the storming of the fortress but it was not one of the great frontier defences for nothing and it still held out. Wellington subsequently told Hill that it had proved one of the hardest jobs he had ever had. Rowland wrote to Maria on 28 September telling her that the enemy had evacuated the town and that Wellington had taken some of 'the out works before the place'. It has been said that his failure to raise the siege of Burgos was the nearest that Wellington ever came to defeat, an unverifiable claim, but it is fair to say that if the corps of Royal Sappers and Miners had been available just a few months sooner than the end of 1812, then Burgos would have fallen earlier. Thomas Noel would later compare it with the siege of San Sebastian with which he would be involved the following year.

Hill was marching towards Toledo and Aranjuez via Navalmorale de la Mata, Oropsa and Talavera. He now had Major General Charles Alten [201] of the King's German Legion under his command, a most excellent soldier with first-class troops. Alten was at Madrid from whence, on 29 September, he sent Hill some intelligence as to the movements of the King and Marechal Suchet, who had now joined together at Almanza. He also enclosed for Hill some information received from Don Carlos d'Espana. [202] Alten wrote that it looked likely that Soult was marching to join forces with Suchet and Joseph.

Wellington told Hill he was not yet clear in his mind as to the plans of the French. In fact, this was a moment of the campaign when things were confused and even the Duke had a problem formulating his strategy. They arranged, provisionally, that Hill would shortly join the Duke on the Tagus.

On 2 October, with two French armies moving against him, Hill had to retreat. The French had 60,000 men under King 'Jo' and Soult. Rowland had no choice but to give way. He drew back to Salamanca where he joined with the Duke on 8 November.[203] Hill and Soult certainly had a long shared hunting history. Twenty six years later, they were to meet face to face in London and Soult is reputed to have said, 'What! Have I found you at last? You, whom I followed so long without ever being able to overtake you?'[204] This is quite probably apocryphal, although true enough.

Rowland had halted to the northwest of Madrid with the bulk of his troops housed in the Escorial – the great, sombre fortress and palace of that dour and fanatically religious King Philip II of Spain – and in Aranjuez nearby. The original plan had been for him to hold Madrid but it was to prove impossible. His force was far too small to take on these approaching armies. All the same, he spent a 'peaceful' three weeks with leave granted to some officers to go and enjoy the delights of Madrid. Three of the brothers, Rowland, Robert and Clement, were together and all of them made visits to the city, which Rowland described as very beautiful. The rest and the 'cultural tours' did not last. Intelligence was soon telling Rowland that the armies of King Joseph, Soult and Suchet acting in co-operation, were indeed approaching and so, after blowing the magazines and taking as much in the way of food stores from Madrid as his army could carry, he withdrew, preparing for a junction with Wellington, who had now retreated from his siege of Burgos.

The weather was terrible during this period and part of Hill's crossing of the Guadarrama mountains proved another epic march not dissimilar to, if not as long, as the terrible retreat to Corunna. Everything was saturated; no fires could be lit. 'The dreadful weather we have had has been very much against us and our army has, I am sorry to say, suffered a good deal, particularly our cavalry.'[205] The main reason for the lack of provisions was the stupidity of the Quartermaster General, Colonel James Willoughby Gordon.[206] This man, unfortunately, had friends in the highest places – including the Duke of York – and he had been foisted on Wellington, who already had the excellent Sir George Murray acting in this capacity. London removed Sir George on the pretext of a promotion, and put Gordon in his place. He was a disaster. He was already in Wellington's bad graces having leaked one of the Duke's secret dispatches to the *Morning Chronicle*. He leaked several more pieces of information over the months he was in the Peninsula but this was one of the most important.

This particular dispatch had been critical of the Whig Government. Gordon also spent much of his time in writing letters to people of influence in England criticising the way that the war was going and the manner in which the Duke was handling it. Officially, it is listed that he went home in 1812 due to bad health; in truth the Duke had finally got rid of him. 'He estimates his own good qualities and acquirements to the highest pitch of self approval ... and he is possessed of

the most inordinate ambition.'[207] This snub on the part of Wellington did nothing
to blight Gordon's career. He held staff appointments at Horse Guards for many
years and was created a Baronet. He was still at Horse Guards when Hill became
Commander in Chief in 1828.

As far as the Duke was concerned, the final straw was when his Quartermaster
General sent the supply column by the wrong road leaving the men with no
rations. Richard Aldington writes that 'it is not necessary to think that Gordon
deliberately sent the army's food on the wrong road from Salamanca; his natural
incompetence would take care of that; but it does seem probable that he omitted
to tell Wellington of his mistake and that his subordinates dared not do so.'[208]

Wellington and Hill covered each other's retreats and joined up at Salamanca
on 8 November. By Sunday 15 November, the Allied forces were in some danger
of being encircled but Wellington ordered a retreat and marched his men along
the enemy flank and across the river Zurguen, with Hill and his column forming
the rearguard. They avoided being outflanked but found the going very tough
with flooded rivers and creeks. Once again, the Allied forces were suffering from
a severe shortage of food. A week later, Wellington decided that the French were
not going to risk an attack in such unfavourable conditions and Rowland withdrew to Coria.

In many ways, 1812 can be summed up as disappointments mixed with occa-
sional moments of good fortune. One of the best results was that the end of the
year saw the French leave the southern part of Spain for good and this meant an
end to the necessity for Sir Rowland's detached Corps keeping an eye on their
movements there. Winter was on them and Hill put his troops into cantonments
at Coria and the men began the 'make do and mend' so necessary to ill-provi-
sioned troops whenever they had the time. The years 1811 and 1812 had seen a
great loss of men to sickness and there had also been an unprecedented number
of deserters. The number sick or unfit for duty was calculated at 13,000.

In October 1812, the Prince Regent had finally been persuaded to part with
some of his Household troops, the Life Guards and the Blues. He requested that
two companies should be added to each regiment so that they could continue
to mount the King's Guard and provide royal escorts in London. Four troops of
each regiment embarked at Portsmouth in October 1812. They formed a small
Household Brigade under General Rebow. Rebow would return to England in
March 1813, when command of the Brigade passed to Rowland's brother Robert
Hill.[209]

One of Hill's first actions after reaching Coria was to write a long letter to his
father. With the enthusiasm awakened by personal victories achieved by a local
'hero', Rowland had been elected, *in absentia,* to serve as one of the two members of Parliament for the Borough of Shrewsbury. The vacancy had occurred
when his cousin, William Noel Hill of Attingham,[210] gave up the seat to represent
Marlborough. Sir John had managed his son's campaign and, in fact, there was

never much doubt that the General would be elected. Rowland wrote to his father from Coria on 30 November, enclosing 'a few lines to the electors of Shrewsbury' and adding, 'I think we shall be here for some time.' The time they spent in the little city of Coria on the banks of the river Alagon was no real hardship.

The Duke was going to wait for the spring to bring the fresh new grass that was so important as forage for the horses and thousands of mules engaged in carrying men, pulling gun carriages and supply carts. It was at this point that Wellington issued his memorable circular about the Army's moral condition and behaviour. Nobody who reads of this war can doubt that many of the soldiers did commit crimes of greater or lesser greed or brutality but the Duke's all-embracing harangue created a great deal of bad feeling because many of the sweeping charges certainly did not apply to everyone.

Life in cantonments was far from dull and gave the men a chance to let off steam and organise a few amusements, which were often highly inventive. The officers of the 2nd Division passed much of their time in coursing, hunting and shooting, none more keenly than their General. According to young Robert Blakeney,[211] Hill was 'as keen at unkennelling a Spanish fox as at starting a French general out of his sleep, and in either amusement was the foremost to cry, "Tally ho!"' Many of the men served as beaters. Hill was obviously a first-class horseman but in the course of one chase, he nearly met his end when a fox hotly pursued by nine of his hounds leapt over a cliff and the General barely managed to pull up his own mount in time to avoid following them over. All the hounds and the fox were found dead below. At Hawkstone, amongst the many follies and points of interest in the celebrated park, there is still today 'The Fox's Nob'. Was this originally named to commemorate Rowland's near escape? It is quite possible since this part of the park at Hawkstone is no country for hunting; it is very suitable for foxes but not for the horses and their riders in pursuit!

In addition to his official duties and his sporting activities, Hill was involved in thinking up and attending all manner of amusements got up for the troops' diversion. Nothing was beneath him. According to a subaltern of the 34th Foot,[212]

He patronised an amateur theatre, which was very well got up. We had amongst us so many regiments, capital actors, scene-painters, and really a first rate company. The female roles were generally taken by the youngest of the ensigns. After the play we all went in our stage dresses to the General's supper table, where we did enjoy ourselves to the full, a singular group of painted actors.

Rowland wrote to Sir John asking for a statement of his finances, 'My KB may look very well after my name but they have a very indifferent effect on my purse … hope Emma[213] has received some melon seeds. Clement sent about a fortnight ago – I got them in Madrid.'

As a sop to the British, on 12 October the Cortes had voted to make Wellington Commander in Chief, *Generalissimo,* of the Spanish forces. Hill described the effects of this announcement in a letter home dated 15 December. The Spanish General Ballesteros had written several letters over the course of the last three years to both the Duke and General Hill saying he was 'anxious to comply with their wishes' and in this Hill had thought him sincere but, on hearing of Wellington's appointment, Ballesteros was outraged and refused to accept it. His efforts to rally support from the Spanish military failed and he was eventually arrested by the Regency.

Wellington, crippled with lumbago, left for Cadiz in mid December leaving Hill in command of the Army until the end of January.

VIII

CHAMBER MAIDS AND THE 'TRAVELLING BORDELLO'

The spring of 1813 arrived and with it a re-energised Duke, who went directly on the offensive. It was well known by now that Napoleon had suffered a crushing defeat in his Russian campaign. Sir Rowland had sent a quantity of newspapers, together with copies of the latest reports to London of Lord Cathcart, the British Ambassador to Russia, to French frontier posts so as to ensure that it was not only the French Marechals who heard the bad news, but the rank and file as well. Morale was not good in the French ranks.

On 12 February, Hill was on the move. Unlike the French Army, morale within his force was high and the general feeling was that there was a fair prospect of success. The weather had also improved, which helped to lift the spirits, the state of the Commissariat was good, for once, and there was no reason to fear for a lack of supplies. 'We are heading towards Pau.'[214] Pau is in south-west France, which may seem a little odd at that moment in the war. In addition to his own Corps, he was to have Picton's 3rd Division[215] for the time being. Picton was to return in May.

The state of the campaign in the Peninsula was debated in the House of Lords in March. The situation was different than at any other time in the war to date; Ciudad Rodrigo and Badajos had been taken and the French had failed to succeed in many of their attempts against the Allied Army. Joseph's government was a 'miserable Government without power, without any authority'.

Lord Wellesley[216] pointed out to London that the number of troops was not necessarily the vital factor; after all, 'that able and excellent officer, Sir Rowland Hill' had kept Soult corralled in the south of Spain with only 5000 British and 12,000 Portuguese. He added that the state of affairs in the Peninsula had taken a turn for the better.

On 23 March 1813, Rowland wrote to his father telling him that the enemy had withdrawn from La Mancha and he gives his father a description of the enemy armies:

The Army of Portugal commanded by the Comte de Reille, ADC to the Emperor, has 8 divisions. 11 Generals of Brigade, 31 infantry regiments making a total of 31,256.

Cavalry consists of one general of division, 2 generals of brigade plus 9 regiments totalling 3256; the Artillery includes 1775 men. This army is currently centred on Avila, Valladolid and Tore and Salamanca and the grand total is 100,552 men.

The Army of the South, formerly commanded by Soult, is now under Comte de Gazan. It has 8 divisions of infantry totalling 30,705 men and cavalry numbering 3,000 plus 500 artillerymen. This army has its HQ at Toledo and IT IS IMMEDIATELY IN FRONT OF MY CORPS.[217]

The Army of the Centre is commanded by Comte d'Erlon and has its HQ at Madrid. He has 7000 infantry and 4000 cavalry with artillery in addition. The Army of Valencia commanded by Suchet has 13,000–14,000 infantry. The Army of the North does not, I believe, exceed 12,000.

These figures including all the sick and wounded were compiled before Soult left for France taking with him selected officers and men to complete the Imperial Guard but Rowland did not know exactly how many men he took with him. 'Our Army, I believe, is in very effective condition, the 2nd Division's infantry was never so strong in the field as we are at present and the cavalry are recovering from their weak state. I am inclined to think the enemy has sent no reinforcements into Spain.'

On 10 May, Rowland wrote to Maria from Galisto, '... I am quite anxious about Edward coming out again so soon but I hope Robert's letters will have reached him in time to stop him.' Once again, we have no explanation as to what Edward's problems are. On 4 May, the 28th Regiment, which had played a prominent part at Albuera two years before, decided to give a dinner to Sir Rowland, although he had been absent himself on sick leave at the time of the battle, and the Staff of the 2nd Division. This was less in the nature of a celebration but more of a commemoration of so many friends lost during that frightful battle.[218] The feast was organised by Lieutenant Irwin who selected the softest and most even piece of turf he could find on which he marked out the due length and breadth of a table for no less than 100 guests. The officers and men of this army were nothing if not imaginative when planning their entertainments.

The turf was carefully lifted off and a trench was dug around it large enough for all the company. The table was formed in the centre of the sods ... and duly levelled and excavated to give ample room for the legs and then the green turf was once more gently laid on and supplied the place of a tablecloth. Each officer invited was desired to bring his own knife, fork and plate, and not to be particular about having them changed.[219]

The food was said to have been substantial, 'the heavy artillery' of field cuisine. There were heavy joints roasted and boiled, with soups and pies baked in the camp kettles. Then came the cordial welcome of the chief guest, 'the man who never had an enemy but on public grounds, whose bland smile put the company at ease, while his genuine dignity prevented in his presence every word and every act that did not perfectly become it.'[220]

Wellington took off with a few members of his staff and crossed the Douro on 30 May – in a basket rigged up on a cable to carry him over! He quickly rejoined Graham and the larger portion of his army. On 3 June, the two armies joined at Toro. The Allied Army was now larger than it had ever been: it numbered 80,000 – it was the French who were the ones stretched. This rapid advance had thrown them into confusion. Joseph was no strategist but together he and Jourdan decided that the enormous number of refugees and the 'loot' from Madrid should proceed 'in retreat' to Burgos. The retreating 'King' of Spain was anxious to take home the treasure from Madrid by way of what was called the Royal Road; perhaps Joseph felt that his brother might forgive him if he presented him with riches.

The Allied Army's men were in high spirits, they had put the second half of 1812 behind them. As they crossed the plains on the march to Salamanca, some of Hill's officers unleashed their greyhounds to course the hares; many were killed alongside the column as it wound its way across the rolling uplands.

Hill had received his orders on 2 June and proceeded by forced marches on Toro via Fuente Sauco. The men crossed the Douro as best they could at fords and over makeshift structures replacing the bridges. Yet again, they were desperately short of food. If armies march on their stomachs, these fellows succeeded with precious little in theirs! On 12 June as Hill's Corps moved forwards in two columns, there was a little skirmishing with the enemy who eventually retired to the heights above Hornillo but apparently alarmed by the numbers of the Allies, they withdrew and joined up with General Reille[221] in command of the Army of Portugal. Their combined forces took the road to Burgos.

Early on 13 June, the Allied *piquets* saw a huge cloud of thick white smoke enveloping the fortress at Burgos, then came an enormous explosion followed very quickly by several more. The great stronghold had been blown up, destroyed by the French. This may possibly have been accidental, arising from spilled gunpowder, nobody seems certain. Suffice to say, the huge pile of stone that had defied the British for so long had vanished. The French drew back.

From Vittoria, an apparently safe defensive position, Jourdan and Joseph planned to send off to the north all the baggage containing the plunder they were carrying, which came mainly from Madrid. The French Generals were concentrating on the idea that Wellington was coming from the west. He was indeed, but not only from the west. He brought some of his army over mountain roads that had never been considered by Jourdan as remotely passable to such large bodies of men. Was Wellington heading for Bilbao? Jourdan and Joseph seem to have been confused and having sent off an entire infantry division as escort to the baggage train, which, after all, was worth a great deal of money, they were left with around 57,000 men. For once, Wellington was superior in numbers.

On the evening before the Battle of Vittoria, Sir Rowland had to ask permission from Wellington to give some food to the Portuguese. The latter had never been very good where their commissariat was concerned and the wretched soldiers had nothing to eat. Hill could presumably have taken it on himself to have supplied them with one day's rations, but Wellington had given such fierce directions that the Portuguese and Spanish must supply themselves, that he felt it necessary to write a short note to the Duke:

> Barquiseda, June 20th
> My dear Lord
> I am sorry to have occasion to address your Lordship again on the subject of provisioning the Portuguese division under my orders, after the instructions which I have received from you; but they are at present in so destitute a state that I feel it my duty to make your Lordship acquainted with it;. They for some days have been on very reduced ration. The day before yesterday they had only three quarters of a pound of meat and yesterday nothing, and have no prospect for this day. To give them bread, I am aware, is out of the question but I beg to know whether your Lordship will permit me to give them some meat?

The Duke's reply was somewhat terse, unusual in his dealings with Hill, but perhaps understandable under the circumstances;

> June 20th, half past 1pm
> My dear Hill
> I have just received your note of this morning. You may assist the Conde d'Amarante as you please, but let the Conde know that it is an exception to a rule to which I am determined to adhere, and that he must make his commissaries exert themselves.

Clement wrote home four days before the battle sounding in high spirits.

> England will, I think, be a little astonished at our rapid march. The whole of our army got over the Ebro yesterday and continues to advance. What Lord Wellington's plans are I believe nobody knows but himself. We all feel confident of great success, and you may expect to hear of the French being fairly turned out of Spain. We have driven them so far almost without the loss of a man and they find themselves completely outmanoeuvred. After they destroyed the

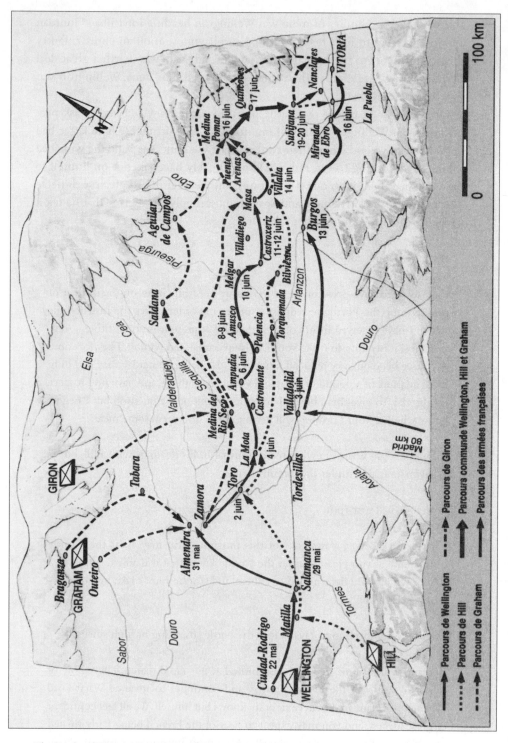

The Battle of Vittoria. (Jean-Francois Krause, *Napoleon I*)

Castle of Burgos, we did not venture to march in the line by which they retired; but by rapid marches to our left by a difficult road which they could not have expected us to attempt, we crossed the Ebro before them, and expect to continue moving, and get between them and their communication with France, which will bother them a good deal.

The Battle of Vittoria was fought on 21 June 1813. It was to prove a turning point, possibly *the* turning point, in the war. . The Allied Army was in three corps: the right led by Hill, the centre under Wellington himself and the left under Graham. The Duke had planned an audacious encircling strategy. The plans drawn up by Joseph, Jourdan, (now serving as '*chef d'etat major* to the fleeing 'King'), Gazan and d'Erlon, were to give battle at Vittoria and then to take the great road to the safety of France and, if necessary, fight again on their own territory. Their second possibility was to take the road for Pamplona and Saragossa. This latter risked the possibility of the great baggage train being attacked and the first plan was adopted.[222]

Hill's troops on the British right were the first to attack. As described by the French, Hill entered the village of Puebla, marched through and then sent Morillo and his Spanish division to climb and take the crest of the ridge, the Heights of La Puebla, which lie to the south of the Zadorra river valley. These heights are much steeper on one side than the other. The Allied forces climbed up the gentler side. The Spanish fought well and were soon reinforced by British and Portuguese troops, led by Colonel Cadogan[223] and the 71st.[224] Morillo was severely wounded. The combined Spanish and British efforts had taken the ridge. It was still only 8.30am as Hill's flanking force on the right was engaged by the enemy desperate to dislodge the British and take possession of the heights, which gave the holder such an advantage. However, they had to attack up the steep side of the hills and arrived breathless at the summit putting them at a severe disadvantage. After some tough fighting the Allies managed to hold their position. The rest of Hill's men were massed below the heights in a gulley under William Stewart, the divisional commander. Stewart, as already mentioned, was impetuous and not entirely reliable, and Wellington had come to an agreement with Hill that he should always act as Stewart's 'overseer'.[225] Sir Rowland then pushed his men on through the narrow valleys below the hillside and proceeded to take the village of Sahjana de Alava in front of the enemy's lines, and the bridges of Nanclaus and Tres Pontes.[226]

Rough old General Picton, despite disobeying his orders,[227] had taken the Mendoza bridge encouraging, it is said, his men with 'Come on, ye fighting villains.' The French never managed to regroup effectively and were soon being pressed by Hill's left.

By this time Jourdan was growing anxious[228] wondering if Hill's actions were just a feint, this was probably due to the fact that Hill had, so far, only had two of his British brigades engaged together with Morillo's Spaniards.

Sir Rowland had fulfilled his orders,[229] whereas Wellington was still looking anxiously for Graham. Unfortunately, this great General had misread his orders, or, unusually, Wellington's orders had been ambiguous, and it was not until just after midday that Graham thought he should advance. One of his orders had been that he was not to permit himself to be drawn into unnecessary fighting and this had led him to halt for some time to see how things were going. It could well be that his failing eyesight was partially responsible.[230] Thanks to the delays by Graham, who was supposed to cross the Zadorra and cut the Royal Road to Bayonne, and also the tardy arrival of Dalhousie, Hill was not supported for a long time and took a lot of casualties. Graham had 20,000 under his command but he had left the French a route to safety and they were not slow to take it once they saw that they were defeated. This road lay towards Pamplona by way of the pass over the mountains at Salvatierra,[231] not an easy route for a retreating army.

Although he had been delayed himself, Graham had sent off Colonel Francisco Longa and his Spaniards at around noon to cut the Royal Road. Graham by now was engaged north of the river but having sent Longa to cut the road, he then proceeded to leave the other escape route for the French intact, which was a serious mistake. To be sure, this was no 'super highway' but a rough road leading in the direction of Pamplona via the pass of Salvatierra through the mountains. Vittoria was not Graham's greatest battle.

Dalhousie was not an especially efficient officer and his position at the head of the 7th Division at Vittoria was unfathomable to many. When he remained in command during the battles of the Pyrenees, there was much muttering amongst the troops and some raised eyebrows from the officers. In fact both he and Stewart were to reinforce the opinions of their abilities already held by their commanding officers; both required supervision.

By 5pm, when Wellington's centre broke through the French lines, the French Army had lost all sense of formation and King Joseph had used all his reserves. He virtually threw up his hands and ordered a retreat towards Pamplona. The soldiers broke and ran, abandoning the huge French wagon train to the victors. Many descriptions have been written of this French baggage because its contents were almost unimaginable in their riches and certainly so to the Allied private soldiers. The French lost about 8000 men, the Allied Army in the region of 4500. Napoleon's brother was no commander and Jourdan, admittedly suffering from a high fever, was no tactician. The Marechal was to be held responsible for the defeat by Napoleon. He was disgraced.

The collection of weaponry, gold and works of art that the French Army left behind in its scramble to safety was simply extraordinary. On the military side, the Allies took all but two of the 153 French guns and apparently the enemy also left 415 *caissons* on the battlefield. The road was completely blocked with equipment, carriages[232] and all the packs of the French soldiers who had just thrown them away as they fled.[233] Of course, there was also a useful amount of ammunition recovered, hundreds of muskets and some first-class horses. The baggage wagons were loaded with silver plate and coin together with many masterpieces which had been cut from their frames in the Spanish Royal palaces and rolled up for easy transport. There was also, of course, food and drink. There were military and state papers, the French Military Chest and, best known of all perhaps, King Jo's silver chamber pot,[234] which led to the regiment, the King's Own Hussars, who found it, becoming known as, 'the Emperor's chambermaids.' Another discovery was Marechal Jourdan's *baton*. It was sent to the Prince Regent who then set about designing a similar one for Wellington. The women, of all ranks and 'occupations' that had accompanied the French were so numerous that they have been described as '*un bordel ambulant*'. What ensued was a veritable orgy of looting with carriages ripped apart in the search for hidden gold. This went on for some time and by the time they had finished celebrating, the men were in no state for a long march in pursuit. It is said that when the bulk of the Allied Army moved on the following day, it was literally hung about with the spoils; there must have been some sore heads.

The inhabitants of Vittoria had also been able to acquire enough loot for themselves to repay them for the 'contributions' that the French had brutally exacted from them. As Oman records, one important piece was never found: the Spanish Crown! It seems strange that this emblem of royalty should have completely disappeared. The only booty that Hill was to enjoy was a couple of hams that his servant managed to get his hands on. They were probably extremely welcome.

Wellington was furious that his men had plundered most of the money and he had to confess to the Secretary for War that nearly half a million pounds from Madrid had passed into the hands of his soldiers. Frequent searches of the men's packs yielded almost nothing; the rankers were very adept at concealing such loot.

Joseph had himself managed to escape, although he narrowly avoided capture, and he did not stop until he reached Salvatierra sixteen miles from the battlefield. Only 2000 French prisoners were taken because the Allied soldiers were far too occupied in looting. Why the cavalry, which had in the main scarcely been engaged, did not pursue the fleeing French is inexplicable. Rowland's brother, Robert Hill, was present at the head of the 1st and 2nd Life Guards, and the Royal Horse Guards ostensibly under the overall command of Stapleton Cotton, though he was on leave and returned three days after the battle. At least 55,000 of the enemy had escaped. Once again Wellington was furious with the indiscipline of his soldiers after the French broke but surely even he realised by this stage in the long campaign that, following a hard fought battle with victory gained, his 'scum' could not be restrained until they had sated their appetite for looting, women and wine. Wellington left Vittoria on the morning of 22 June in pursuit of the enemy. Most of his army was severely hungover as it marched out.

The battle was of wide significance because it forced the European powers to admit that Bonaparte was no longer invincible. It also consolidated Wellington's reputation as he was now once and for all recognised to be much more than a 'Sepoy' general. The battle also brought the affairs of the Peninsula to prominence on the European stage once again.

Moyle Sherer had been assigned a most unpleasant but essential duty following the battle. A captain's detachment was left behind by each regiment. These men were responsible for looking after the wounded and seeing that the dead were listed and buried. It was hard work and also involved collecting the heavy *caissons*[235] and guns. He describes the ground as thickly strewn with papers, some of these were highly important army records but were not, of course, of any interest to the looting soldiers who had ransacked everything in their crazed search for gold.

There was, however, one Allied officer who profited from the capture of the wagon train, but in a very different way; this was Lieutenant Colonel George Scovell, a most interesting officer. A clever man, he thought himself despised by the Duke owing to his relatively lowly birth. Snob he may have been but Wellington certainly recognised merit. Scovell had made himself extremely useful by a combination of brains and sheer hard graft. He first came to notice in Moore's campaign. He established a small ad hoc group known as The Guides.[236] This was an odd group of men, principally foreigners, many were criminals or ne'er do wells, hired for their knowledge of the terrain and for their languages.

Working under the QMG, George Murray, Scovell had become fascinated by codes and this eventually led him to being put in charge of the Army's communications employing this motley crew, which was a fairly thankless task but of the greatest importance. He was responsible for sending messages, for example, when Hill was in command of his Detached Corps, messages flew between him and Wellington several times a day. Many of the messages and letters that were intercepted on their way from one French Army to another in the Peninsula were, of course, written in code. Scovell applied himself diligently to deciphering these. What made the capture of the French baggage after Vittoria so very special was Scovell's discovery of the King's leather paper case in Joseph's impressive coach. When Scovell opened the case, he found Joseph's personal copy of the Great Paris Cipher's decoding table. Elsewhere, he found the booklet for enciphering with its alphabetical listing of words, letters and phrases.[237] The luckless Joseph had to confess this loss to the Minister of War, in Paris, who already despised Napoleon's brother. A new cipher was immediately created but this took some time.

Meanwhile, Joseph was deposed from his 'token' position at the head of the French forces. He was strictly forbidden to go to Paris, he no longer had a kingdom! Soult, old enemy of General Hill, was appointed to rally what was left of the

French Army in its retreat to the Pyrenees and back into France, although before embarking on his march through the mountains, he tried to raise the Allied siege of Pamplona.

Moyle Sherer records how a bookseller in the town of Vittoria told him that he had sold more books to the British in the two weeks following the battle than he had sold to the French during the two years during which the French had constantly marched through Vittoria. You have to ask yourself what sort of stock the man kept since the average British officer was not known for his erudition! As recorded by Sherer, it was largely made up of books written by the best-known French authors and published in Parisian editions and all going very cheaply. The bookseller expressed considerable surprise that so many British officers were reading men.[238] The victory was recorded not only in books but in music with Beethoven composing a piece. His Battle symphony is known as Wellington's Siege or the War by Victoria.

Wellington had gained an extraordinary strategic victory, one could even say that if Graham and Dalhousie had not been so late in taking their places in the battle order, then the battles through the Pyrenees might possibly never have been fought. On the other hand, should that have been the case, Sir Rowland would never have had the chance to fight and win a general action entirely on his own.

The victory was also very timely for Britain's position in Europe. Castlereagh had been trying to establish a coalition amongst Sweden, Russia and Prussia while the Austrians still remained undecided; the victory of the Allied Army at Vittoria forced them on side. The former Marechal Bernadotte, who was now the Prince Royal of Sweden, was fiercely opposed to his brother-in-law, the Emperor, despite having achieved his 'royal' status entirely thanks to Napoleon. Bernadotte founded a dynasty in Sweden that exists today whereas all the other kings that Napoleon created fell by the wayside almost immediately.

The news of the defeat at Vittoria finally reached Napoleon's camp on the Silesian border on 30 June, at the very moment when the Emperor had been about to attack the Russians and Prussians once again. The dire news made him change his mind and he agreed to a six weeks' extension of the truce. The Austrians were delighted as this gave them some time to prepare. Unknown to these great powers far away to the northeast, Wellington was already on the march for the Pyrenees, although he still remained uncertain as to whether he should actually 'invade' France immediately. He certainly did not intend to advance until he was sure he had secured his rear.[239] Soult, sent back by the Emperor to take charge of the crumbling armies in Spain, 'to re establish the Imperial business', had formed a daring plan, he thought, to turn the tables on Wellington and relieve San Sebastian.

Wellington did achieve one further welcome 'victory' of a different sort, in 1813. He received a letter from Torrens at Horse Guards saying that the Duke of York would accede to his request to recall several of his most inept generals. These included Slade, who had the nerve to ask the Duke for a letter of recommendation and Erskine, who shortly therafter committed suicide by jumping out of a window in Lisbon. The Duke's query to Horse Guards as to Erskine's suitability when he had heard that he was being sent out, seems to have been well justified. The others that were sent home were Robert Long,[240] Victor Alten[241] and, a few weeks later, Tilson Chowne.

IX

BATTLING IN THE HIGH PYRENEES

Whe Wellington marched out of Vittoria taking the road to Pamplona on the morning of 22 June, following one of the most decisive battles of the whole campaign, he left behind the 5th Division and Robert Chambré Hill's cavalry brigade. Rowland's younger brother was now Lieutenant Colonel of a new brigade of cavalry composed of two squadrons each of the 1st and 2nd Life Guards and the Royal Horse Guards. This had ranked as the 3rd Brigade, 2nd Division but was transferred to the 1st Division on 5 February with Robert having taken command in March.[242] Robert had joined the Blues as a cornet aged 16 in June 1794. In 1797 he purchased his lieutenancy and his captaincy in 1800. By 1805, he was a major and by the age of 35, in 1813, he was Lieutenant Colonel and in command of the regiment. All the Hill boys' promotions would have probably been paid for by their uncle, Sir Richard, since their father, John, being a younger son, was not a rich man at this point, although his wife, Mary Chambré, of another old Shropshire family, had brought some money with her to the marriage; five sons in the Army must have cost a fair penny.

The 6th Division was expected to reach the city of Vittoria within the next 24 hours. Wellington rode with the centre column together with his HQ staff while Graham and Hill took their columns off the main route using minor roads that were not much more than mule tracks. Graham rode by way of Arzubiaga and Audicana while Hill passed through El Burgo and Alegria.

Hill's division arrived at Salvatierra on the 23 June and Clement wrote another letter home to reassure his family of the brothers' wellbeing:

> On the road from Vittoria to Pampeluna – I hope you will receive this in good time to assure you of the safety of the four brothers after the battle of Vittoria. We are all at this moment together in the same room and in perfect health …

Never was an Army more completely routed and defeated than the French. Rowland's corps were principally engaged during the first part of the action, and have suffered more than any other. The Blues were in the fire but not engaged. Tom had a good deal to do which was well done.

Hill's next mission was to establish the siege of Pamplona. He began by cutting off all water supplies to the city by severing an aqueduct. Next, he established *picquets* along the river bank opposite. The men manning these posts fired at anyone rash enough to venture to the bank of the river for water. Wellington also suggested to him that all the corn in the fields surrounding the city should be harvested and taken away and if this was not possible, it should be burned.[243] As soon as all these plans had been effected, Hill left the wearisome job of blockading to the Spanish of Morillo and the Portuguese of Silveira while he took the road north towards the frontier with France, the great barrier of the Pyrenees.

From just outside Pamplona on 1 July, Clement wrote

… the army we so gloriously beat at Vittoria has been in France some days. They ran so fast, having lost every incumbrance, even their last gun, that we made but few prisoners on their retreat … we are in the most delightful part of Spain I have ever seen for summer, but it must be bad in winter. The weather has been quite cold even now, and for the last fortnight almost constant heavy rains. The country is very mountainous with fine valleys covered with corn and good villages. We get well supplied with everything: amongst the luxuries, excellent French butter. The Blues are at Logrono on the Ebro, and I fancy will not move up at present, as cavalry are not of much use in the country we are in.

Hill pushed his troops on and wrote to Maria from Lanz, 'three leagues from France' on 3 July. He tells her that the mails will now be going from Santander on the north coast of Spain, which shows that the centre for supplies arriving from England had shifted north from Lisbon. In fact, the principal port for supplies was to be the sheltered harbour of Pasajes – inevitably written as 'Passages' by the English. This is in an almost concealed inlet just east of San Sebastian. The only drawback to using Pasajes was that it was tricky to navigate the entrance in rough weather. With the arrival of more and more ships bearing troops, guns and supplies, Pasajes was transformed from a small fishing village to a hub of commerce. Apart from the difficult entrance to the harbour, it was a small place and often the quays were full of ships, which meant that new arrivals had to drop anchor in the middle of the harbour and offload into small and often rather fragile boats which were certainly not intended to transport great guns. Some of these boats were rowed by muscular women, which much surprised the men of the British Army.

Tomorrow, I expect to be with my corps on the border of France. Some of my people are at this moment at Arriege, which village is in France ... I have now the pleasure to inform you that your four brothers in this country are well. Tom, as usual has had his share of the fatigues and fighting; he and his regiment have invariably conducted themselves well. Clement is with me ... he is not looking very stout but is well. Robert whom I saw about a week ago, is in perfect health. Lord Wellington is much pleased with the conduct and appearance of the Blues. This not being cavalry country, Robert and his brigade are, I believe, to remain for the present in the neighbourhood of Vittoria.

Sir Rowland was about to begin many weeks of fighting and manoeuvring in the mountains. It was to be a different sort of war that they would fight amongst the valleys and peaks of the Pyrenees. If you consider the physical state of the entire army on the march, you realise how incredibly tough, how fit they were by this stage of the war. Some of them had spent five years in the field, often under unspeakable conditions, which had served to make them into first class troops – just so long as they had something to pursue and attack! Throughout the war, once victory had been gained, they could only too often turn into brutes, totally out of control, the worst examples probably being at Ciudad Rodrigo and Badajos. This breakdown of discipline always came after an especially bloody battle and, of course, with the free availability of unlimited wine; it was one of the senior Generals' worst problems and not one that was easily dealt with despite every effort being made and salutary examples being made of many of the men who were found plundering and raping; if they were caught in the act, the Provost Marshals would have them strung up.

The mountain range of the Pyrenees forms a natural barrier between France and Spain. They stretch for 400km from the Atlantic to the Mediterranean. If the highest peak in the Pyrenees, Pic d'Anet, is not as high as Mont Blanc in the Alps, the mountains and deep valleys make for just as rugged a region and with a harsh climate.

The news of the great victory at Vittoria only reached London on 3 July and, needless to say, resulted in wild celebrations. The 'frightened leopard' of Napoleon's imagination, was now in possession from Roncesvalles west to the Atlantic and was driving King Jo's army back to France. The Prime Minister, Lord Liverpool, was delighted as the news came at a most timely moment. Napoleon had appeared to recover from the disaster of the Russian campaign with quite extraordinary resilience and despite the death of something akin to 250,000 soldiers.[244] He had been victorious at Lutzen and Bautzen and an armistice had been arranged to discuss peace terms with the Russians, Prussians and Austrians. Austria dithered; she was not sure which side to support. Napoleon had tried to keep word of the British victory at Vittoria from the other leaders while the British Government broadcast the news as widely as possible, printing copies of Wellington's dispatch in German, Dutch and French and distributing copies at all the continental ports they could reach.[245] A few days later, Austria realising that she would now be wise to switch her allegiance, joined the coalition against the Emperor; weaknesses were appearing in the once invincible Corsican.

The Emperor had fallen into a wild rage when the news of the defeat at Vittoria finally reached him. Joseph attributed much of his troubles to the war minister in Paris, the devious Henri Jacques Guillaume Clarke, Duc de Feltre, who would correspond with Joseph's generals in the Peninsula by going over his head, without consulting him. Since Paris seems to have been completely out of touch with events in the Peninsula, such instructions as were received were frequently simply ignored, since they were often out of date. By the time that the battles were being fought in the Pyrenees, 'King' Joseph was already in France; he would never return to Spain. Napoleon was dismissive: 'If there was one man wanting in the army, it was a real general, and if there was one too many with the army, it was the King.' The Emperor's supreme self confidence was, by this date, such that he appears to have never paused to question his own judgement.

On 6 July, the French Army began its retreat through the mountains via the Bastan valley. The question was where would they turn and fight. Nobody believed that they were just slinking away; they were not. Nor did Sir Rowland imagine that he would be pushing directly on into France even should he manage to dispose of the immediate threat of Soult and Gazan.[246]

Sir Rowland and his Corps had to push Gazan slowly back in a number of skirmishes but with minimum loss of life. Rowland then halted at Elizondo, an historic city of the Basque country which is now a thriving centre of tourism. Here he was joined by Wellington on 5 July to discuss tactics. Rowland on the right (post of honour)[247] continued to occupy the mouth of the Bastan valley. Under Hill was Stewart commanding the 2nd Division;[248] Major General Pringle of the 2nd Division together with Walker's brigade guarded the Passes of Maya on the right while the Col d'Arriette and the Col d'Espequi were watched by more of Sir Rowland's 2nd Division and by Colonel Ashworth's and Brigadier Da Costa's Portuguese brigades. Brigadier General Campbell's Portuguese held a strong position on the mountain to the right of Los Aldudes while keeping contact with the Vallee de Bastan.

With his numerical inferiority so vast, Hill wanted to avoid a major battle until he had been reinforced by the promised arrival of Clinton with the 6th Division and Picton with the 3rd. He knew that Lowry Cole was at Roncesvalles, the city on the road to Compostella where the Breton soldier, Roland, fought in Charlemagne's army and was killed, his memory for ever preserved in 'La Chanson de Roland' one of the oldest French works of literature. As one wit of the 34th, Cumberland Regiment said, 'Plenty of help was coming to us, but never came.'[249] Doubtless the difficulties of maintaining communication were one of the greatest problems during the battles in the Pyrenees. At one point, Hill was in a very dangerous position, hopelessly outnumbered, when suddenly he found himself in dense fog. One of the French divisions even found that they had walked around in a circle.

Initially, d'Erlon had some success when he attacked Sir Rowland's[250] forces in the Passes of Maya. At the same time Soult, who had returned to Spain on 11 July to take charge of the Army of Spain[251] as it was now to be known, with his eventual goal to try and break the blockade on Pamplona, attacked in the Pass of Roncevalles dislodging the Spanish in the ravine of Orbaicete. He then pushed Byng's brigade back after fighting that lasted nine hours. Lieutenant General Sir William Stewart had gone to Elizondo some ten miles in the rear where Hill, his commander, and Wellington were conferring. This was a serious error on Stewart's part and when he received word that the French were pushing through the Maya passes in great numbers, he had to return as fast as possible. His men were in very difficult positions; some had expended all their ammunition and were reduced to hurling rocks down on the enemy. As the French advanced, the British were forced to push some of their guns over the mountainside and retire. Stewart's report to Hill on this rather dismal affair was published in the Royal Military Calendar[252] in 1815, the original seemingly having disappeared, although there is a record of Hill having sent it to the Duke. Stewart commended the bravery of several of his generals and rounded off his report:

> A very spirited charge by the 6th Regiment led on by Major General Barnes … enabled us to close an inauspicious day in a manner that imposed upon our enemy [and] left us in an eligible situation, for which had such been your orders and had succour arrived, we might this day have regained that ground, the loss of which I have been detailing with much pain to my feelings.

Stewart was indeed to feel this loss very keenly. Perhaps he was fortunate that his report to Hill had not been inserted in the *Gazette* at the time, as his conduct and direction of his men had received considerable criticism. There is no means of discovering how John Philipparts got hold of the report and published it. There is no copy of it, today, in either the Wellington Archive or in the Hill Papers. The failure festered in Stewart's mind.

Hill, who had hastened up after Stewart, together with Major General Barnes, had put a stop to d'Erlon's advance and had ordered a retreat under cover of night. The troops had taken a considerable beating, not helped by the fact that Cole had not, as Hill had hoped, managed to hold on and when that General retreated and met Picton coming to his assistance, persuaded the latter to retire as well saying that the French had enormous numbers with them, which was not entirely true.

Meanwhile, although Hill with Major General Barnes had put a stop to d'Erlon's advance, they too were compelled to retire as a direct result of Byng being forced back. They withdrew first to Elizondo and then to a position on the Bidassoa. Campbell withdrew through Roncevalles and joined the rest of the right wing at Zubiri. Thus the French, under Soult, cleared both the pass of Maya and that of Roncesvalles and it seemed that they might even reach their goal, Pamplona, but the British together with their Portuguese allies rallied at Sorauren and forced Soult's retreat after the second battle there on 30 July. It was all scrappy, difficult fighting and included several different battles[253] with the action lasting from 25 July to 2 August 1813. As Wellington wrote, 'it was bludgeon work.' The Allies lost about 2600 men, the 2nd Division being the hardest hit, whilst the French are estimated to have lost something in the region of 4000. Soult did not retreat immediately into France but tried to sever Wellington's communications with Graham who was still taken up with the siege at San Sebastian. He failed in this and eventually retreated into France on 2 August. Pamplona was ultimately starved into surrendering on 31 October.

The Michel Papers in the Dorset Records Office contain papers of Captain, later Colonel, Churchill, Military Secretary to Hill in the last couple of years of the Peninsular Campaign. They serve to illustrate the system of exchange that went on between the enemy armies. These requests were usually made at the top level – by Generals to Generals. Sometimes, they concerned the exchange of prisoners or enclosed money for prisoners that could not be exchanged. Each side always asked for a receipt! A letter to Lieutenant General Stewart in August of 1813 contains an anguished plea from Lieutenant Colonel John Fitzgerald. He is a prisoner having been captured when he got lost, knocked down, stabbed twice and plundered of everything. He needs clothes at the very least if he cannot be exchanged. He has also found two other of his officers, Lts Power and Bartley, both of the 50th Regiment.[254]

Another rather touching incident demonstrates the more compassionate side of the war; General Foy wrote to General Hill on 6 September 1813, saying that a Captain Joseph Guillet, attached to the staff of Soult (now also created Duke of Dalmatia) has gone forward to the English advance posts to fetch his daughter who has 'been in your care'.[255] This little girl had been found, lost, wandering in the British baggage train following the Battle of Vittoria and had spent nearly three months with the British Army before being restored to her father, who gave effusive thanks for her care. A similar tale, but without, as far as records show, the same happy ending,[256] was that of another Frenchman, Captain Floquerel. He wanted to know if there was any news of his wife, Maria de Las Navas from Alcala la Real who had vanished on 21 June, the date of the Battle of Vittoria. We have no record as to whether or not she was ever found and returned to her French husband. Another communication from General Foy on 27 November 1813 informs Sir Rowland that an officer of the 13 Regtiment Light Dragoons has been given a horse to go to St Jean Pied de Port, Wellington's HQ at that time and that there an exchange will be arranged. Sudden movements between the two armies led to a delay and the man mentioned, together with his servants, had been taken 'deeper' into France near Pau. These are but a small sample of the correspondence, much of which deals with money for prisoners and the exchanges that could sometimes be arranged.

Churchill's time was also much taken up by requests from officers who considered that their bravery in action had not been sufficiently recognised, or who grumbled that they were overdue for promotion. Wellington was often sparing with mentions in dispatches, which sometimes led to considerable resentment. He could also be extremely harsh and is known to have reduced several senior officers to tears.

A letter from Hill's old friend, Thomas Graham, written from Ozarzun, reached him by the hand of a doctor.

> I profit by Dr Ferguson's passing here in his way to the second division to send you two lines. You have had a great deal of fag and fighting of late which I was glad to hear you had escaped safe from. We are waiting for ordnance ships to bring ammunition and more guns to enable us to renew the attack against San Sebastian, which we tried to storm unsuccessfully on the 25th ult. But the defences were untouched and the enemy made too good use of them against our column of attack, confined to a very narrow front between the river the foot of the left line wall, where it was left dry by the falling tide.

Sir Thomas continued in a postscript, 'I hope you received the box sent by Lieutenant Colonel Colburn[257] of the 52nd safe with the coffee essence from Lord Mulgrave, in the top of which I sent an old map of yours which has been travelling about with me for years, in order to be returned. Remember me to Currie.[258] I have been suffering again a good deal from my eye and stomach.' This eye trouble was obviously quite severe and soon resulted in Graham going home again.

Whilst Sir Rowland and his Corps were high in the Pyrenees, the first storming of the town and fortress of San Sebastian down on the coast, almost on the frontier with France, was underway on 25 July. If Wellington had a fault as a commander, it was that he never appears to have learned how to handle a siege; Ciudad Rodrigo, Burgos, Badajos, San Sebastian and Pamplona all took far longer and involved greater loss of life than was probably necessary. One reason, for which he cannot be held culpable, is that he did not have the right equipment until the very end of the war. Endless badgering of the War Office frequently failed to produce results and, if equipment was eventually forthcoming, it took a very long time to arrive. Even then when he did have some 100 engineers and sappers, plus a strong siege train, which he had lacked throughout most of the campaign, the

engineer-historian John T. Jones pointed out that the operations were still 'irregular ... not enough science, not an effective enough blockade by the Royal Navy.'[259]
Wellington's career came at the very beginning of what could be termed 'modern'
military engineering. He distrusted Colonel Congreve's rockets,[260] not without
some justification in the early days and a few years later was to show what he
thought of trains – not much! The siege of San Sebastian kept Hill's young brother,
Thomas Noel Hill, and his Portuguese regiment busy until the fortress finally fell
on 9 September. Thomas described San Sebastian as an 'abominable place'.

Rowland wrote to Maria from the camp at Roncesvalles on 17 August. He
described Soult's efforts to relieve Pamplona and continued, 'We had a good
deal of fag and fighting[261] and managed to withstand the huge numbers brought
against us.' Hill had now briefly returned to the blockade of Pamplona. This
was one of the moments when Wellington was asked by the War Office if he
would release Hill to take command of the army (British, Spanish and Sicilian
troops) in Catalonia on the eastern coast of Spain. He would have replaced
General Sir John Murray who had been mishandling[262] a diversionary operation
against a French army under Marshal Suchet. Wellington refused. The British
Government asked him at least three times to release Hill but always received
the same reply, to the effect that he could not spare him. Other men in Hill's
position might have been resentful considering that their careers were in jeop-
ardy but Hill does not seem to have been upset by this highhanded approach.
One hopes he accepted it as a compliment. The Commander was not about
to part with his only completely reliable senior general when eventual victory
finally seemed to be in sight.

On 29 July, Soult, who had twice been foiled in attempts against the Allies
during the two previous days, decided to try to relieve Pamplona by an attack
on Sir Rowland. He was repulsed. Rowland managed to establish himself on a
mountain ridge about a mile in his rear where he held his ground and thoroughly
discomfited the French, who retired during the night. Rowland followed them
the next morning and came into contact with two hostile divisions in the Donna
Maria Pass. He dislodged these together with Dalhousie and the 7th Division;
Byng also managed to gain revenge on his recent opponents by capturing a large
convoy in the town of Elizondo.

On 1 August, Rowland and his two supporting divisions pursued the retreating French into the valley of the Bidassoa and took a large number of prisoners
together with much useful baggage. Thus this part of the Allied Army found itself
back on the frontier in much the same position as it had been at the start of hostilities at the beginning of July. Rowland wrote to Maria on 17 August that he was
sure that Pamplona could not hold out for much longer; the French Commander
of the garrison was a brave man but without relief from Soult or d'Erlon, there
was nothing he could do after the population had finished eating the last of the
cats and dogs!

The front now stretched from near to St Jean de Luz on the coast, south of Bayonne, to Maya about sixteen miles east. Sergeant Joseph Donaldson, who was at Maya, was ordered to take a letter to Sir Rowland who had his HQ at Roncesvalles. There are many stories such as this that illustrate Hill's sympathetic behaviour towards enlisted men. Donaldson confessed in his 'Recollections' that he felt nervous:

> Judging from the proud and haughty bearing of some of our ensigns, in coming into the presence of the general second in command of the British Army, I expected to be annihilated by his look, and I was ushered into the room to deliver my message with a palpitating heart; but I no sooner saw the humane and benevolent-looking countenance of the general, than my apprehensions vanished. Having read the letter, he questioned me concerning the health of the commanding officer, and asked me questions concerning our regiment (of which he was Colonel) in the kindliest and most unaffected manner; then calling one of his servants, he ordered him to provide me liberally in meat and drink. Some time after, seeing me standing outside the tent, he called me, and asked whether the servants had paid attention to me. Next morning, on giving me a letter for my commanding officer, 'I did not intend,' said he, 'that you should have returned so soon but we are going to remove down to the valley, and as it would be only taking you out of your road, it will be as well for you to proceed; but there is no necessity that you should go farther than the small village two leagues from this. I will give directions to my orderly dragoon to procure you a billet there, and tomorrow you can join your regiment.' He then ordered his servant to fill my haversack with provisions, and when I was going away, he said 'Remember now what I have told you, – don't go farther than the village and here is something to get yourself a refreshment when you arrive there.'

He handed Donaldson a coin or two. This kindly treatment made a great impression on Donaldson who could well understand why General Hill was so popular with the men; they respected him as a clever, brave commander but they also held him in affection for his humanity and concern for their welfare.

The Allied Army was exhausted after the nine days of fighting in the mountains and Hill occupied a camp at Roncesvalles for some days. From here, he could observe the movements of the French Army and he spent much of each day with his telescope following their movements and trying to deduce their intentions. Pamplona somehow was still holding out but Hill knew that it could not do so for much longer; there was no food and the inhabitants and the garrison were struck down with sickness.

On 15 October, Rowland wrote to Maria from his HQ at Roncesvalles. He was replying to a question from a Dr du Gard:

re Dr du Gard's enquiry respecting R. Holland – it appears he has been reduced to the ranks for drunkenness. I have to beg you will have the goodness to inform Dr du Gard that although I shall at all times be most happy to comply with his wishes … the object of the present application is contrary to my ideas of what is right, that I feel myself obliged to decline asking Lord Aylmer to reinstate R. Holland as Sergeant.

Sir Rowland was no soft touch! He was a stickler for the rules and not to be swayed by either friendship or kinship. Further on in the letter he acknowledges the receipt of two pipes of port which he cannot recall ordering but for which he is most grateful. He notes with pleasure the course of events in Germany and doubts that they (the Peninsular Army) will move into France but rather 'halt to refit our troops and to be ready to act according to circumstances'. He also asks Maria to send him some brawn, which he thinks should keep well as the weather is so cold. Cheese, he added, would also be most acceptable.

On 29 October he wrote to Sir George Murray, QMG, that they had already had heavy falls of snow and that he did not think he could keep his troops so high for much longer being without any form of shelter. He had instructed one of his divisional commanders, General Pringle, to make his own report on the state of the countryside in his neighbourhood. 'I am expecting General Byng down from the mountains; I shall then be able to judge what is best to be done.' The weather on the mountains was so wild that it was impossible to erect tents and the men were terribly exposed. A rendezvous was arranged: 'in front of Colonel Browne's[263] quarters at Urdax' for 7 November when Sir Rowland would meet Wellington to discuss future movements. Rowland added in his note to Sir George 'In a letter I wrote to you a few days ago, I mentioned that we had buried three of Captain Maxwell's guns on the mountains owing to the impossibility of withdrawing them on account of the snow. I am happy to say that we have, by the great exertions of the artillery and troops, been able to extricate them.'

X

VICTORY AGAINST ALL ODDS

It was now mid-autumn but the Allied Armies' operations were not yet finished for the winter. Wellington had reorganised his army somewhat. Thomas Graham had gone home because of his failing eyesight and several other senior generals such as Picton, Leith and Dalhousie were all on leave. It seems, today, bizarre that so many very senior officers would be given permission to go home before the season's campaigning was over and it leads one to suppose that Wellington did not expect much action before the real winter set in, or surely he would have refused these furloughs. Beresford was in command of the left hand Corps with Wellington accompanying him,[264] Hill had the right-hand Corps, which included the usual brigades plus also the 6th Division (General Clinton) and an independent Portuguese Brigade under General John Hamilton. Together, these amounted to about 55,000 men. Wellington's intention was that they would, together, make a concerted attack in the early morning of 10 November. The British knew that Soult was spread very thin as he 'held' a front stretching from the Atlantic Ocean on his right as far east as the pass of Roncesvalles, a distance of 20 miles. Wellington was superior in numbers, Napoleon had been steadily taking men from his armies in Spain to shore up his wavering position in north-eastern Europe, from whence the news arrived on 3 September that Austria had joined with Russia and Prussia to turn the tables on him. Three weeks later, the word came that Napoleon had been routed at the Battle of Leipzig. Wellington pushed his men across the Nivelle; Hill had brought his men down from the mountains by moonlight and fell on the French at about 7am. He took several French redoubts and pushing the enemy from before Ainhoue, he forced them to retreat. In spite of the time he had had to prepare, Soult was completely out manoeuvred. He withdrew towards Bayonne.

Sir Rowland did not seem to think there was much prospect of another fight in the immediate future: '... the glorious news from the North, I trust, will ere long settle Napoleon. The people of France receive us well. I never met with so much attention. The mayor of Ustaritz prepared an excellent dinner for me yesterday, and the people run out of their houses to give our people wine.' A couple of weeks later he wrote to his brother John:

> Our future depends a good deal upon what is going on in other quarters. We are perfectly prepared to act on the offensive; and if our Allies on the Rhine continue to do so, we shall not be idle. On the other hand if Bonaparte is not kept well occupied either by internal commotions, or by our northern friends, perhaps it may be well for us to maintain a safe and threatening position. This latter situation we have at present. At the same time, we are very much cramped; and although we may be able to get our men under cover, the total want of forage for the animals is a serious inconvenience … the rains which fell about a fortnight ago rendered the river Nive a formidable barrier: the last week's fine weather has, however, made the river fordable in many parts, in consequence of which both parties are kept on the alert.

Four days later Hill was at St Pe. On 11 December he received a letter from Marshal Beresford.

> Lord Wellington says we must not be surprised if he should turn his attack against you [Hill] in which case the 6th Division, now at Ustaritz, will pass over to your support; and, at all events, if you want it send for it, and Sir W Clinton has directions to conform to your wishes. Lord W says the enemy yesterday brought from your side [of the river] three, some say four, divisions; and it is not quite certain if one division was not left in their entrenched camp on your side.

Hill was completely cut off from Wellington by a sudden rise in the level of the river Nive, which carried away the remaining bridges. He established his HQ on the height of the Horlopo from where he had an excellent view over his front, which stretched for some three miles and included three hills; the heights of Larralde with its Chateau, Mouguerre, and Horlopo, each separated by deep, water-filled gullies. These gaps could not be taken advantage of by the enemy thanks to the water, which meant that the French could only attack through a narrow front.

Soult, ever the opportunist, transferred the major part of his force – five divisions – which had been in front of Wellington, across the Nive by way of bridges in Bayonne. On 13 December he fell on Hill, who had only two divisions; his force being made up of his old 2nd Division troops plus Hamilton's Portuguese. During the night of 12–13 December, Hill had heard the ominous rumble of Soult's artillery as it crossed the bridges out of Bayonne. Thanks to a rapid rise in the water level during the night, the pontoon bridge at Villefranque, by means of

Rowland, Viscount Hill
as a young man. (Author)

General Hill in his later
years. (Author)

Above: 'Rowland Hill, 1st Viscount Hill' by John Romney after Meycon, 1815. (National Portrait Gallery)

Left: 'Rowland, 1st Viscount Hill' by Henry William Pickersgill (1782–1875). (The Royal Collection © 2011 Her Majesty Queen Elizabeth II)

Sir Robert Chambré Hill, KCB, Lieutenant-Colonel commanding the Royal Horse Guards, Blue at the end of the Peninsular War and at Waterloo. (Author)

Major-General Clement Delves Hill as a young man, as shown by the fact that his hair is still worn in a queue and powdered. He was ADC to Rowland throughout the Peninsular War. He was Lieutenant Colonel, Royal Horse Guards, Blue, Silver Stick in waiting. (Author)

Clement as an older man wearing the Waterloo medal, which was added after the portrait was originally painted. (Author)

James Thomas
Brudenell, 7th Earl
of Cardigan by Sir
Francis Grant, *circa*
1841. (National
Portrait Gallery)

'Comrades in Arms'; Thomas Graham (Lord Lyndock), Lord Hill, Sir Thomas Picton and
the Marquis of Anglesea. (National Portrait Gallery)

The family seat of the Hills in Shropshire, Hawkstone, 1860.

The salon at Hawkstone today. (Courtesy Father Denis McBride)

'The Grotto Hill and Red Castle in Hawkstone Park' by W. Williams, 1783. (Author)

'The Red Castle at Hawkstone Park' by W. Williams, 1783. (Author)

Top left: Freedom box from Shrewsbury. Top right: Freedom box from Plymouth. Bottom left: Sir Robert Chambré Hill's helmet worn during the Peninsular War and at Waterloo. Bottom right: A French cuirassier's breastplate found on the battlefield at Waterloo.

The Hill coat of arms. (Author)

A commemorative 'election jug' for Shrewsbury, 1796. The candidate John Hill had it made in advance but was beaten by William Noel Hill. (Author)

Marshal Soult
by G.P.A. Healy.
(Victoria & Albert
Museum)

Marshal Blücher
by George Dawe.
(Victoria & Albert
Museum)

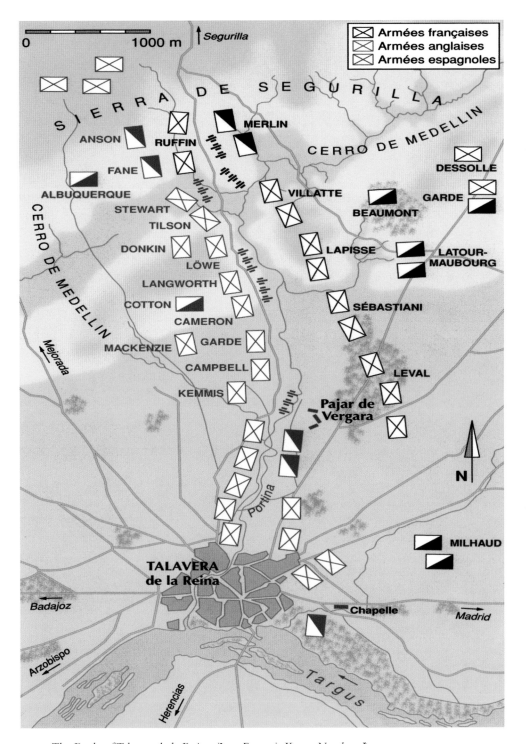

The Battle of Talavera de la Reina. (Jean-Francois Kraus, *Napoleon I*)

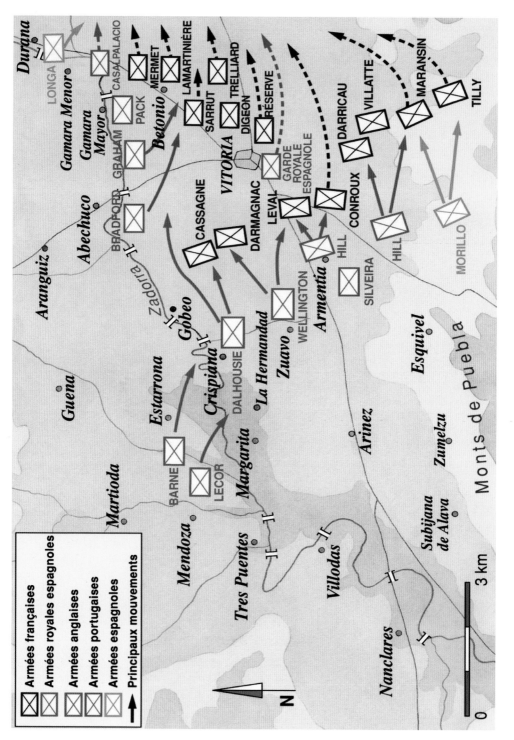

The Battle of Vittoria. (Jean-Francois Krause, *Napoleon I*)

'Hussars at ease, being supplied with provisions' attributed to Henry Thomas Alken.

'Fording the river Mondego' by Thomas St Clair.

'Waterloo. The Duke of Wellington's Head Quarter' by Charles Turner, after a drawing by Captain George J. Jones. (Wellington Museum, Waterloo)

'The Morning of the Battle of Waterloo: The French await Napoleon's Orders' by Ernest Crofts. (Sheffield Galleries and Museum Trust)

'Prince Blücher under his Horse at the Battle of Waterloo' by M. Dubourg, after a drawing by
J.A. Atkinson. The incident actually happened at the Battle of Ligny two days earlier. Blücher was
trapped for several hours beneath his dead horse. (Wellington Museum, Waterloo)

The Waterloo Medal. On the front a winged Victory holds a laurel palm in her right hand and an
olive branch in her left. The reverse shows the Prince Regent.

A nineteenth-century depiction of the column at Shrewsbury erected in 1816 by public subscription to commemorate Lord Hill's exploits. At the time it was the tallest Doric column in the world. (Author)

which support was expected, gave way. Hill was cut off. As soon as Sir Rowland heard that the bridge had gone, he knew it would be some hours before he could expect reinforcements from the 6th Division under Beresford. Early in the morning, he could clearly see dense blocks of soldiers advancing towards him.

The leading division, commanded by General Abbé, headed towards Hill's centre, where the 2nd Division was under the command of Lieutenant General Stewart, while a second column approached General Pringle holding the Chateau Larraldia. At the same time, General Byng's brigade on the right was pushed back by Chassée under General Foy; for the present, the Portuguese, now commanded by Le Cor (Hamilton having succumbed to illness) were held in reserve. The difference in numbers on either side was once again enormous; where Hill had only 14,000 men, Soult had 35,000. Pringle did sterling work in the Chateau, which he barricaded, keeping 5000 men at bay with his meagre force of 1800. Taking only 130 casualties, his attackers suffered at least 450 and he held them off for four hours. Hill was everywhere; his right flank was threatened and Colonel William Bunbury of the Buffs ordered his regiment to retire to the protection of Byng's brigade, although Sir Rowland maintained he should have resisted for longer; apparently Byng had already marked Bunbury[265] out as 'shirking responsibility'. On this occasion, his conduct on the Mouguerre ridge where he had been sent forward by Byng was considered 'feeble to the verge of criminality.'[266] St Pierre was certainly one instance when Sir William Stewart, commanding the 2nd Division, distinguished himself by his bravery and sense in the face of fierce attacks by General Abbé.

Rowland was aghast to find a large gap appearing in his centre where the newly arrived commander of the 71st Regiment, Lieutenant Colonel Sir Nathaniel Peacocke, ordered his regiment to retire. One can only imagine that, although an officer of many years service, he had never before experienced such bitter, close combat; he would be remembered as a tyrant in barracks and a coward in the field. He ordered the 71st (Glasgow) to retreat at a crucial moment and when Sir Rowland went to discover the reason for this gap in his centre, he found Peacocke in the rear making pretence of inspiring the Portuguese ammunition carriers to advance while carefully keeping himself well out of danger. Rowland was furious and immediately demonstrated his own bravery by personally leading forward his final reserves, Da Costa's reliable Portuguese, while General Stewart put himself at the head of the 71st in the place of the cowardly Peacocke. The 71st (Glasgow) Highlanders were very happy to be able to restore their reputation. The fierce 92nd (Gordon) Highlanders also counterattacked, with their piper, suffering with a broken leg, playing 'Cogadh na sith.'[267] This brave regiment, led by Colonel Cameron, took a terrible beating yet again. They were regarded with fear by the French who called them the *sans culottes* because they had hung on to their kilts, most other Highland regiments had now given them up in favour of trews.

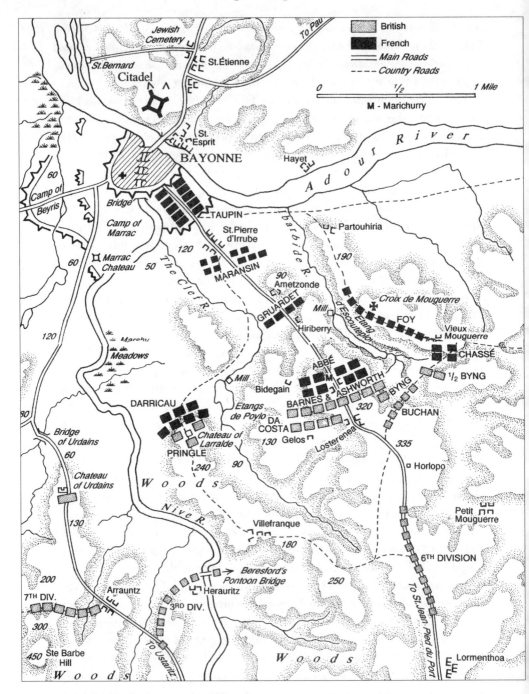

The Battle of St Pierre, 13 December 1813.

Hill fed his last reserves into the battle, 'with skill and spirit' beating back each French attack with detached companies holding on in the face of terrible odds; 'dead or alive, we must hold our ground.'[268] Hill evidently made masterly use of his reserves leading them forward quite early, which was probably because he knew that help would be coming – although he could not have known how soon. Stewart's report to Hill and Hill's to Wellington can be found in the Scovell papers.[269] Stewart's was very long and either his, or Hill's – which would have been the version sent on to the Duke – contained an enclosure describing the cowardly behaviour of Bunbury and Peacocke.

Wellington's dispatch to London makes no mention of these two men but that action was subsequently taken against them is confirmed by a letter written from the Allied Army HQ at St Jean de Luz on 2 January 1814 to Colonel Torrens at Horse Guards sending a Lieutenant Colonel's resignation with the request that he might be allowed to sell his commission. This must have been Bunbury, although a blank space is left in the copy letter.

> Sir R. Hill was very much dissatisfied with his conduct in the action of the 13th of last month and had determined to bring him to trial before a General Court Martial, the result of which the Colonel had first determined to stand but he has since thought it better to resign and I send his resignation ___ recommends that his place be filled by a Lieutenant Colonel from another regiment.

Wellington wrote further on the subject to Lord Bathurst on 22 February saying that his report of the events of 13 December had been more detailed than Sir Rowland's but that he had not enclosed a very long report from ___ (obviously Sir William Stewart) as 'in mentioning some names in it, he might do injustice to others.' This is frustrating so long after the event.

Sir Rowland's actions in command also appear in the Scovell papers, which consist in the main of codes.[270] The fact that Soult was comprehensively beaten in the end was certainly partially owing to the fact that he did not support General Abbé in his attack on Hill's centre early on in the battle. With their vast numerical advantage, surely the French should have crushed the British with ease. Wellington was probably right when he said that Soult could bring a fine army onto the battlefield but he could not fight a battle. In Hill, Soult had found his nemesis.

At the close of the battle, Hill was incensed to find that Peacocke had retired a second time, suffering from shock when a musket ball passed through his coat tails! The Colonel was subsequently cashiered. To be cashiered was the most severe penalty with which an officer could be punished. To demonstrate how rarely this penalty was imposed, throughout the entire campaign, it was done only 30 times.[271]. Only twice was it the result of shirking or cowardice, as in the case of Peacocke. In January 1819, five years after the event, Peacocke wrote to the Duke in an attempt to justify his behaviour. You imagine that the shame of being dis-

missed in such a way must have preyed upon him and his family. In his letter to
the Duke, he wrote that he wished to have the 'opportunity of explanation or justification, observing that nothwithstanding the severe penalty inflicted upon me,
I am at this moment uninformed of the cause or of the charges which have led to
this severe punishment with which I have been visited.'[272] A second letter written
immediately after the above is very interesting. Did Peacocke really believe what
he writes in this letter or has his memory clouded and led him to put down what
he would have liked to believe his actions had been?[273] His recollections of events
on 13 December 1813 are very different from both Stewart's and Hill's dispatches.
According to him, he had led the 71st forward in the teeth of enemy fire, when
in fact he had retreated. He had been found beating the Portuguese ammunition carriers in the rear when, as Colonel in command, he should have been at
their head, as he wrote that they were advancing and he could have sent a junior
officer to chivvy up the ammunition carriers in the rear if necessary. He writes
that he saw Wellington, Hill and Beresford beside the mules loaded with ammunition. This would have been impossible since neither the Duke nor Beresford had
even crossed the river by that time and Hill was far too concerned with what was
happening to his centre, where Peacocke had left the great gap, and his right wing
where Bunbury had forfeited his forward position.

Conspicious bravery was, however, demonstrated by many other officers, especially Major General Edward Barnes, Colonel John Cameron, Major General Byng,
Captain Hew Dalrymple Ross of the artillery and 'Auld Grog Willie', the often
erratic Lieutenant General Sir William Stewart. Stewart reported that all the ADCs of
Barnes, Byng, Buchan and his own had been wounded and Generals Barnes, Le Cor,
and Ashworth had been hit. After four hours of desperate fighting, the French withdrew just as Wellington arrived having crossed the pontoon bridge at Villefranque,
which had finally been repaired. The 'thin red line' had held throughout the day and
to give Wellington his due, he rode up to Sir Rowland when victory was certain
and catching his hand, said, 'Hill the day is your own.' Wellington wrote to Sir John
Hope, who had replaced Graham on the left, 'Sir Rowland Hill has given the enemy
a terrible beating.' The Duke wrote in the same vein to Spanish General Castanos
adding, 'It is a long time since I saw so many dead on a battlefield.' A gunner who
was present described it as a 'murderous day' and at places the principal road was
described as 'literally running with blood'.[274] For a short time, in the middle of the
battle, things had looked desperate; the cause was quite exceptional, and previously
unrecorded – the cowardice demonstrated by a battalion commander who had panicked. Sir John Fortescue wrote of the incidents, 'It was a rare thing in any army to
have on each flank a regimental commander who lost his nerve.'

Sir Rowland had won the only general action, St Pierre d'Irube, which he
fought entirely on his own and with all the odds stacked against him. He would
not have been human if he had not taken some pride in his achievement. His
men, just as they had been after Arroya, were truly gratified for him. It makes one

reflect again as to what he might have achieved in the field if he had not always been kept at Wellington's side. Although the Duke lavished praise on Rowland in his letters to other officers; he failed to designate the Battle of St Pierre as a major victory, which must be considered an oversight. Although enclosing Hill's report in his own dispatch, he seems to have made very little of Hill's victory when communicating with London. This was noted by several people, including John Colborne of the 52nd and even modest Sir Rowland himself had expected to see his own dispatch in the *Gazette*. Wellington's dispatch appeared in the *London Gazette* of 30 December. However, Wellington did give a nod of approval to Hill when he sent Clement with the dispatch to London. Lieutenant General Sir William Stewart, anxious to redeem his reputation tarnished in the events of Albuera (in Sir Rowland's absence)[275] had expected to be mentioned more fully in Wellington's dispatch. He attributed the reason that he did not receive much official praise to the fact that Wellington disliked him. This was to be an ongoing battle between the two men with Sir Rowland a neutral.

Hill might well have been surprised not to have received more official recognition but he was not the man to dwell on such a supposed 'slight'. To some, today, it might sound pompous or anachronistic, but he was a man who first and foremost 'did his duty'. Hill was only heard to swear twice during the entire campaign; the first time when he was nearly captured by the French on the eve of Talavera and on this occasion, when he found Peacocke in the rear, frankly his 'swearing' was so mild as to hardly merit the term! Fortescue wrote, 'there is no escape from the conclusion that the British General [Hill], though his name is unknown outside the British Isles [not quite true by this date] was a Commander indeed, while the French Marechal, though his fame is deservedly worldwide, was no more than an admirable chief of Staff.'[276]

Clement, now a Major, set off for London and suffered a wild passage on the way as he crossed the Bay of Biscay. Rowland wrote to him from Vieux Maugerre on 31 December:

> By this time, I hope you have reached London in safety. You must have had tremendous weather about the 20th … With respect to our future operations, nothing so far as I know, is yet determined upon, though we are looking for the best communications for our pontoons towards the Adour. I enclose you a letter from Egerton [Richard Egerton who had joined the Hill 'Family'] who no doubt sends you all the family anecdotes and events. Should it appear that the year 1814 is likely to turn out another year of campaigning in this country for us, I think you will do well to bring out some canteen dishes and anything else you know will be acceptable.

He also told him to bring at least three complete sets of saddlery with all its accoutrements. His final request was for his brother to bring him some lavender water from a shop in Bond Street! This letter was not finished for a couple of days as he had to involve his men in an expedition to prevent the French from constructing works on the 'island' of Urt. This was not in fact a true island but a piece of high ground almost surrounded by the rivers Adour, Jouyeuse and their tributaries. He pushed out a half battalion established there by Foy and placed some captured guns above the village to target boats passing on the river.

Thomas Noel, who had had home leave after San Sebastian was finally reduced, had returned to his regiment and spent Christmas of 1813 with his elder brother.

> I came here a few days ago to spend Christmas with Rowland. The brilliant victory of the 13th secured us from any further attempt on the part of Soult .... I enclose you a plan of the Battle of the 13th which you certainly should get framed and placed in the most conspicuous place at Hawkstone – every Body is delighted that Rowland had it all to himself and that his own Corps only were engaged.

Hill, once again, did his best to amuse his troops and keep them occupied during the cold, damp winter days. The theatre that had been such a success previously in the war, was revived. 'Our dear rosy-faced Farmer Hill entertained the whole dramatis personae at supper after the play. There was nothing about the war except in some comic songs composed for the occasion, of how, He [Hill] leathered the French.'[277]

In the early days of 1814, Rowland was kept busy adopting measures to prevent enemy boats from navigating the river Adour. When he found muskets were not effective, he proposed using rockets, which he felt, even if most inaccurate, would at least confuse and terrorise the boatmen. Wellington was still sceptical where Congreve's rockets were concerned. Eventually Hill was forced to send to General Fane for some heavy guns. At the same time he mentioned to the General that he was becoming concerned over the fraternisation of the two opposing forces on either side of the Adour and that it had increased to such an extent that he felt forced to put a stop to it. Officers and men had become quite intimate with each other and the men carried on a regular traffic upon a river running between the two armies (the Adour or more probably a smaller stream). A great stone was placed in the river and on it a canteen was put containing money. After a time it would be found to have been filled with brandy. One evening the French sentry failed to supply the brandy to a private named Patten who was, as he supposed, tricked out of his liquor. He dashed across the stream in the morning, seized the French sentry, stripped him, and carried his accoutrements in triumph to the picket house. A flag of truce appeared soon afterwards and the French captain who came with it begged hard for the return of the things taken from the sentry, on the grounds that if they were retained his own commission and the sentry's life would be undoubtedly forfeited. 'I have got them in pawn,' said Patten, 'for a canteen of brandy.' He gave them up and flatly refused to accept the money offered him by the officer. All the same poor Patten was sentenced to receive 300 lashes. The General had the delinquent led out with all due solemnity before the whole division to undergo this severe punishment. Sir Rowland then remonstrated with all the regiments concerning the indiscretion and probable consequences of such conduct. He then unexpectedly enumerated many acts of gallantry performed by the prisoner and, in the midst of faces beaming with admiration, remitted the sentence. Hill did believe that flogging had a place in the discipline of the Army as can be seen when he was at Horse Guards. He only resorted to it in the most extreme cases and was certainly not a 'flogging' General, but with an army composed of thieves, crooks and many men from the gutters of the big cities, he felt it was the great deterrent and was to continue to hold to this point of view in company with Wellington. The French did not flog but then their army was composed, in the main, of conscripts.

Wellington now found some of his 'scum' came in useful in an unexpected fashion; he was desperately short of money, as indeed were both the Spanish and the Portuguese; some of the muleteers had not been paid for 26 months. The British infantry were at least six months in arrears. Eventually, Wellington did manage to obtain silver from England only to find that the French peasants would not accept payment in silver[278], nor would they accept dollars as they had no concept of their value. Ever resourceful, Wellington set up his own mint in St Jean de Luz to strike Napoleonic 5 franc coins. Word was circulated that any professional coiners[279] could apply to work in the new mint; there was no shortage of applicants!

As the enemy boats continued to use the river, some method had to be employed to prevent them. The Duke suggested firing red hot shot against them from both the heavy guns and the four-pounders. At Hill's order, General Fane obtained two boats and taking some men from General Barnes' brigade under the command of Lieutenant Law, an intelligent young ex-naval officer, prevented all but the smallest boats from passing. On the night of 26 January, a large boat was captured.[280] Colonel Dickenson was also directed to send some rockets. These offensive precautions led to the cessation of most boat traffic.

Soult knew that Wellington had sent the bulk of the Spanish troops back to Spain. They could not be prevented from plundering and they refused to pay for anything; they just took what they wanted in the form of forage, meat, women. Soult even went so far as to sound out Morillo, one of the few reliable Spanish generals, who was still with the British in Hill's division, as to the possibility of getting the Spanish on his side. Morillo forwarded on to Sir Rowland some strange letters on this subject including one from General Paris stating that he had orders not to attack Spanish troops. Did he really think that the Spanish would make an alliance with the French after all that their country had suffered? These letters were, of course, sent on to Wellington.

Off the battlefield, even Morillo knew that he could not control his men who were not only seizing provisions but also revenging themselves brutally in other ways on the French for the treatment that they and their fellow countrymen had received during the long French occupation. The French peasants, on the other hand, were quite bemused by the fact that, with few exceptions, the British not only paid for everything but usually a much higher price than was warranted. Soult circulated proclamations exhorting the locals to raise partisan bands to prevent the invaders obtaining supplies; the peasants refused to do anything so unprofitable![281] It must have been highly galling to Soult to know that his countrymen were welcoming the enemy so warmly when he found his own troops absconding. The news had been received that the armies of Austria, Prussia and Russia had crossed the Rhine before Christmas and this meant an invasion of France was underway. The French people, certainly those in the south west, no longer supported the Emperor; Bordeaux was openly pro-Bourbon. Wellington, however, was sure that Napoleon would not capitulate tamely.

Another factor was now in the equation. In November, Napoleon had begun making overtures to his prisoner, Ferdinand of Spain. He offered him his 'own' throne back but, of course, with many provisos. Once Ferdinand was back in Madrid, the wretched Spanish were soon to find that they had traded one sort of oppressor for another. The Emperor despised Ferdinand; he had not seen him since he had lured him treacherously to Bayonne in 1808 but he felt that if he should restore him to his throne in Spain, then the French would have one certain ally in Europe. The fortress and harbours of San Sebastian, Santander and Pasajes, would then be closed to the Allied Army and six weary years of fighting in the Peninsula would have been wasted by the Allies. What became known as the Treaty of Valencay[282] was brought to Ferdinand by the Comte La Forest, formerly ambassador at Madrid, on 17 November 1813. Ferdinand was quite cunning and knew enough to refuse to sign the Treaty in the form that it arrived without some negotiation. One of these terms was that he would keep Spain neutral and pro French. Needless to say, he had not the slightest intenton of adhering to this. He rapidly reverted to absolutist rule. He cut his brother, Don Carlos, out of the succession. Don Carlos had never renounced his rights to the Spanish throne at the time that Napoleon had forced his father and elder brother to do so in 1808.[283] Historically, this has proved a problem for Spain with the 'Carlist' faction existing until the present day.

Things warmed up a little during the month of February. On the 12th Sir Rowland wrote to Maria from Marshal Beresford's house in Ustaritz, telling her that the weather had now improved and that they were very well supplied. He added that some sort of action in the immediate future was likely and that Wellington was collecting men including Rowland's own Corps in the neighbourhood of Hasparren; he also has Sir Thomas Picton's division with him. 'With respect to the handsome present of beef, I am sorry to say it has not yet reached

Passages ... I do, however, hope the next packet will bring this present.' A variation in diet was always eagerly anticipated and this one had been a long time in coming, too long as it would transpire.

> It is said the French princes (presumably the Comte d'Artois, brother of Louis XVIII and later Charles X together with his son, Louis Antoine, Duc de Lorraine) are at St Jean de Luz and have been waited upon in a private manner by many respectable people, and have received assurances of support when the moment shall arrive. This is indeed a most interesting time, and a few weeks will in all likelihood produce great events. God grant they may be for the best.

On 14 February, Wellington moved his army again. Sir Rowland marched his men on the right. For perhaps the first time in the entire campaign, Soult was not at a numerical advantage. Napoleon had taken so many men from him to bolster his Imperial Guard and the armies in the north that the French were now lacking seasoned troops. Conscription was, not unnaturally, more and more unpopular. Hill was acting as a diversionary force at this time, concealing from Soult Wellington's immediate design, the crossing of the river Adour below Bayonne in the estuary with Sir John Hope and his left to take Bayonne. These manoeuvres left Soult very puzzled. Sir Rowland's Corps rested at St Palais on the 16th and then started very early on the 17th with a view to following Wellington's instructions to push the enemy back as far as he could. The French held a bridge at Arriverayte but there were some passable fords above and below the bridge which Hill seized without much trouble. The 92nd found an unguarded ford a little above the bridge and crossed with little opposition and then fell on the French who were holding the bridge against a frontal attack.[284] The bridge fell almost undamaged into Sir Rowland's hands and allowed for the passage of the guns.

Having crossed the Saison, Rowland was now between that river and the Gave d'Oloron. He stayed there for four days before he joined in Wellington's scheme to turn Soult's left wing. Soult wrote to the Minister of War in Paris that he was being attacked by an army of 100,000 men; you might have thought by this late stage in the war, Soult would have known roughly the size of Wellington's army – it certainly never amounted to anything approaching 100,000. On 24 February, Wellington's columns appeared at several different places including at the fords of the Gave d'Oloron; here General Picton's men were more or less decoys and, despite explicit orders to the contrary, the General engaged with some of Harispe's troops and lost some men. The other columns crossed the Gave with virtually no opposition and very little loss of life. Rowland had thrown a pontoon bridge across at Villenave and his 2nd Division together with, as usual, the Portuguese of Le Cor, crossed without any problem. Sir Rowland's central column lost only two rank and file, both of whom were drowned. By the evening, more than 20,000 men had crossed but it had taken longer than Hill had hoped and none of his divisions got close enough to Harispe to cut him off from the road to Orthez, as had been Wellington's intention. Finding that he had been out-manoeuvered, Soult ordered a retreat on Orthez to defend the line of the Gave de Pau.[285]

Rowland arrived before Orthez on the south side of the river. Soult was in a fine defensive position on the north bank, on the heights above the village and does not seem to have thought of immediate action. Foy wrote in his personal journal, of the 'council of war' that he had attended with Soult, d'Erlon and Clausel together with four other generals of division. General (later to be Marechal) Bertrand Clausel had distinguished himself in the Pyrenees and the south of France, although he had the reputation of sometimes being rash and here he was the only one of the senior officers who advocated attack. On this occasion, Soult even thought he had finally got General Hill. He apparently exclaimed, '*Enfin, je le tiens!*' As Cole wrote, he exulted too soon.[286]

A message sent to Hill by Sir George Murray[287] on 26 February gave him Wellington's instructions, which were to establish a bridge near Orthez as early as possible the following morning and to report how the enemy appeared to him. The Quartermaster continued with a postscript: 'If we get into Orthez every exertion should be made to repair the bridge that our pontoons may become again disposable for other service for which they will immediately be wanted.' The river in front of Sir Rowland's corps was spanned by an impressive Roman bridge.[288] This bridge was completely blocked with stones placed in the arch of one of the towers and the entrances under the towers were, in any event, too narrow to permit more than one wagon at a time to pass through. Rowland chose to cross about a mile farther on, at the fords of Souars where the river bank was less steep and the water not so deep. His object was then to turn the enemy's flank. Hill left a brigade of Le Cor's Portuguese to show their strength opposite Orthez and marched east; he then forced a passage across the Gave and threatened Soult, who retreated. In his dispatch, the Duke wrote, 'It is impossible to express my sense of their merits, or of the degree in which this country is indebted to their zeal and abilities for the situation in which the army now finds itself.' This referred to Beresford, Hill, Cotton and Hope, Wellington's senior generals. Sir John Hope had quite often misjudged events in the past but when it came to crossing the mouth of the broad estuary of the Adour and besieging Bayonne, he made a good job of it; he was taken prisoner not long after.

Following the battle, Hill's corps bivouacked above Sallepisse; they were very tired and many did not bother to try and pitch their tents. The French occupied a strong ridge of hills with their right flank on the Adour, thus covering the road to the town. Soult had written to Clarke in Paris on 28 February:

Saint Sever could be defended, but behind it there are the worst defiles possible – the line of retreat completely commanded from the enemy's side of the Adour ... unless I get positive orders to the contrary, I shall not manoeuvre in the direction of Bordeaux, where I should have much trouble in passing the Garonne and should leave the whole of the south of France exposed to the enemy. I shall base myself upon Toulouse, and take my first position at Aire and Barcelonne where I shall be able to prevent the enemy from moving on Bordeaux no less than upon Toulouse. If the enemy does not attack me for several days, I shall be in a state to fight again.[289]

On 2 March, Sir Rowland advanced towards a French corps resting near Aire. It was thought likely that it was placed there to protect a magazine. The only opposition he encountered in the course of the march was in the region of Aire itself. Soult had decided to move southeast to Tarbes, abandoning his efforts to keep in contact with Bordeaux; he was to have sharper fighting than he had anticipated.[290] Marechal Clausel, completely deceived as to the numbers in Hill's force, was to find himself in a position from which he could not retreat. Sir Rowland approached around 2pm in two columns; his faithful 2nd Division nearer to the river and Le Cor's Portuguese about a mile to the south. Hill did not wait to form proper lines of battle but fell on Clausel and his five brigades. The French Generals Harispe and Villette were driven off, many of their men throwing away their arms as they did so. It was another victory for Hill even if only a relatively minor one; Wellington commented on it as 'another instance of the conduct and gallantry of the troops under Sir Rowland Hill.'

Success in the field was to be followed by the receipt of sad news. Rowland's elder brother, John, had died. He wrote a hasty letter to Maria on receipt of her letter giving him the news. He was still at Aire. That he was most shocked is very evident in his letter; the two brothers had been close.

> ... if I had ever so much time I could not express my real feelings on this melancholy occasion but under present circumstances, I am sure you will not expect me to say much. I am only this moment come into this town and I understand Lord Wellington will send his dispatches off early tomorrow morning. You will see that in the midst of my affliction, I have had to attend to important military matters. Scarcely a day has passed without our being in the presence of and in contact with the enemy: all our operations have been attended with success, and the enemy are now retreating towards Toulouse. Surely Bonaparte cannot hold out much longer.

He also told her that the long awaited baron of beef had arrived but that, alas, its journey had been so slow that it was inedible! He wished it to be known, however, that he was immensely grateful to the citizens of Shrewsbury for having sent it to him. He told her that the local French people were anxious to know what England and the other Allies' intentions were with respect to the Bourbons. There was little doubt in Rowland's mind that much as the people wished to rid themselves of Napoleon and the swingeing taxes he levied to pay for his endless wars, for the most part, they were not anxious to see the return of the Bourbons.

The last skirmish with the enemy before the final Battle of Toulouse in April came at Tarbes on 20 March. Rowland approached via the town of Vic Bigorre scattering the French in all directions. Soult retreated via St Gauden in the direction of Toulouse. The French Marechal was suffering from an ever increasing number of deserters and he had also been told that the city of Bordeaux had pronounced in favour of the Bourbons and had received Marechal Beresford with open arms; the white cockades were now the order of the day in that city. However, there was still no official word of the Emperor having abdicated so Wellington pushed his army on to take the most important city of southern France, Toulouse. The passage over the Garonne was never going to be an easy one for an army and Sir Rowland's crossing was rendered more difficult because the pontoon bridges were not long enough. He was therefore temporarily unable to fulfil his orders to take control of the main road from Toulouse to the east towards Carcassonne.

During the night of 30 March, they tried to lay another bridge across the river at Pansaguel. On this occasion, they lacked just one pontoon to reach the other bank – this necessitated the engineers dismantling all their work and beginning again at a slightly narrower point in the river.[291] Hill crossed with two divisions of infantry on 4 April. They were now about eleven miles from the city and on the west bank of the broad Garonne. Sir Rowland was next detailed to create a diversion in the suburban area west of the city known as St Cyprien. Picton and Alten were on the north-western side of the city with the main part of the Army to their left (east) between the Garonne and the Canal du Langudoc. Soult had only left one division to face Hill and hostilities began early on the morning of 10 April. Rowland's men fought in the streets and took a few casualties but were not heavily engaged. Rowland had fulfilled his orders to divert the enemy's attention. Meanwhile, after a desperate struggle, Beresford and Freire had taken the strategic Heights of Calvinet to the east and managed to bring guns to bear on the city below.

Soult was aware he could not withstand the guns pouring shell on the city from these heights, and on the 11th he withdrew to the east towards Carcassonne. Rowland and Beresford chased the retreating Marechal some way down the road to Villefranche de Lauragais, Rowland was instructed by Wellington to make sure his cavalry kept sight of the enemy.

XI

CELEBRATIONS AND A PEERAGE

Everyone was waiting for news from Paris: had Napoleon really abdicated? Word had been coming in for some time by means of deserters or intercepted messages that he had done so but the British Army had received no formal confirmation. Wellington entered the city of Toulouse on 12 April to a rapturous welcome. Rowland wrote to Maria: 'The joy and enthusiasm of the people of Toulouse when we entered, was, to all appearance, more sincere than any thing of the kind I ever witnessed. Robert is at Toulouse: I have not yet seen him. I have this instant a message from my outposts to inform me a flag of truce is there … it is really most gratifying to find that we have got rid of Bonaparte. My troops did not have too much fighting at the Battle near Toulouse.' The wretched Soult, after fighting the 'hideous leopard' for so long, was now about to admit defeat.

The day that he rode into Toulouse, entering, with unusual modesty by a small gate, Wellington announced that he would give a ball at the Prefecture that evening. At 5pm, Colonel Ponsonby, messenger from Lord Dalhousie in Bordeaux, rode into the city bearing the news that the Emperor had indeed abdicated at Fontainebleau on 6 April and that Bordeaux had declared for the Bourbons and everyone was sporting white cockades. Wellington apparently called for champagne and quietly proposed the health of Louis XVIII. The only person in the French camp who did not accept the abdication was Marechal Soult (with the exception of General of Division Thouvenot, who caused pointless loss of life on the 14th in the Battle of Bayonne because he refused to accept that the abdication meant the end of the war). It took Soult a few days to realise that the days of Napoleon were done and he was then most anxious to protect his personal belongings; they could be more accurately termed his loot. When Colonel Cooke first delivered the news of the abdication to Soult, the General declared that he was not convinced that the message was genuine and was shocked that the new acting War Minister was General Pierre Dupont de l'Etang[292] replacing Clarke.

He initially offered to sign a temporary armistice until he received what he considered official notification of the Emperor's abdication. Wellington refused to accept an armistice until he had 'made his submission'. The Duke was afraid that Soult might cause a civil war if he retained his army and he sent Hill, Freire and Beresford, whose pursuit of Soult had been halted on the 14th, to advance on the Marechal on the road to Carcassone once again.[293] On 17 April, Soult received an official dispatch from Marechal Berthier and conceded defeat.

On 18 April, Rowland received a letter from Sir George Murray, QMG, confirming that terms of an armistice had been agreed to and that all hostilities were at an end. One has to wonder whether the chief protagonists felt a sense of anti-climax at this moment, or was it just relief? More than six years of continual fighting were at an end. What would follow now? The Bourbons were not popular and the King, Louis *dix huitres*[294] as he was often labelled, not an inspiring figure. He was old, not well, very fat and extremely greedy. In the meantime, Wellington established his HQ in Toulouse and the city began to fete the victors in earnest.

Many books have assessed the relative merits of the generals under Wellington's command but one of the most succinct appraisals comes from the pen of a junior cavalry officer, who wrote home, 'Apart from General Hill there is scarcely a general officer in this army of any talent and very few of any activity, except for Sir S. Cotton and I suppose no commander ever had so few clever men on his staff, almost all of them being cox comical and old women.'[295]

On the 30th, Roland wrote to Maria that Wellington had set off for Paris leaving him in charge. He also told her that part of the Army was to be made ready to sail for America. 'The General Officer commanding it is not named, but should it be offered to me, I shall not accept it. Indeed, I am as you may imagine, truly anxious to get home, and as soon as I can with propriety, I shall be with you. I send this letter by Lord W, who is just going off.' Rowland doubtless felt that his presence at home would be of assistance to the family, with his brother John so recently dead, his nephew Rowland and his brothers so young, and his father, Sir John, now an elderly man. He planned to go first to Paris and thinks that Robert will accompany him. 'Tom has a return of his bowel complaint and it has been recommended he goes home – I think you may expect him as soon as you receive this or soon after.' He writes, too, of the dinner he gave to some French officers which was the first chance that the two opposing sides had had to talk together in many years; the evening had evidently passed in a most amicable manner.

Wellington's highly trained and experienced Peninsular Army was now to be disbanded. The Commander in Chief even went so far as to say he did not think there could be another force equal to his army, which was most complimentary when you consider his usual comments on his troops. A number of men marched to Bordeaux to take ship for America. The cavalry was sent home overland. Sir Robert rode from Lectoure north-west of Toulouse on 31 May and embarked for England at Boulogne on 23 July. The regiment rode almost the entire length of France, a six-week journey that most of them appear to have enjoyed enormously. There were only two horses unfit for duty at the end of it. They passed through Cahors, Brives, Limoges, Nantes and Abbeville on their long ride.

Hill was in London by 27 May. He had been told that it was the particular wish of the Government that he should go to America, which was the reason he went to London to speak to Lord Bathurst. Although Hill did not wish to go, Wellington told Bathurst that he was sure Hill would agree if pushed.

Peerages were conferred on five of the British generals: Hill, Graham, Beresford, Hope, and Combermere together with a pension of £2,000 per annum. Some of the public considered this sum to be derisory after all that these men had been through. Graham grandly refused to accept this payment, he did not have need of it, but one is sure that it was very welcome to Hill, who lacked private income. The Government of Spain awarded him gold clasps for Roliça, Vimeiro, Corunna, Talavara, Vittoria, Pyrenees, Nivelle, Nive and Orthez.

On 20 May he received advice from Lord Bathurst that he would probably not to be called on to go to America. Rowland was most relieved; events there had changed and a much smaller force than originally planned was now to be sent.

On 1 June, Rowland took his seat in the Lords. He had never had the chance of taking his seat for the borough of Shrewsbury in the Commons. London was *en fete* with visits from the Tzar, old Marshal Blücher and the King of Prussia. Although the new Lord Hill was longing to go home, he understood that it was expected of him, as one of England's heroes, to attend the receptions in honour of Napoleon's downfall. He was to go to the Guildhall to receive a sword that was being presented by the City of London. At a ceremony on 11 June 1814, he and Lord Beresford were presented with their swords, worth 100 guineas apiece, together with the Freedom of the City. The speeches were long and one of the civic dignatories ended by reminding the assembled crowd:

> I am happy in this opportunity of declaring in the presence of the noble Lord whom I have had the honour to address, that the civic chair, which is so ably filled by the present excellent chief magistrate,[296] was, nearly three centuries ago, graced by an ancestor of the noble Lord, Sir Rowland Hill,[297] who was the first Protestant Lord Mayor of this City, a man who was not only eminently useful as a Citizen of London but who has left lasting monuments of his piety and munificence by his extensive and liberal endowments in his native county.[298]

Both of the new peers were presented with gold boxes which contained their Freedom of the City. The first Sir Rowland had been a member of the Mercers' Company, the most senior of all the great Livery Companies in the City of London. It was he, born in Shropshire, who had set the Hill family on the path to wealth and status in the sixteenth century.

Any free time that Rowland had in London, he spent with his aged uncle, the Reverend Rowland Hill, and the Tudway family[299] telling his sister that he was still taken up with engagements for a further two or three weeks, much as he wished to get home 'It [was] an interesting time to be in the Capital of England' and he suggested that she come to join him there.

Rowland finally returned to Shropshire in mid July. On the way he stopped at Birmingham. The city was anxious to honour him and he was presented with another sword: 'Take it My Lord and it will not fail you.' Hill replied 'Trust it to me and I will not disgrace it.' He was welcomed on the whole of his long ride to Shropshire and his arrival was a triumphal entry into the town of Shrewsbury. The streets were packed with thousands of people who had come in from the country, the fronts of the houses were decorated with bunting and flowers and women lent out of the widows waving their handkerchiefs. The yeomanry paraded for his inspection and formed part of the procession as he rode into town accompanied by the Lord Lieutenant of the County, Lord Kenyon. Rowland was accompanied by all his soldier brothers together with Colonel Richard Egerton, one of his aides de camp. Rowland's horse was dressed in black trappings for his recently deceased brother, John, in marked contrast to the bright uniforms of the fourteen troops of cavalry that followed. A grand dinner was given at the Guildhall.

Shrewsbury was evidently determined to honour its soldier hero and the Freedom of the City was given to all the Hill brothers. Presentation of the Freedom was made outside in sight of the assembled crowds. When the ceremony was over, Lord Hill addressed the populace but this was not enough; the shaking of hands that had worn poor Blücher out in London had now reached the provinces and everyone wished to grasp his hand. In the end he was obliged to retreat saying, 'I never did fly from the fury of my enemies but I have been obliged to do so from the kindness of my friends.' The public subscribed to the purchase of sheep, which were roasted and fed to an enormous company of people.

Shrewsbury had already, in December 1813, decided to raise a permanent memorial to Sir Rowland. There was considerable debate as to what form this should take until it was finally decided to erect a column in the Abbey Foregate. This column, which still stands, is surmounted by a statue of the General as if he is keeping watch over the town, and at the time of its construction was said to be the tallest Doric column in existence; at 15 feet in diameter, it is equal to the Monument[300] in London and larger than both Lord Nelson's column in Dublin, at 13 feet, and a foot larger than that in Paris erected by Bonaparte, 14 feet in diameter. It also exceeds the height of the Emperor's column by one foot, being 133 feet in height including the platform on top and the figure of Lord Hill. Deliberate one-upmanship? The design was drawn by a Mr Haycock with a few alterations made by Mr Harrison, a well-known architect builder of Chester.[301] The first stone was laid in Masonic order by the Salopian Lodge of Freemasons[302] and 'within a cavity of the foundation stone (which weighed four and a half tons) a bottle was deposited containing gold and silver coins of George III, accompanied with a copy of the *Shrewsbury Chronicle* of the preceding Friday.'[303] The plans were presented to Mr Straphen, the principal assistant to the contractors, who completed the column, and who generously personally made a gift of the staircase within the column; there are 172 steps. The last stone was laid in June 1816 on the Anniversary of the Battle of Waterloo. The total cost came to £5,972.13.2d, which sum excluded the cost of the staircase, stone plinth and palisading round the base of the column.[304] On the east side are listed Lord Hill's battle honours: Roliça, Vimeiro, Corunna, Douro, Talavera, Busaco, Arroyo dos Molinos, Almarez, Vittoria, Pyrenees, Nivelle, Nive, Hillette, Orthez, Aire, Tarbes, Toulouse and Waterloo. On the north side is a sort of paean of praise to the General and on the south, a list of his full titles in Latin.

A small cottage was built beside the column to house its guardian. This was also constructed in the Doric style. Lord Hill put forward the name of the first occupant himself; Sergeant Thomas Davies[305] of the Royal Welsh Fusiliers, who had served as his orderly Sergeant in the Campaign of the Netherlands in 1815. In 1962 the cottage was removed to make way for the New Shirehall.

With most of the celebrations both in Shropshire and also in neighbouring Cheshire having drawn to a close, Lord Hill was for the first time able to enjoy his house at Hardwicke Grange. Lord Bathurst had written to Hill on 10 August 1814, in the most flattering terms:

I find that the collecting of such a force as would be fit for your Lordship to command, is attended with much more difficulty than I had imagined, having a regard to the great demand for troops to be stationed in Ireland. Under all these circumstances I am inclined to give up the thoughts of availing myself of your Lordship's zeal to serve in an expedition, which, I am afraid, would have exposed your health more than, from the little opposition to be expected, it would have added to your glory ... I shall probably do nothing more than detach a very small force to be placed under the command of Major General Ross, now in America.

General Ross was subsequently killed at Baltimore. Lord Hill was most relieved since he had no wish to go to America so soon after his return home. Another letter from HRH Frederick, Duke of York in September 1814 offered him the command of the Army in Scotland. This he also refused. He was offered the Governorship of Gibraltar but this he declined explaining that due to the death of his elder brother and the extreme age of his father, he felt that he was needed at home for a short time at least.

Peace did not last for long and just a few months later, in the spring of 1815, Lord Hill was back in harness.

XII

CLASH OF THE TITANS

Were you at Waterloo?
I have been at Waterloo.
'Tis no matter what you do,
If you were at Waterloo.

In late March 1815, Rowland took his sister Emma to London. Clearly, he must already have heard the news of Napoleon's escape from Elba and his landing in the south of France, at Golfe Juan, with approximately 1000 followers. The Bourbons had done nothing to improve their popularity in France in the short period since Louis XVIII had been put on his murdered brother's throne. Now, the majority of Napoleon's generals had flocked to their old chief's side, never dreaming that their Emperor could be defeated a second time. These Generals even included Marshal Ney, Napoleon's 'bravest of the brave'. Ney was Minister for War in the Bourbon government, and he had left Paris assuring the King that he would bring the Corsican back 'in chains'. However, he was soon to rejoin the ranks of his old master, such was Napoleon's charisma. Ney was to pay with his life for his 'treachery'.

Napoleon and his feats still hold a place in the hearts of the French 200 years after his second and final abdication. He bankrupted the country on the one hand with his grandiose and martial schemes but he has also left enduring legacies in his reorganisation of the country: his Code Napoleon, creation of a Public Audit Office, the *Banque de France*, the Penal Code, the *Legion d'Honneur* and many other civil reforms. Today there are societies where not a word dare be spoken against the fallen hero; there are dinners with speeches devoted entirely to his memory. Yet the Corsican – about whom more words have been printed than any other figure in history, by some margin – was a player on the world stage for fewer than 20 years. Was it just that France had been looking for a major 'royal' leader ever since the death of Louis XIV? Whatever the reason, the 'Napoleon' factor was at least as important to the French as the 'Wellington' factor was to the British during the Peninsular War and at Waterloo. As statesmen, they both lacked some of the right qualities and often demonstrated poor judgement. While Napoleon died in exile only five years after his last great battle, Wellington lived on to be an old man who saw the arrival of steam trains and mechanisation. Together with other elderly personages, he did not understand the necessity for either; at his death, he could be said to have outlived his generation. Hill, on the other hand was somewhat unexpectedly interested in modern inventions such as photography and engines, although he too was certainly of an older generation with regard to his opinions and philosophy of life.

While Hill was in London, he unexpectedly received an urgent summons to the Cabinet Office. He was told that there was a real danger of an action being fought on the frontiers of the Netherlands.

> Two gentlemen arrived last night from Ostende. Their account is very bad. The King of France has lost Lille etc and is in Ostende. Bonaparte is on the frontier but no large body of his troops yet arrived. [The] government is anxious you should go out immediately as it is of the greatest importance that you prevent any rash action, and also that you should persuade Louis to retreat upon Holland, rather than come to England. Pray call in Downing Street at three o'clock.

England was to be more or less forced to take in Charles X in 1830 during the July Revolution, but certainly did not want his elder brother in 1815.

The Government's greatest concern was that the impetuous young Prince of Orange, anxious for glory, would do something rash and Hill was charged to recommend to the Prince, 'the utmost caution on the part of the forces under his command'. The Prince was to be urged not to take up too advanced a position or to involve himself in any serious engagement. On receiving the news that Napoleon was once more at the head of an army, the Sovereign Prince Willem, father of the Prince of Orange, had proclaimed himself to be King of the United Kingdom of the Netherlands.

King Willem did not get on very well with his heir, the Hereditary Prince Willem of Orange Nassau. Having sent him to Oxford University and then to serve in the British Army under Wellington in the Peninsula, he was now annoyed that the Prince had become 'too British'; it should have come as no surprise! The Prince of Orange Nassau, often irreverently referred to by his brother officers as 'Slender Billy' or sometimes the 'Young Frog,'[306] was an impetuous and not very competent officer, certainly not fit to be at the head of a large body of troops, unless under capable and tactful supervision. It was not the first time that Lord Hill was to find himself cast in this role! Undoubtedly he was chosen for two good reasons, the first being that he was already in London and therefore able to receive instructions from the Government immediately, and secondly, because he was respected by and got on very well with the young Prince. His short stay as a country squire was already over; he was returning to the battlefield.

Rowland told Emma that he could not, after all, escort her to the opera that night, and set about preparing for his departure early the following morning. What were his feelings at this moment? Was he full of anticipation at once more taking on the French? After all, until the last few months, his whole adult life had been spent in the British Army; he was first and foremost a soldier. After so many years spent crisscrossing the Peninsula and southen France, he had certainly enjoyed his few months in Shropshire living in his new house and catching up with his friends and the large Hill family. However, such a call to arms must surely have given him a surge of adrenalin; could the Allies finally finish off Bonaparte for good?

Lord Hill collected Captain Digby Mackworth. They boarded the *Rosario*, commanded by Captain Peake, in the Downs on the morning of 30 March at 12.30. Lord Hill had his valet but they had no horses or other servants. Clement was to follow him with the horses a few days later. The small party reached Ostend around 5pm the following day after a long but pleasant journey. Here they found the whole town in the greatest confusion

> … from the number of English Troops lately disembarked, all of whom true to their English nature, were wandering about with their hands in their pockets, and their eyes and mouths wide open, staring at the wonderful sight of a few dozen heavy stupid Flemings. I was so much occupied in procuring horses etc. for the continuation of our journey to Brussels that I had no opportunity of viewing the fortifications. Lord Hill who visited them said that they are tolerably strong. We met here Captain Colin Campbell, the officer who had been staying so long with Napoleon on Elba … he passed through the Prussian army on the Rhine who were in full preparation for opening the campaign. … The King of France had left this place two days ago for Gand, [Ghent] where he now is with not above 200 soldiers who have remained faithful to him. Marmont is the only Marshal who has not left him and he dare not.[307]

A messenger had, of course, been dispatched to Wellington in Vienna and the whole Congress was turned upside down by this unexpected turn of events. Why everyone should have been so surprised that Napoleon had escaped from Elba is a mystery.[308] He had been permitted to take 400 men with him, had acquired up to 1000 more on the island, which he ruled more or less as a monarchical state, and was constantly assured by his old lieutenants that many, if not most, of his former army would rally to his cause should he return to mainland

France; they did so almost without exception. Meanwhile, the French King, who had 'run away' from Paris just as Napoleon was approaching, had installed himself at Ghent. Poor Louis was now a fat and miserable old invalid who was highly unpopular with most of his subjects. From the moment that the Emperor had landed in Golfe Juan, word had spread like wildfire and men, most of them his old soldiers, had flocked to join him all along what is now known as the Route Napoleon.

The news of Napoleon's escape and the size of his rapidly increasing army had concentrated the minds of the leaders in Vienna as perhaps nothing else could have done; for once they could agree on joint action. The Congress confirmed the Kingdom of the Netherlands[309] under the rule of Willem, Prince of Orange, Wellington was appointed as Commander in Chief of the British and Dutch/Belgian forces in Flanders. Ferdinand was put on the throne of Spain, a decision that the Spanish people were shortly to regret. The Prussians agreed to send Marshal Blücher with a large army. The Russians and the Austrians, both victims of Napoleon's military aggression in recent years, were also sending armies, although neither of these two was to arrive in time for the decisive battle.

Meanwhile, the War Office and Horse Guards in London were frantically engaged in trying to find suitable troops to serve. This was made much more difficult since many of the Peninsular veterans had been shipped off to fight in America and Wellington was to have to make do with often untried recruits, 2nd battalions and militia soldiers. The 52nd Regiment[310] had been ordered to America but fortunately the ships carrying the troops had twice failed to leave Plymouth because of unfavourable winds. This gave the British Government the chance to redirect them to Brussels where the regiment arrived on 4 April. Money was a pressing concern but the Government was eventually saved by the Rothschild family who opened the vaults of their banks to help the British subsidise their Allies.

Lord Hill arrived in Brussels on the evening of 1 April and immediately requested an interview with the Prince of Orange in order to impart to the young man Lord Bathurst's instructions, tactfully couched as 'suggestions'. Hill found that the Prince had established an HQ in Brussels; the Dutch troops were at Genappe and the British and Hanoverians at Tournay. The General impressed on the Prince that he must evade any direct confrontation and should withdraw if necessary. Hill was not very satisfied with his interview with the Prince although he was most cordially received. It appeared that a great deal of flattery had turned the 'young frog's' head, considering himself, according to Mackworth's diary, 'as great a general as some of the ancient princes of his house; which judging from the present state of the army under his command and from the mode in which everything is carried on by him, does not appear to be the case.' The only point on which Lord Hill succeeded was inducing the Prince to withdraw the troops from the advanced position they occupied between Tournay and Ath 'to Enghien where they are to remain at present.'[311]

On 3 April, Mackworth spent the whole day in looking for a house for Lord Hill and in the evening His Lordship dined with the Prince of Orange. 'We had a snug party by ourselves at the Hotel d'Angleterre, and went to a play in the evening which was so bad that I mentally vowed not to go to it again unless on duty as ADC walking stick to my good little man [Lord Hill], who likes going there though he does not understand two words of what is said.' The following day they moved into their house, which fronted on the Parc Royal and was only a short distance from the King's and Prince's respective palaces. One must bear in mind that Mackworth's diary was written for himself – at least one imagines so – although occasionally when he is being 'clever' you have to wonder. Mackworth, rather surprisingly, seems to have been a bit of a prude and he apparently took good note of the forwardness of some of the young ladies when he accompanied Lord Hill to Lady Charlotte Greville's; apparently even 'my good natured little Man observed it and remarked to me: "it is quite a shame for Young Ladies to be so forward."' Mackworth was thoroughly bored with all the grand fetes, reviews and the rest and was quite happy to leave Brussels to search for an HQ for Lord Hill out at Grammont.

The Duke arrived late on 4 April from Vienna and began to organise his forces. Clement arrived with the brothers' horses on 10 April[312] and Rowland wrote to Robert to say that all of these, with the exception of one of Clem's chargers, were in good shape. Clement had applied to Wellington for permission to rejoin his regiment, the Royal Horse Guards Blue and thus, on this occasion, he was not to serve on his brother's staff. Robert had embarked his men, two squadrons of the Blues, at Dover and Ramsgate on 2 May. They had landed at Ostende and then ridden from there to Bruges and on to Ninove, the HQ of the British cavalry. The regiments of Life Guards, the Royal Regiment of Horse Guards and the King's Dragoon Guards were then formed into one brigade under Major General Lord Edward Somerset.

Lord Hill's HQ was at Grammont. Here he found a former enemy, now an ally, the Prince d'Aremberg whom he had taken prisoner at the Battle of Arroyo dos Molinos and who had subsequently spent some time as a prisoner near Shrewsbury. Following his capture, the Prince had been sent off to Lisbon, en route for England, under the guard of young Robert Blakeney. Blakeney has described that journey with colourful and probably somewhat embellished details of their trials and tribulations.[313] He had been personally selected for this duty by Hill who had already taken note of the rather cocky young man who was to be especially useful on this mission thanks to his fluency in French, Spanish and Portuguese. Escorting a senior French officer[314] and his entourage through 'enemy' country was quite a charge since the Spanish and Portuguese very naturally harboured enormous ill will towards any and all Frenchmen. The

Prince was all too recognisable, according to Blakeney, and this meant that they could never leave their lodgings of an evening without a military escort, which then drew more hostile attention to them. As a result, Blakeney told the Prince that if they were to enjoy any freedom and have any fun on the march, he must sacrifice his magnificent cavalry mustachios. The Prince was crushed but finally agreed and sent one of the long, silky, curled mustachios to his fiancée, a Mlle Tacher who was a niece of the Empress Josephine. Blakeney was to remain in touch with the Prince and visited him at his home in 1819 when he was most graciously received and royally entertained by the Prince's father, Prince Prosper d'Aremburg.

On 20 April, Hill was at Ath on an inspection of the cantonments of his Corps and together with the Duke of Wellington, reviewed the 2nd Division under Sir Henry Clinton. All was found to be in excellent order except for the artillery, with which the Duke found fault. Wellington was never very keen on the artillery; it was a necessary evil so far as he was concerned. They continued on to Tournay, a magnificent town surrounded by strong works but a place that would take a large number of men to defend. On the 21st the party slept at Oudenaarde,[315] near to which, at Courtray, work was going ahead to put defences in place. They returned to Grammont on the evening of 22 April. Sir Digby is evidently very fond of Lord Hill but spends a lot of time in mocking him, albeit gently, in his Waterloo diary. For example, when Mackworth says that he is going to take a journey 'incognito' in the hope of seeing more of the ways of the people than if he travelled 'en grand Seigneur,' he writes,

> I should be still more incog [sic] as I should not be *reconnaisable*; but I can tell him [we don't know who] that as ADC of the Rt. Hon. Lord Hill (he ought to have taken the title of Lord Mountain because he is a <u>great hill</u>), is not to be accounted as small beer in a country where the true value and importance of an Officer is better known than in that odious England.

No wonder, with such feelings about England, Mackworth eventually married a Frenchwoman!

Rowland wrote to his sister-in-law, Elizabeth, Mrs John Hill, his brother's widow. He told her that he had been in communication with Lord Bathurst concerning his peerage, which he had requested should be entailed on his nephew,[316] her eldest son, yet another Rowland, 'your excellent son'. At the time of Waterloo, this Rowland was only fifteen years old. Bathurst promised to attend to this. Hill seems to have been most concerned in case he was killed. It does not appear that he was afraid of dying, but that he wished to ensure that the laurels he had won should be inherited by the family since he had no children of his own. He was very close to this nephew and there are a number of letters between them in the Shropshire archives. There is no other mention in any of his numerous letters written home before an impending battle of any fear of death but perhaps this time he felt he had something to lose in the form of his peerage. Following Waterloo, when further battle honours were being distributed, this right of succession to his peerage was confirmed.

Rowland told Elizabeth that the Duke would have an army totalling around 150,000, including the Prussians, of which he would have command of nearly 30,000 in his own Corps. Wellington had divided his army into three columns, one to be commanded, at least nominally, by the Prince of Orange – under strict supervision and some excellent staff – the second by Hill, which included his 2nd Division, together with the 4th Division and young Prince Frederic of the Netherlands Dutch/Belgians, some Hanoverians and West Indians. The third Corps, the so-called 'Reserve' Corps' was under the Duke's own direction; although, needless to say, the Peer kept an eagle eye on everyone! Blücher was bringing his Prussians and the Russians were also expected. Was the net finally closing in on the Emperor? Hill and the Prince's Corps were posted to the west with Hill on the extreme right flank at Ath and the Prince at Braine le Comte nearer to Wellington. Prince Frederic of the Netherlands, the 18-year-old younger brother of the Prince of Orange, was put under Lord Hill. According to Mackworth, this young man made a very good impression although he was a little shy, which, as Mackworth wrote, 'is an error on the right side in a Prince!'

Wellington has been criticised for posting Hill's Corps so far to the right but his strategy was designed to prevent a flanking movement by Napoleon. It did mean that Hill took part mainly in the second half of the day's fighting at Waterloo and has led some accounts to infer, wrongly, that he took virtually no part in the battle at all; the Duke's justification was that he could count on Hill as on no other, to hold the lines of communication to Ostende and Antwerp.

The other three brothers, Thomas Noel, Clement and Robert Chambré, were also in the Netherlands. Thomas was serving as Assistant Adjutant General, while Clement was now back in his own Regiment, the Royal Horse Guards, Blue, of which Robert had command, the regiment being in Lord Edward Somerset's brigade. It is not known whether the elusive youngest brother, Edward, was with Robert and Clement but since it has often been quoted that five Hill brothers took the field, he probably was. He certainly served in the regiment as first a Cornet and then a Lieutenant, without the necessity of purchasing the latter, according to the Household Cavalry Archives at Combermere Barracks, Windsor, which also show that he left the regiment in mid July 1815, in other words almost immediately after Waterloo. There is, however, no W.M. (Waterloo Man) in red ink beside his name, which would have designated him as having served at the battle. (The composition of Lord Hill's Corps is given in Appendix II.)

Hill, having established his HQ out at Grammont, was living in the Chateau Cambresis owned by an evidently charming lady, Madame Annette de Portemont.

It is not likely that Rowland was a 'ladies' man' in the generally accepted sense[317] but from many comments made about him, he obviously had excellent manners and was always a welcome figure in the smartest drawing rooms. He was of necessity doing a certain amount of entertaining of fellow officers and he was also responsible for a large staff. In perhaps a rare show of sensitivity, the Duke wrote to Bathurst in London. 'He is' wrote Wellington, 'again at the head of what is really an army, composed of troops of different nations, with a large staff attached to him, and great expenses to be incurred, and he is paid only as a Lieutenant General,[318] of whom he has several under his command.' The Duke asked for an increase and it was ordered that Hill should receive the pay and allowances of a General on the Staff.[319]

On 30 April 1815, Wellington issued his instructions to his Corps commanders, the Prince of Orange, Lord Uxbridge in command of the cavalry, and Lord Hill, commanding the 2nd Corps. No. 4 of these instructions was that the garrison of Ghent was to flood the country if necessary by opening the sluices. Shortly after this meeting, a rumour was circulating to the effect that this had been done. Fortunately, before panic could set in, Rowland was swiftly able to establish that it was not true. On 8 May, Wellington sent Hill a letter he had received from Lieutenant General Sir William Stewart, dated 30 April. In Wellington's words, it 'appears to have been written in the anguish of mind … he had in his actions and by his own sufferings and does not do justice to himself or his troops, and I did not send it home or communicate it, I believe to anybody.' This was probably in connection with the publication of Stewart's report to Sir Rowland Hill of the actions in the Pyrenees on 26 July 1813. His account had just been published by John Philipparts in The Royal Military Calendar and had drawn considerable criticism on his head. (see page 121). It is unclear how Philipparts had obtained a copy but Stewart certainly felt hardly done by and bore a considerable grudge against Wellington.

The tourists and sightseers who flocked to Brussels that spring were shocked to find that the Corsican 'ogre' was coming to take the city. Some took both fright and flight, quickly returning home, but a large number of stoic English remained enjoying a frenzied round of parties, picnics, routs and reviews. Even Rowland had written to his diplomat brother, Francis, suggesting that he might find it interesting to come to Brussels. He did so in the company of the Honorable Charles Shore. The Shore family were close friends of the Hills and a few years later Sir Thomas Noel married Anna Maria Shore, Charles' sister. Once it was certain that there was shortly going to be a battle, the General packed them off to Antwerp.

When writing about Waterloo, it seems churlish, if not impossible, to avoid mentioning the Duchess of Richmond's famous ball. The Duke of Richmond had brought part of his very large family to Brussels; he had himself served as a senior officer in the Army and was very interested in Wellington's plans. Wellington told him firmly that being the father of so many children, he must stay away from the fighting. The Duchess, who sounds as if she was a fairly formidable *grande dame,* had asked Wellington whether it was safe to throw a party on 16 June. He had said that he thought it would be fine. Was this based on what he 'knew' or did he think it would serve to steady the nerves of the people still in Brussels? Everyone left in the city was trying to obtain an invitation.

One of the Duke's daughters, Lady Georgiana Lennox[320] was largely responsible for organising the ball which was held on the eve of the Battle of Quatre Bras. A carriage house adjacent to the family's rented house had been turned into a ballroom with the walls, Lady Georgiana writes, originally covered in a rose patterned paper, but now hung with draperies. Invitations had been sent out to the upper crust amongst the Allies. Four Hills were on the invitation list[321] but there are no references to any of them actually attending in the available sources.[322] The General certainly did not; he was with his Corps at Merck Braine. Thackeray wrote in *Vanity Fair,* 'There were almost no nobodies there.' An abrupt end to the festivities came with the arrival of a message for the Duke. He withdrew to read it and then to consult a map provided by Richmond. The Duke said 'Napoleon has humbugged me.' This news spread throughout the city like wildfire and naturally led even more panicked English families to take the road to Ostende, choking it with their baggage and carriages. You could not procure a horse, a mule let alone a carriage or even a cart, for love nor money.

A serious problem for the Duke was that he did not have the same level of intelligence available to him that he had had through the years in the Peninsula and he could not decide which road Napoleon was going to take. Marshal the Prince Blücher at the head of his Prussians was engaged with Napoleon himself at Ligny on 16 June. He had concentrated his men too far forward and suffered badly when attacked by the Emperor. The Prince Blücher was, however, a tough old man. He was well into his seventies, and was unhorsed and trampled on by the French cavalry – one of his staff said that it was fortunate that he had such a thick head! He was defeated there but he still managed to get himself up and even, with help, onto a horse. He was forced to retire to Wavre to reform his army. Although his Prussians had been forced to fall back, they had maintained good order.

Lord Hill's Corps was not engaged in the Battle of Quatre Bras, which was also fought on the 16th. Here Wellington took on one of the old enemies, Marechal Ney. This conflict had resulted in a 'draw' and the retreat of part of the Allied Army on Waterloo.[323] (For the full story see *The Battle of Quatre Bras* by Mike Robinson.) This retreat was in fact made in order to keep open his lines of communication with Blücher, now at Wavre, following Napoleon's heavy defeat of the Prussians at Ligny. These two battles had certainly boosted morale in the French Army and must have given Wellington considerable food for thought.

Hill called on the Duke at Wellington's HQ on the following morning. McBride described Hill's arrival in his memoirs:

We all stood up and gave him three hearty cheers, as we had long been under his command in the Peninsula and loved him dearly, on account of his kind and fatherly conduct towards us. When he came among us, he spoke in a very kindly manner and inquired concerning our welfare.

McBride belonged to the 71st (Glasgow) Regiment, part of General Sir Frederick Adam's brigade, which had served under Hill through the Peninsular War and made an especial mark at the Battle of St Pierre,[324] where Hill had retrieved them from the rear where their cowardly commander had taken them in the midst of the fighting. The men's affection for Hill had only grown in the years when the regiment had served in his 2nd Division. On hearing the noise, Wellington rushed out from the hut that was his HQ and when he saw the cause of the cheering was not that the French were coming but that the Army's favourite General had arrived, he laughed. Wellington, himself, did not seek popularity or the love of his soldiers but he recognised that they held Hill in both great respect and affection.

The night of the 17/18 June was wet. Why did it always rain heavily on the eve of so many of the Duke's most famous battles? It was absolute misery for the men in the open, who found it difficult to light cooking fires. (The French were ordered not to.) The General and his staff fared a little better in a small 'cottage' to the right of the Nivelle road at Merck Braine. His Corps formed Wellington's principal reserve on his extreme right flank; to ensure that Bonaparte did not try and get around the Allied Army. Adam's brigade eventually formed a right angle with the 1st Foot Guards. The Hanoverians were on Hill's extreme right.

On the day of the great battle, Hill's Corps remained for some time unengaged, covering the general line. Hill had put a stopwatch in his pocket and could therefore always pronounce with authority that the exact time when battle commenced, the first gun fired, was 11.50am. Some hours had passed and things were not going too well for the Allied Army when Wellington called on Hill to bring up part of his reserves to support the embattled centre. Hill first sent forward Colonel du Plat's brigade of the King's Own German Legion and personally brought up General Frederick Adam's brigade including the 1/52nd led by Lieutenant Colonel John Colborne. The 52nd, the Oxfordshire Light Infantry, was the central and largest battalion of Adam's Brigade of Light Troops, a part of General Hill's Corps. The other battalions were the 71st and the 95th.

There appear to be almost as many versions of the last hour of the battle as there were soldiers fighting, but as Nigel Sale pointed out,[325] few but Peninsular veterans could have carried out the manoeuvre that followed. Colborne having carefully watched the Imperial Garde, wheeled his men into parallel with their column. He then caught them entirely by surprise by firing on the move, on their flank and then advancing with the bayonet. The Garde were brave men but they were overpowered and broke. The Duke then ordered a general advance and the

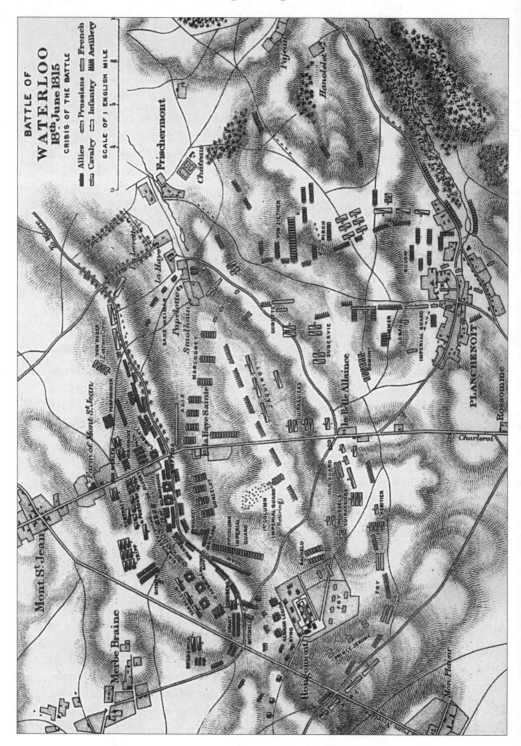

The Battle of Waterloo, 'crisis of the battle'. (Samuel Rawson Gardiner)

panic that ensued spread to the remainder of the French Army causing it to retire in confusion. According to Mallinson[326] as Wellington's signal was heard, Lord Hill on the right, shouted, 'Now come on drive them back Thirteenth'[327] and the much reduced ranks of Grant's brigade[328] surged forward. They could only move at a trot, so thickly did the dead and wounded lie on the ground.

The Prussians had arrived around 4pm. The battered old Marshal, having apparently dosed himself with rhubarb and gin, was to advance personally in support of Wellington as he had previously promised to do. Blücher was a fiercely brave soldier and his IV Corps, under the command of General Friedrich Wilhelm von Bülow, took on Napoleon at Plancenoit, with the Marshal himself arriving a little later. At the final crisis of the day, Muffling[329] brought up the Prussian troops of General Thielmann commanding the III Corps to give support to Wellington's threatened left wing. Without these brave Prussians, the outcome might have been very different.

Uffindell in his *Great Generals of the Napoleonic Wars* points out that 'for much of the day he [Hill] was in the thick of the action but he barely features in accounts of the battle.' No doubt he was content with Wellington's simple yet sincere praise in the Waterloo Dispatch: 'I am also particularly indebted to General Lord Hill for his assistance and conduct upon this as upon all former occasions.' Others were not; many felt under-appreciated.

Digby Mackworth, ADC on the staff of General Hill, has left a personal record of the great battle, written that very same evening in the hovel in which the exhausted General and his staff were sheltering.

He [Hill] placed himself at the head of his Light Brigade, 52nd, 71st and 95th, and charged the flank of the Imperial Guard as they were advancing against our Guards. Here Lord Hill's horse was shot under him, and, as he ascertained, the next morning, was shot in five places. The General was rolled over and severely bruised but in the melee this was unknown to us for about half an hour. We knew not what was become of him; we feared he had been killed; and none can tell you the heartfelt joy which we felt when he rejoined us, not seriously hurt...

The cavalry and infantry repeatedly charged in masses under cover of a tremendous fire from 240 pieces of artillery. Four times were our guns in possession of their cavalry, and as often did the bayonets of our infantry rescue them. For upwards of an hour our little squares were surrounded by the elite of the French cavaliers: they gallantly stood within forty paces of us, unable to leap over the bristling line of bayonets, unwilling to retire, and determined never to surrender. Hundreds of them were dropping in all directions ... at about 6 o'clock we saw heavy columns of infantry supported by dragoons returning for a fresh attack. It was evident it would be a desperate fight, and we thought probably a decisive one. Everyone felt how much depended on this terrible moment. A black mass of the Grenadiers of the Imperial Guard with music playing and the great Napoleon at their head, came rolling onward from the farm of La Belle Alliance. With rapid pace they descended. Those spaces in our lines which death had opened and left vacant, were covered with bodies of cavalry. The point at which the enemy aimed was now evident; it was an angle formed by a brigade of Guards[330] and the light brigade of Lord Hill's corps.[331]. Lord Hill was there in person. The French moved on with arms sloped, *au pas de charge*. They began to ascend the hill. In a few seconds, they were within a hundred paces of us, and as yet not a shot had been fired. The awful moment was now at hand. A peal of ten thousand thunders burst at once on their devoted heads. The storm swept them down as a whirlwind which rushes over the ripe corn; they paused; their advance ceased; they commenced firing from the heads of their columns and attempted to extend their front; but death had already caused too much confusion among them; they crowded instinctively behind each other to avoid a fire which was intolerably dreadful. Still they stood firm – *la garde meurt, et ne se rend pas*[332] [the Guard dies, and does not surrender]. For half an hour this horrible butchery continued. At last seeing all their efforts vain, all their courage useless, deserted by their Emperor, who was already flown, unsupported by their comrades who were already beaten, the hitherto invincible Old Guard gave way, and fled in every direction. One spontaneous and almost painfully animated 'Hurrah' burst from the victorious ranks of England.[333]

It is difficult to know how much of Mackworth's high-flown account to take at face value. He was there, being one of Lord Hill's ADCs. Why should he fabricate any part?

It is certainly difficult not to question the 'official' account that it was the Foot Guards alone, under General Sir Peregrine Maitland, who led the last furious charge against the Imperial Guard. Even Sir John Byng, who commanded the Brigade of Guards in the 1st Division, told Colborne that he knew the vital charge had been made by the 52nd. In the History of Lord Seaton's (Colborne) Regiment, the 52nd Light Infantry, there are many accounts by people both present and not present. Siborne who wrote an extensive history was not there and made many mistakes, which caused much bad feeling; he was not alone. When the Allied Armies had reached Paris, Byng even said to Colborne, 'How do you fellows like us getting credit of doing what you did at Waterloo? I could not advance when you did, because all our ammunition was gone.'[334] However, there is no doubt from Mackworth's journal – written on the very day of the battle – that Hill's 2nd Corps was engaged to the last, if not from the first, and that Colborne at the head of the 1/52nd had pursued the fleeing grenadiers with brigade commander General Sir Frederick Adam and the remainder of the Division galloping after them. This, together with an account by William Leeke, an Ensign in the 52nd who carried the regimental colours, and at least three

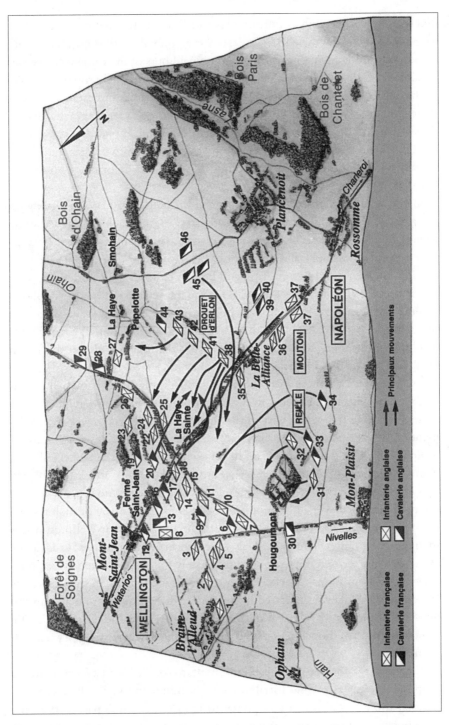

Adam's brigade (5) of Hill's II Corps forms a right angle with Maitland's Foot Guards (10) before taking the French in the flank.

different French accounts confirming his words, attributed the final death blow to the flank attack by the 52nd. Was it, however, only the 52nd? Further confirmation of this regiment's major role in the final hours of the battle is borne out by Colonel Colborne having led his 52nd across the battlefield roughly parallel to the Allied Line and meeting the Duke, Lord Uxbridge and their staff. 'Well done Colborne, well done!' cried the Duke, 'Go on, don't let them rally.' Seeing three squares of the Garde were standing firm, the 52nd advanced to chase them off. The enemy fired before retiring southwards to melt into the general confusion. It was one of these shots that famously hit Lord Uxbridge[335] above the knee, taking off his leg.

In 1833 Colonel Gawler, who had been at the battle as a Captain serving on the right of the 52nd, told Colonel Brotherton[336] 'An attack was made by the Imperial Guard and reserve. For some time the combatants (3rd Foot Guards) were enveloped in smoke and the event of the day was in suspense. The [French] column however, was taken in flank and broken by the 52nd. Assailed on every side it became a flight.'[337] One is left with the impression that perhaps nobody recorded the exact truth; everyone who was present on the day and who later (often much later) recorded their thoughts, had seen events from different angles. The only thing about which we can be sure is that the Guards got too much credit and the 52nd too little.

Even so, with all these eyewitness accounts, including his own shout to Colborne to pursue the enemy in flight, is it not bizarre that Wellington failed to acknowledge the 52nd's part in the final rout? Colborne never received a mention in dispatches despite General Adam having submitted a full account to Lord Hill, who duly passed it on in his own dispatch to the Duke. Hill had, in any event, seen Colborne's clever right wheel and flank attack for himself. Was it just that the Duke felt that it should have been he and no other who gave the coup de grace? If so, it would have been an act unworthy of such a great commander. On the other hand, it is well documented that Wellington was sparing in his praise where individuals were concerned and not always accurate. His dispatches, written in the hours immediately following a battle, were prone to errors and omissions especially with regard to individuals. In the years after Waterloo, the Duke was irritated by anybody who presumed to bring up the question of the 52nd's role at Waterloo. On one occasion, he dissembled, 'Oh, I know nothing of the services of particular regiments, there was glory enough for us all.'

Nigel Sales, a former Greenjacket himself, makes at least two errors in his proposal. He refers to the distribution of honours and says, when suggesting that there was a sort of conspiracy to ignore the 52nd's part in the final push in favour of the Guards, that Hill, the Corps Commander, was party to it. Apart from the fact that there were many other witnesses, it seems unlikely that Hill would have deliberately agreed to suppress an account of one of his battalion's exploits, since he was a man known for his integrity and for rewarding good service. In addition to all the above, it is certain that Hill's dispatch must have reached Wellington[338] since Colborne was invested both as a Knight of the Order of Maria Theresa of Austria, and of the Russian Order of St George, 4th Class. One can hardly say that his service went unremarked or unrewarded. It points indirectly to the fact that, although he receives few mentions in accounts of the battle, Hill and his Corps played a vital part at the crucial moments of the bloody fighting leading up to the hour of victory.

Sir Frederick Adam, brigade commander in Hill's Corps, was also awarded the Order of Maria Theresa and appointed a Knight Commander of the Military Order of the Bath. Rowland was created a Commander of the Order of Maria Theresa in company with the Marquess of Anglesey. He was also, again together with Anglesey, given the order of St George, 2nd Class, by the Russian Emperor. Hill may well not have minded – too much – that he and his Corps had not received more specific praise, although he would certainly have sympathised with Colborne, for whom he held a high regard.

What of the three other brothers? Sir Robert had had command of a part of the Household Brigade, the Blues and the Life Guards, and these troops had performed bravely. The men had breakfasted on gin and biscuits and were held in reserve for a frustratingly long time but, eventually, feeling that they had been in that position long enough, they joined the rest of the cavalry out in front. Robert was wounded through 'the fleshy part' of his right arm but it was not too serious. He was created a Knight of the Order of Maria Theresa of Austria and awarded the order of St George, 4th Class, by the Emperor of Russia. He was also created a Companion of the Most Honourable Military Order of the Bath, KCB. The bullet that had passed through his arm is in the Museum of the Royal Horse Guards.

A serendipitous tale: at Waterloo, Robert had a trooper in the regiment called Thomas Evans. When Tom had returned to his wife at the end of the war in the south of France in 1814, she had been shocked by the amount of weight he had gained and when the men were selected for service in the Netherlands a few months later his name was not included because he was too fat! He was desperately disappointed. It was suggested to him that he approach the Colonel when he was feeling mellow after a good lunch. He did so and, Sir Robert relented. This was to prove very fortunate for the Colonel. At one point in the battle he was totally surrounded by five French Cuirassiers and cut off from the rest of his men. Tom barged his way through, killing four of the French with his sword; Tom's own sword then broke and he used the hilt to pummel the fifth. When the Regiment was paraded in 1816, Sir Robert acknowledged his debt to Tom by calling him out of the ranks. Tom retired in 1829 and opened the pub the 'Oxford Blue' in old Windsor. The regiment had got its name from their blue coats and their 1st Colonel, Aubrey de Vere, 20th Earl of Oxford.

In addition to the honours mentioned above, Rowland also received from the Prince of Wales the Guelphic Order for leading his Hanoverian troops in the battle and soon after, the Duke of York, Commander in Chief, announced he was to wear a gold clasp in commemoration of the Battle of Orthez. His chest was now well covered with medals.[339]

Clement received nothing. This staunch companion of his elder brother throughout the long Peninsular years was to command the Royal Horse Guards a few years later.[340] His wound at Waterloo was no more serious than Robert's. In his haste to dress in the early morning hours of the 18th, he could not find a shirt to put on and so went into battle wearing a dressing gown. He was pinned to his saddle by a sword thrust through the thigh and was to claim that he had been saved by that dressing gown. Brother Thomas Noel Hill was invested with the Order of Maximilian Joseph on the orders of the King of Bavaria.

On the other side, the Prince de Moscowa (Marechal Ney) wrote his own account to the Duke of Otranto[341] following the defeat. Otranto, better known to most people as Joseph Fouche, was a cold and cruel, although very clever man who was to be exiled in 1816. Although implicated in the death of Louis XVI, he was in favour of the return of Louis XVIII. Ney was much criticised for his conduct during the battles of the Netherlands and he wrote a fierce defence of his actions to Fouche:

> ... the most false and defamatory reports have been spreading for some days over the public mind, upon the conduct which I have pursued during this short and unfortunate campaign. The journals have reported those odious calumnies, and appear to lend them credit. After having fought for twenty five years for my country, after having shed my blood for its glory and independence, an attempt is made to accuse me of treason; an attempt is made to mark me out to the people, and the army itself, as the author of the disaster it has just experienced.[342]

Ney describes how Napoleon had put him at the head of the 1st and 2nd Corps of infantry, commanded respectively by d'Erlon and Reille, and also some divisions of light cavalry. On 16 June, during the Battle of Quatre Bras, he writes that when he received orders to attack the English, he had advanced towards the enemy and his troops were infused

> ... with an enthusiasm difficult to describe ... The battle became general and victory was no longer doubtful, when, at the moment that I intended to order up the first Corps of infantry, which had been left by me in reserve at Frasnes, I learned that the Emperor had disposed of it without adverting me of the circumstances ... the shock which this intelligence gave me confounded me; having no longer under me more than three divisions in my position instead of the eight upon which I calculated, I was obliged to renounce the hopes of victory.

Ney continued with a description of his part at Waterloo when Marechal Grouchy, being at Wavre, failed to arrive in support

> … which to us was the same as if he had been a hundred leagues from the field of battle … at the same time, the Prussians continued their offensive movements, and our right sensibly retired, the English advanced in their turn. There remained to us still four square of the Old Guard to protect the retreat. The brave grenadiers, the choice of the army, forced successively to retire, yielded ground foot by foot, till, overwhelmed by numbers, they were almost entirely annihilated. From this moment, a retrograde movement was declared, and the army formed nothing but a confused mass. There was not, however, a total rout, nor the cry of 'Sauve qui peut' as has been calumniously stated in the *Bulletin*.

Unfortunately for the Prince, too many people believed that he had let his master down, although the reverse was probably the truth, and when he came to trial some months later, there was no protest in Paris against the sentence that he receive a traitor's death.

XIII

OCCUPATION AND FINANCIAL TROUBLES

The 19th was a terrible day of reckoning. Lists of dead and wounded had to be made; it was a dire business. Bodies were strewn for miles and the scavengers were already hard at work long before the sun rose, removing anything of value from the corpses and even from the wounded. The slaughter had been enormous. Hill had lost his much loved Lieutenant Colonel Currie who had served on his staff for nine years. He sent Thomas Noel to try and find Currie's body so that they could bury it decently, or to see if he might only be wounded; sadly, his good friend was dead. Rowland was to go to great lengths after Waterloo to see that Currie's wife was looked after adequately; he tried in vain to have recompense made for the Colonel's charger that had also been killed in the battle but he was told that this was only available to living officers! Thomas also found Rowland's own charger on the battlefield; he was dead, shot in five places. The General had only been badly bruised in his fall; like Wellington, he seems to have led a charmed life.

On 23 June, Sir Thomas Noel wrote to his sister from Cateau:

My dear Maria
Robert and Clement are going on as well as possible; but I dare say you will get later accounts from them than this. Rowland and I are quite well and have only to regret that our brothers cannot witness the finishing stroke of Master Boney … Rowland is gone with the Duke of Wellington to pay a visit to old Blücher, who is within a few miles of us. The poor old fellow was terribly maltreated in one of his affairs with the enemy.[343] His horse was shot, and they rode over him; but he takes a deal of killing. His head being tolerably thick, he received but little harm.

Rowland wrote to Maria from Cateau on the 24th:

My dear Sister

Before this time you will have heard, in various ways of the glorious result of our battle of Waterloo, on which occasion I am really inclined to think that the fate of Europe was decided. Bonaparte is still retreating and we are following him. It is possible he may endeavour to collect at Laon, where there is a position; but in my mind he cannot again make any serious stand against us …

Yesterday I rode with the Duke of Wellington to see Blücher. We found the old Marshal amusing himself with Bonaparte's hat, stars and personal baggage, which with his carriage was taken by some Prussian cavalry … the King of France is coming to this town today: the people seem rejoiced at the event.

The Prussian Army's Major von Keller had captured a great quantity of Napoleon's baggage including the *necessaire* which included more than 70 pieces in silver and gold. The carriage was in itself a work of art; built by Symonds of Brussels according to Buonaparte's order for the campaign in Russia, in which he travelled and returned. It contained numerous secret compartments,[344] various articles for the table, mostly 'massy' gold and even if the jewellery and gold found inside did not quite amount to the horde that had been captured after Vittoria, it was certainly impressive. The carriage was put on display in London but some Waterloo veterans did not appreciate the sight of members of the public paying their two shillings to be permitted to clamber all over the vehicle; they felt it was demeaning as the British Army had a healthy respect for Napoleon.

A grand coach, together with seven other 'state carriages' had also been captured. Evidently, Napoleon had brought them for his state entry into Brussels; his personal state carriage was to have been drawn by eight cream-coloured Arabian horses. Apart from diamonds and other precious stones, the Prussians found Napoleon's travelling library of 800 volumes. Yet another coach was captured by the same Major Keller. He was pursuing the fleeing Emperor and met up with his travelling carriage at Genappe.

The British Army marched after the Prussians towards Paris and met with virtually no opposition. There was precious little to take; the pursuing Prussian Army stripped everything in its path and had not spared the people. The British were initially quartered at Nanteue outside the city and reinforced by remounts from England. When the Army lay before the city, the French Provisional Government entered into negotiations, the main object being to save Paris from ruin. Some Prussians had been set to blow up all the bridges over the Seine but this was avoided. The President of the interim government endeavoured to obtain a general pardon for each and every Frenchman regardless of what they had done but this was refused by the Allied generals who had expressly added 'If the King desires to adopt more severe measures against his unfaithful subjects, they, the foreign generals, had not to interfere in it.'[345]

On 22 July[346] a scheduled review of the British Army 'under the walls of Paris' was postponed as being possibly too provocative, but Lord Hill reviewed the 1st Corps in the Champs Elysee. The troops consisted of three regiments of the line, one of *carabiniers* and two of light horse. It was reported that Blücher had promised that all his soldiers would behave and commit no excesses and that all supplies would be paid for. 'I only make war against Bonaparte and his accomplices; the peasant shall not have to complain of my Army.' The same edition of the newspaper reported that French Generals Puthod, Curial and Montfort 'have arrived in Paris as deputies for Marshal Suchet to make their unconditional surrender to the King.'

Rowland had had another of his narrow escapes in July when the posts (gates) of Paris were being given up by agreement between the French Government in Paris with the Allies. These posts were surrendered on successive days as per article VIII of the Commission drawn up between the French and the representatives of the Allies. On the evening of 3 July, Lord Hill marched to take possession of the 'Barrier'[347] of St Denis, accompanied by his Staff. Just as Lord Hill approached close to where a French soldier stood on duty at the barrier, the soldier levelled and discharged his musket at the English party but, fortunately, the shot was wide of the mark. A French officer galloped up apologising profusely and saying that the solder was intoxicated. A similar outrage had also been committed against the officer sent into the city just ahead of the Duke. This man was even carrying a white flag but he was not so fortunate, being shot through the body. Lord Hill apparently carried on as if nothing had happened.

The Allies in Paris were celebrating. There were brilliant fetes, grand reviews and Hill gave a ball. The expanding form of the General does not seem suited to dancing but he surely beamed with pleasure as he saw his guests enjoying themselves. His sister[348] was acting as her brother's hostess. She was by all accounts a formidable lady and Creevy commented to General Barnes that she looked more suited to the role of Second in Command than did her brother. Barnes laughed and said that one could not have a better Deputy Commander of the Army than Hill.

With the second surrender of Napoleon, who was now at the start of his journey to a remote rock in the South Atlantic, the English flocked to Paris. After all, the delights of the city had not been enjoyed since before the start of the Revolution. Everyone wanted to make up for lost time and also to see the heroes who had finally defeated the Emperor. Senior officers were given big houses to live in and Rowland occupied the grand Hotel de Montesquieu for a few weeks while friends and family came flocking to visit. Rowland was longing to go home but he had commitments at the very least until after the grand review of the Russian Army on 12 August. Quite why the Russian Army should have been reviewed in this manner is unclear since they had been absent from the final battle, though they had certainly played their part in subjecting

Napoleon to his terrible defeat in the winter of 1812. Rowland hoped to be at home by the middle of October. It was not to be. He got as far as London to be told that his services were required as second in command to Wellington of the British forces of occupation and in command of the infantry. Back he went to France.

The terms of the Treaty of Paris were punitive toward France but then she had cost the whole of Europe dearly in blood and treasure. The terms negotiated back in 1814 following Napoleon's first abdication were adhered to in the main, although made somewhat harsher. France's frontiers were pared back to where they had stood before the Revolution. The heaviest burden on France was the sum of 700 million francs in indemnities, and the maintenance of a coalition army of occupation for up to five years. It was also laid down that all the works of art looted during the deposed Emperor's reign must be returned to their rightful owners. The French were incensed when the great bronze horses, the Triumphal Quadriga or Horses of St Mark, were returned to Venice. Lord Hill approved of this policy but it caused consternation at the Louvre, where M. Denon, the 'aimiable and intelligent' Director saw half his recently acquired and much treasured collection vanishing. As Croker recorded, the collections were being 'plundered of their plunder' by Marechal Blücher, who was described by Denon as that '*animal indecrottable*'.[349] A large number of the most valuable paintings had come from Spain. Ferdinand, in a grand gesture, gave them all to Wellington.

The final significant event of 1815 was probably the execution of Marechal Ney. Lord Hill had fought against numerous French generals of greater and lesser ability but it was only at Bussaco, the French retreat from Torres Vedras and at Waterloo that he came up against Napoleon's favourite general, Ney 'the bravest of the brave'. Ney, Prince de Moscowa, (which had turned into a rather unfortunate title since 1812), had risen from quite humble origins, as indeed had so many of his fellow marechals. On Napoleon's first abdication in April 1814, he had sworn loyalty to the Bourbons, falling on his knees before the King and covering the King's hands with kisses. In the following year, when the King told him that he had raised 6,000 men, Ney put himself at their head vowing to bring the Ogre back in chains and then marched without hesitation to join Napoleon.[350] Ney was to pay for this with his life. When Louis XVIII returned for the second time to his capital, he was to pardon almost all the old Napoleonic marechals and even permitted them to keep both the spoils and the imposing titles they had amassed; perhaps he hoped that this generosity on his behalf would keep them loyal this time. Not so with Ney. Ney had quietly disappeared to live on a country property belonging to a cousin of his wife.[351] He stayed there undetected for several months until someone recognised and denounced him. This time there would be no escape; after all, he had proved himself beyond doubt a traitor to the King. He was tried and found guilty of treason. His wife wrote to Wellington begging him to intercede on Ney's behalf. He refused to take any action, saying that it was not up to him what happened in the French Army. Ney's lawyer had, in a last ditch effort to obtain clemency, argued that since an amnesty had been granted to all those not born on French soil, this should be extended to Ney since he had been born in Sarrelouis. This region of Alsace had been returned to the Prussians in 1815 and is known as Saargebiet. This technicality did not sway the court and Ney was shot by firing squad on 7 December 1815. He refused to have his eyes bandaged and personally gave the order to fire.

In December, the Allies moved out of Paris and the British troops went into cantonments at Cambrai and Valenciennes. They were now no more than a day's journey from the port of Calais and so it was that, even if he could not go often to see his family, Hill could receive them at his HQ in France. The new organisation of the Army gave Lord Hill the command of 25,000 infantry and Lord Combermere 3500 cavalry,

Rowland remarked in a letter to Maria that Ney's execution 'has caused very little sensation in Paris, and the Act of Amnesty, which has been passed since that event, seems to give general satisfaction ... Upon the whole, the Duc de Richelieu's conduct and appearance are much in his favour; and I hope he will be able to make the poor Bourbons more esteemed than they appear to be at present.' The politically astute 5th Duc de Richelieu had left France during the Revolution. He returned in 1814 and accompanied Louis XVIII on his flight to Lille in March 1815. Here he left the King to rejoin the Russian Army with which he had served, in exile, under Catherine the Great. He was largely instrumental in obtaining the agreement of the Allies' armies of occupation to quit France in 1818, which was earlier than had been agreed in the Treaty of Aix la Chapelle. He became, on the urging of Talleyrand (who always managed to turn his coat as often as self preservation demanded), Prime Minister but found the role impossible and resigned for the second time in 1821.

Louis XVIII was not fitted to fill the role in which he had been placed by circumstances. His brother, the Comte d'Artois and later Charles X, was to do no better. It is scarcely surprising that both Wellington and Hill were terrified that the French 'disease' of revolution might spread to England when the number of civil disturbances increased.

Thomas Graham, now Lord Lynedoch, had proposed forming a club for Peninsular officers in London. He wrote to Hill saying that he thought it was very important to have a place where officers could meet in convivial circumstances and that the club should be provided with maps and books.[352] Wellington had of course been invited to join and had replied to Lynedoch from Brussels on 5 May 1815 agreeing to do so. In the beginning, the club was to be restricted to senior officers only but it was quickly apparent that a more general military club was required on a permanent footing. The first Secretary and Treasurer was Archibald Campbell. There was to be an entry fee of 20 guineas and then an annual subscription of 5 guineas. Members were to be elected by ballot and officers serving overseas would pay a lower subscription. The total membership was not to exceed 1400 and no dogs were to be allowed! Hazard and games of dice were also to be forbidden. A branch of the club was established in Paris in July 1815 with Lord Hill as its Chairman. In London the club started life in Albermarle Street and the Royal Navy quickly asked if they could be part of the venture. This was agreed to and Lynedoch began to look for permanent premises large enough for a 'United' Services Club. The Club's original purpose-built site, at the corner of Pall Mall and St James's, is now occupied by the Institute of Directors. The Club would eventually become the Naval and Military Club and is in a handsome house in St James's Square.

On 13 February 1816, Hill wrote to the Duke asking for a leave of absence so that he could go home to try and resolve a very difficult financial problem that had arisen. His father old Sir John had stood as a bondsman to one Thomas Eyton of Wellington. Eyton had now died and the Treasury was demanding an enormous sum from his bond holders. The loans/guarantees to Eyton seem to have gone back many years. Eyton was quite an important figure in Shropshire being, apart from his official role as Collector of the Revenue, a Deputy Lord Lieutenant and Lieutenant Colonel Commandant of the Wrekin regiment of local militia. Sir Richard Hill (Rowland's uncle) had given a bond in 1787[353] for Eyton's 'performance of duties as receiver general', together with his cousin, Lord Berwick, and in subsequent years numerous others. It seems probable that Sir John Hill, Baronet, Rowland's father, inherited these obligations on Sir Richard's death together with another Shropshire landowner, Sir John Kynaston Powell, who had also stood as a guarantor to Eyton of Wellington. It sounds even more extraordinary when you know that Eyton was the local tax collector! With Eyton dead, the bonds of the 29 July 1813, 6 August 1814 and 16 June 1815[354] in the amounts of £92,000, £92,000 and £98,000 respectively, were due.[355] Eyton's role had been to collect tax due on inhabited houses, servants, land tax, coaches, windows, lights, horses and other goods.[356] Once the Government had discovered that imposing such taxes was highly profitable and efficient, there was hardly anything that they did not tax. On Eyton's death, naturally, everything he had possessed had to be sold with the Government expecting its due share. Ironically, Rowland's brother, Sir Francis, formerly of the diplomatic service, had now been appointed Collector of the Revenue in the County as successor to Eyton; this appointment had, of course, been made before the problem of the money and his family's ties with the former Collector had emerged.

The Duke replied in a letter from Paris dated 20 February 1816 in warm and generous terms. He was serving as a rather unpopular ambassador in the French capital, which many considered a tactless and unnecessary appointment.[357]

My dear Hill

I received only yesterday evening your letter of the 16th and I am very much concerned for the unfortunate circumstances which has occasioned the necessity for your return to England. I consent to it as well as to that of Sir Noel. Let him apply through the official channel, but he need not wait for the answer.

In the existing state of public and private credit in England, I am apprehensive that you will find it difficult to procure the money which you will require. I have a large sum of money which is entirely at my command; and I assure you that I could not apply it in a manner more satisfactory to me than in accommodating you, my dear Hill, to whom I am under so many obligations, and your father, for whom I entertain the highest respect, although I am not acquainted with him. I trust, therefore, that if you should experience the difficulty which I expect you will, in finding money to settle the disagreeable concern in which your family is involved, you will let me know it, and I will immediately put my man of business in London in communication with yours, in order to apply it to you.

The Duke could scarcely have offered more practical help. It underlines his personal appreciation of Hill. It was not, happily, necessary for Lord Hill to call upon the Duke for financial help but the case dragged on for several years. Indeed, on 26 February 1821 the Duke wrote to Rowland returning his 'memorial' about liability as security for deficiencies in tax accounts and recommending that all judicial means should be used to pursue the case, and, in the event of failure, that it should be brought before Parliament. The Duke suggests a petition to the House of Commons, although, as it touches on financial matters, the King would have to consent through a Member of the Privy Council. If that should fail, then Hill should get some of his friends in the House of Commons to 'move for the papers' and then have them referred to a committee. The Treasury had earlier assented to the family's request that it be represented by Lord Teignmouth, eventually to become father-in-law of Sir Thomas Noel. As Sir John Shore, Lord Teignmouth had been Governor General of India in the 1790s. The Chancellor, Nicholas Vansittart, wrote to Mrs Hill (daughter-in-law of Sir John) saying the he would 'be happy to communicate with Lord Teignmouth on the claim of the Treasury on Sir John.'[358] Teignmouth's dealings were eventually fairly successful and matters were settled with Sir John only being required to pay £5,000; a very considerable sum in those days but much less than the original demand.

When Hill returned to Cambrai from England, he moved into his new house, the Chateau Maniers. This was free for him to use, he wrote to his sister, although he needed some new furniture to make the part he planned to occupy more comfortable. Life now being altogether more settled, Rowland was able to reduce his staff and thus almost halve his expenses. During his absence, Richard Egerton and his wife had done their best to render the Chateau comfortable. The house was about four miles from his HQ at Cambrai and had excellent gardens. 'I think Noel will approve when he comes out, which I hope will be soon.' He continued wryly, 'I very much fear that Mackworth[359] is going to be married to a French woman ... he has said nothing to me but some officers informed me.' Mackworth did indeed marry the woman. When a prisoner for a short time during the Peninsular War, he had been lodged with one of Napoleon's generals, General de Richepanse. He had fallen in love with the General's daughter, Baronne Julie de Richepanse, and returned to marry her. Rowland was obviously not now short of some funds since Creevey[360] describes taking his stepdaughters to a ball given at the Chateau, where a large tent had been erected for the dinner and dancing.

In January 1817 he was ill again, the same sort of fever that he had had in Portugal, which virtually confirms that it was a recurrence of malaria. He had been bled 'copiously'. He was obviously quite seriously ill and the Duke again invited him to come and recuperate in his house in Paris but this invitation was soon followed by the instruction that he should go home to recover as soon as the doctor said he could travel. This he did and tried the waters at Cheltenham, which were said to be most beneficial.

Back at Cambrai, apart from his official duties, which were not too onerous, consisting as they did mainly of reviews and ensuring that the Allied troops did not pillage or otherwise trouble the locals, he enjoyed hunting, especially boar hunting, which can be a very dangerous sport, similar to the pig sticking that was so popular in India. On one occasion, he was waiting on the outskirts of a wood when a vast boar, flushed by beaters, erupted from the trees and rushed towards him; he calmly awaited its arrival and gave it 'a thrust on its nose' that turned it onto its side, whereupon he plunged his spear into the poor beast. The spearhead broke off and a few days later Wellington sent him the present of a replacement. The skull and tusks joined Hill's other 'trophies' at Hawkstone.

Another diversion was a tour taken by several members of the family, George Hill, his nephew, Emma, his sister and brother Clement, together with the Egertons and Colonel Abercromby, son of Sir Ralph,[361] to visit the battlefield of Waterloo. Apparently the woman who lived in the hovel where Lord Hill and his staff had spent the nights before and after the battle, was delighted to see them. Emma made a number of sketches of the battlefield[362] and surroundings and also dug up some plants to take home to the Citadel at Hawkstone. The Citadel is a house built in the form of the family crest. It stands on an eminence in the Park with wide ranging views out over the landscaping to the Grotto Hill, the Red Castle Hill and south towards Shropshire's own mountain, the Wrekin. It had originally housed the family's steward fairly modestly but had long been a sort of romantic folly, an 'eye-catcher', giving the appearance of a twin-turreted, fortified building. In 1824 it was enlarged and formed a handsome Dower House to the Hall and it now has three turrets. It still stands there, a solid, handsome and unusual building to find in rural Shropshire.

XIV

SIR ROBERT'S 'BLUES'

I818 saw the end of the occupation of France by the Allied armies. Hill returned home and set about planning alterations to his house at Hardwicke. His farm and the planting of the gardens took up part of his time but he also hunted and fished when possible. He was a welcome guest at some of the great houses of England such as Woburn and Belvoir. The entire Hill family were bruising riders to hounds and one especially good anecdote has come down to the present day. It was reported in the local paper under the heading, 'Extraordinary Fox Chase'.[363] It took place on a morning when there were five members of the family, including Sir John aged about 80, and Rowland in the field, with the hounds being hunted by 'Mad' Jack Mytton of nearby Halston. After a run of some two hours, the fox, hotly pursued, ran into the house of a spinster lady called Miss Langford in the village of Dodington. He raced up the stairs and hid himself in a cupboard with the entire pack of hounds hard on his heels. The owner was terrified and her maid is said to have dropped the chamber pot she was carrying in her state of shock! Mytton made haste to compensate the two ladies. The brush was awarded to one of the late Colonel John Hill's sons – probably Frederick. Mytton was an extraordinary man, completely without any self-control or judgement, the perpetrator of often cruel practical jokes. He was unkind to his wives and spent some time in King's Bench Prison for debt before fleeing abroad in 1821 to die alone, penniless and an alcoholic. One of Sir Robert Chambré Hill's sons, another Clement, was to marry one of Mytton's daughters.

Hill was now given the Colonelcy of the 53rd Regiment,[364] The Kings Own Shropshire Light Infantry. His papers relevant to this period are in the British Library[365]. Such an appointment was much sought after and only awarded to officers of high standing. What better man to invest with the honour than a General from the Regiment's own county and one who had first served in it as an Ensign. He held the role of Colonel until 1830 when it was taken on by his Military Secretary at Horse Guards, Lord Fitzroy Somerset, with the General becoming Colonel of the Royal Horse Guards, Blue.

It was at this time that Rowland's brother Lieutenant Colonel Sir Robert Chambré Hill, KCB of the Royal Horse Guards, Blue, engendered some rather unwelcome publicity for the family. Robert had served with as much distinction as any member of a regiment of heavy cavalry could have expected to during the last two years of the war in the Peninsula, not cavalry country. However, in 1822, one of Sir Robert's captains, John Jebb, was subjected to a regimental court martial. It was the start of an unpleasant series of exchanges between Sir Robert and Jebb. At the court martial, Jebb objected to two officers who were to sit on the committee, these being Colonel Clement Hill, brother to Sir Robert, and a Colonel Drake MP. It does seem strange that Clement should have been appointed to sit on a court martial that so closely involved his own brother. Jebb was accused of various infractions including refusing to comply with a regimental order dated 18 April 1821 to settle his regimental debts although frequently applied to by the clerk of the troop; for 'disgraceful conduct' in giving two drafts to the messman of the regiment that were dishonoured in June and July 1822; for being repeatedly absent from his regiment without leave in the year 1822 – such conduct being highly prejudicial to good order and military discipline and unbecoming the conduct of an officer and gentleman. The Judge Advocate pronounced that it was an unusual case in that it was the Commanding Officer who brought his own Captain to trial but that the Court having found Captain Jebb guilty 'do sentence him to be removed from his Majesty's service'.[366] The Captain begged to be permitted to transfer to another regiment but this was not allowed. In June 1823, Sir Robert told the Duke of Wellington as Colonel of the RHG that he wished to resign and he did so on 18 July 1823. The Duke of York and the Duke of Wellington both wrote to him that they regretted his resignation.[367] Shortly after this date, brother Clement was promoted to the rank of full colonel and took his brother's place as Commanding Officer of the Regiment.

In February 1823, after he had been sentenced and left the Army,[368] Jebb wrote to the Duke of Wellington, as Colonel of the Regiment, accusing Sir Robert of various offences. Sir Robert wrote to the Duke replying to the accusations and saying that he wished that Jebb had brought these matters up at the time of the court martial so that he could have refuted the charges. One accusation was that Hill's Adjutant, Simeon Hirst, had drawn forage for one of Hill's horses as a troop horse. Hill assured the Duke that this was untrue. A second was that Hill had permitted Corporal Robert Turner to retire from service a very short time in advance of the regular date. Robert explained that this was because Turner had been offered the opportunity of taking over a public house, which he was anxious to do. Hill admitted it was a little irregular but that Turner was a man of 23 years service and that it was in consideration of this that Hill excused him from resuming active duties, following a broken leg, until he was formally discharged.[369] Hill was merely told that it had been irregular. All other charges were dismissed; they all appeared to be both trivial and spiteful.

Jebb had not yet finished with Sir Robert. He must have been plotting revenge and eventually was to put his plan into action. His next attacks came soon after Lord Hill had become General Commanding in Chief in 1828 and must have caused him some embarrassment. Why Jebb had waited so long to begin writing the series of anonymous letters accusing Sir Robert of all manner of extraordinary acts was not explained at the trial, which finally took place in December 1829 in the High Court. The case was one of criminal libel brought by Sir Robert against John Jebb. For some time, numerous anonymous letters had been sent to people in high office, amongst others Robert Peel who received two, Lord Hill, who received five, and to several of Sir Robert's fellow magistrates in the county of Shropshire.

Some of the letters accused Sir Robert of profiting financially by fraudulently buying and selling regimental horses together with a Colonel Hammer. Sir Robert replied to this charge that in order to obtain the very best chargers for the regiment, they often bought promising young horses and Colonel Hammer kept them at his own expense until they were fit to come into service. They were then sold at public auction, where Sir Robert bought back the best for the Blues. There were many other allegations in the letters, accusing Sir Robert of stealing young officers' wine, of leaving the Regiment in July 1823 because he knew that his dealings had been discovered. and another, a most bizarre accusation dating right back to 1810. Sir Robert had appeared, so Jebb claimed, in the rooms of Lieutenant Fenwick in the Barracks at Windsor, where the Lieutenant was entertaining friends and some young ladies, 'entirely naked except for a dressing gown … for an improper purpose'. He was threatened with beng kicked down the stairs by Lieutenant Fenwick, of whom, afterwards, 'he humbly begged pardon.' Learned Counsel stated that Lieutenant Fenwick had denied most distinctly in his affidavit that he ever made such a charge against Sir Robert, 'or that he ever cast an imputation of any kind upon the character of Sir Robert.'[370] In his evidence Sir Robert said that he had merely gone to Lieutenant Fenwick's apartments where some officers were carousing and making a lot of noise and ordered them to their own quarters. The other two officers who had been present had sworn affidavits to the same effect.

The Attorney General confirmed that he had ample proof that Jebb was the author of the malicious letters since, quite apart from the content, there were similar errors and spelling mistakes in all the letters, and a great many of them. All of the witnesses, ranging from Peel and Lord Hill to the regimental paymaster and Jebb's tailor had recognised the handwriting as being that of John Jebb without any hesitation. Lord Tenterden summed up, the jury retired and returned a verdict of guilty after examining the letters.[371]

This must have all been most unpleasant and the case had taken a long time to be resolved because Lieutenant Fenwick, a prime witness, was abroad and had to be contacted for his sworn affidavit. One will never know whether any of Jebb's accusations had any foundation but he certainly did his best to ruin the career of his Commanding Officer.

It was quite common for officers holding senior positions such as that of Commander in Chief to take all their papers with them when they left office. Some have ended up in private archives or in the National Archives; many were destroyed. It is hard to know if Hill took any of his. The author has not been able to track any down but then finding papers of the Hill family became very difficult after the end of the nineteenth century when all possessions were dispersed in the great bankruptcy sales. From his own correspondence, we do know that Hill personally destroyed a large quantity of correspondence during or following his fourteen years at Horse Guards. Fortunately, a substantial amount remains in other archives, particularly those of Brown, Lynedoch and Somerset. He was also asked to supply information for the history of the Peninsular War that was in preparation by Southey. He immediately forwarded the solicitation to the Duke since the request had been made by 'a nobleman of rank' and which, erroneously, intimated that Wellington had himself already furnished information for Mr Southey to use:

> If this is the case, I cannot give him fresh information, and if it is not the case, I am sure I ought not to supply him with any memoranda I may have. I have destroyed, since I came home, many papers relative to our operations in the Peninsula. I have, however, several papers still in my possession, and amongst them the valuable instructions I received from your Grace at various times. I beg to state, however, that I would not on any account allow them or part of them, to go out of my hands particularly for publication, unless it is your wish that I should do so.

Lord Hill ends his letter in saying that the Duke may be pleased to know that Rowland's nephew, young Sir Rowland, has been elected to Parliament for the County of Salop. Wellington replied saying that he had not personally been approached by Southey although he had heard that he was engaged in writing a history.

> If I had received such an application, I would have told him what I have told others, that the subject was too serious to be trifled with … I think, however, that the period of the war is too near; and the character and reputation of the nations, as well as individuals, are too much involved in the description of these questions for me to recommend, or even encourage, any author to write such a history as some I [fear] would encourage at the present moment … this is my opinion upon the subject in general and I should have conveyed it to Mr Southey if he and his friends had applied to me.

The Duke added that he would be grateful if Hill did not give Mr Southey any of his, the Duke's original papers, 'as that would involve him in the work without attaining the object which I have in view, which is a true history.'

Rowland wrote back to assure Wellington that he had no intention of letting any of his papers pass out of his hands unless they were to be given to the Duke. In the event, a large part of the papers referred to have been published in Wellington's Dispatches and Additional Dispatches edited by Colonel Gurwood. The Hill papers in the British Library contain a large number of the letters.

In 1820, Lord Hill was awarded an Honorary Degree, a DCL by Oxford University. He would now spend some relatively quiet years at home. He was evidently a father figure to the sons of his dead brother, John, and tried his best to set them on the right path in life. He also took care of their mother Elizabeth Hill, a woman of great religious fervour. He was busily occupied in setting his own property in order and arranging for the refurbishment of his house at Hardwicke. Typically, he did not want the house to be turned into anything 'fancy' or 'grand' and one detects that his requirements were probably rather a disappointment to the architect, Thomas Harrison of Chester, who had probably imagined his illustrious patron would want something more flamboyant! Harrison had more luck with his rebuilding of the 'castellated' Citadel, which was now to serve as the dower house to the Hall at Hawkstone He wrote a letter to the local builder, John Carline:[372]

> His Lordship appears to wish a useful rather than an ornamental mansion, the same plan [he had already submitted one that Lord Hill found too fancy] might be executed at much less expense by preserving the old front and adding the dining room etc. in a way more or less to agree with it.

The work was carried out between 1822 and 1824 and the total outlay was £7,482 with 'chimney pieces and bells' costing two-thirds as much as the new lodge. He spent a further £1,027 on the grounds. The house was demolished in 1931 but a Gothic lodge remains plus a stable block and the outline of a landscaped garden. The General had taken great pride in his property.

Hill was constantly pestered by requests for help, having his attention drawn to the progeny of friends, family and persons unknown. This was to get much worse when, in 1828, he became General Commanding in Chief. In fact, he found it quite difficult even to help his own nephews, young men trying to get commissioned into regiments that had suffered severe cut backs. After Waterloo, most regiments had lost their second battalions, some were disbanded. It has been said that there was always a war somewhere in the world in which Britain was involved but, following Waterloo, the Army at home in Britain[373] was extremely small, too small as it was to prove when civil unrest threatened. Many people looking back from today's standpoint, see Wellington's role as a politician as a failure; it is certain that, although a colossus of his times at the head of an army, he often appeared as a muddled, old fashioned leader when elected as Prime Minister. The evolution from soldier to statesman was a common but not necessarily smooth transition. The truth was that England was very different from how it had been at the beginning of the Napoleonic wars – as was the world.

The Peterloo Massacre of August 1819 and the Cato Street Conspiracy in 1820 were but the first two major events demonstrating social unrest. The first, in Manchester[374], was a horrible affair arising from a 'peaceful' civil protest in favour of parliamentary reform that escalated and eventually involved calling in, first the local yeomanry, who only made matters worse, and then the 15th Hussars, who eventually dispersed the gathering. The dithering on the parts of the magistrates and the mayor and the fear of Colonel Brotherton, commanding the dragoons, of any violent actions resulting from the presence of his men, led to a long delay before any real measures were taken. There were several hundred wounded and at least eleven people killed. It caused uproar in the country.

The Cato Street Conspiracy of 1820 was an ambitious plot by an extreme radical group to kill the entire Cabinet while at dinner at a house in Grosvenor Square. The plot was discovered and the conspirators were surrounded, in the last stages of preparation, in the hayloft of a stable off Edgware Road. Several of them escaped during a bungled operation but those that were taken were dealt with most severely. The idea of a regularised police force was mooted once again. Old fashioned Tories such as Wellington and Hill were beginning to get a little out of their depth; revolution in Britain now seemed not altogether impossible. However, they could see that crushing any demonstration or insurrection by the use of the Army was going to make them very unpopular. London was to have the first police force in the country, to which the public was initially most hostile and the Home Secretary conceded that for the time being the Army was going to be required to continue to take responsibility for public order.[375] 'In my opinion the Government ought, without loss of a moment's time to form either a police in London or a military corps, which should be of a different description from the regular military force or both.'[376] It would take another eight years before the then Home Secretary, Robert Peel, formed what was to become the police force.

In 1824, Rowland's father died. He had reached the advanced age of 83 and was succeeded by his grandson, Rowland, referred to above, who inherited the estates at Hawkstone and his grandfather's baronetcy; alas he was also to put the family on the road to bankruptcy thanks to his enormous extravagancies. A few years before Sir John's death, the Duke of Wellington had visited Hawkstone expressly to meet Sir John 'the father of so many brave soldier sons'.

In 1824, Lord Hill was appointed a Governor of St Paul's School. This gave him two nominations of boys to attend the school. He wrote to his old uncle, the Reverend Rowland Hill, for some suitable candidates. He was also Treasurer of the Shropshire Royal Infirmary from 17 July 1825 and a Governor and Trustee of the Shrewsbury Free Grammar School.

Rowland did not go to London very often in the early 1820s,[377] but he was in frequent correspondence with Wellington who put him forward for several positions of high office. These he refused, partially because he did not wish to live permanently in the city, which taking on either the Lieutenant Generalship of the Ordnance, or subsequently the Master Generalship would entail. These were prestigious posts but both required the incumbent to reside in London. The Master General was usually a man of high military accomplishment and the position was of great importance up until around the middle of the nineteenth century, when much of the responsibility was handed over to other departments. The Master General was in charge of all artillery, fortifications, supplies and engineering in the British Army and it was often a Cabinet post. It was a role held by many of Britain's finest soldiers including both John, 1st Duke of Marlborough and the Duke of Wellington. It was a real compliment to Hill but he declined, to the Government's surprise, as he also declined the command of the Army in India when it was offered to him in 1827. This he did partially because he knew, after several summers in the torrid plains of Spain, Portugal and Egypt, that his health would not tolerate the Indian climate. Had he also heard a whisper that an even more prestigious position might soon be vacant? Such a vacancy could only arise if Wellington took on another role, should the government fall. Perhaps the idea never crossed his mind, since for one thing he was a very modest man and secondly, he was nowhere near the most senior general officer on the Army List.

XV

'FROM THE HORSE'S MOUTH'[378]

When Lord Goderich[379] resigned early in 1828, it was Wellington who was offered the post of First Lord of the Treasury. 'Goody' Goderich, who had succeeded to the role of Prime Minister on the death of Lord Liverpool, had been fiercely opposed to any kind of reform or Catholic emancipation and had forbidden the introduction of bills for either into Parliament. His successor, the Duke, held much the same opinions.

If Wellington had thought to hold onto his role as Commander in Chief, he rapidly realised that this was not possible when all twelve members of his Cabinet told him that he must relinquish it. In offering the post to Hill, he knew he could be sure of a staunch Lieutenant at his back and one whom he could trust to accept most of the advice he might give him. All the same, it was a great honour for Rowland and what true soldier could pass this offer up? On 2 February 1828, Rowland replied to Wellington accepting the position and, instead of sending it by post, took his letter to London where he stayed, as usual at the time, at the Hanover Hotel in Hanover Square. He then dispatched his letter of acceptance with a short note saying that he had come to London to discuss it with the Duke. The latter expressed his great pleasure and proposed a meeting but warned Hill not to speak of the appointment for the present as there were numerous other more senior generals who were going to be extremely frustrated. Thanks to the seniority system of the Army at that date, Hill had only become a full General in 1824, as mentioned earlier. The Duke opined:

> There is no doubt that your appointment will be highly satisfactory to the country as well as the army; but it has occurred to some of the government, that considering the place in which you stand on the list, it is better in relation to the senior officers of the army, some of whom have high pretensions, that you

should be senior General upon the staff, performing the duties of Commander in Chief. The only real difference is in the pay, which is not of much importance to you.

The official announcement by Wellington was made with a General Order issued on 15 February 1828. Lord Hill issued his own first General Order the following day. Hill seems to have got on quite well with George IV – which was not easy – and it is difficult to find two men who could have been more different in temperament: the frivolous, showy monarch, who had even convinced himself that he had fought (and won) the Battle of Waterloo, and the tried and true soldier. However, George IV's approval of Hill had already been noted when Rowland had carried the Royal Standard at the King's coronation.

George IV spent an inordinate amount of time designing new uniforms for his Household troops. He had been responsible for the enormous and extraordinary helmets worn by the Blues at the time of Waterloo, which fortunately did not last too long in service.

The serious work of Horse Guards now began. Hill's correspondence during this period is constantly punctuated with consultations with Wellington; his old commander held strong opinions and did not hesitate to draft letters for Rowland, whom he still regarded as his *protegé*. Disagreements between them as to how to resolve a problem or a tricky appointment seem to have been few. The bulk of Hill's remaining correspondence during his tenure at Horse Guards is to be found in the Raglan papers – a very large and interesting archive – and in the Brown and Lynedoch papers.

The most tiresome aspect of Hill's work was certainly the relentless stream of supplicants for honours, pensions or positions. The Duke also still received an endless flow and to these he could now reply with relief that the applicant must contact Lord Hill as he, Wellington, was no longer in a position to dispense patronage. Very occasionally, Wellington would forward a letter to Hill with a note saying he felt the writer was worthy of some assistance. Rowland eventually devised his own method of cutting short some of the more tedious personal visits to him in his office at Horse Guards. When all else failed, he retained only a single chair in his room. He would then courteously show his visitor to this chair and remain standing himself. Naturally, this soon led the supplicant to feel embarrassed and his visit would, as a result, be curtailed. A cunning strategy.

Much of Lord Hill's first years in office were taken up with civil disturbances; the winter of 1829–1830 was particularly severe and brought much suffering amongst the poor. The following summer yielded yet another bad harvest. These were two of the factors that began to stir people to action, especially in agricultural areas, and which led to the riots.

Another violent eruption of civil unrest followed in 1831. This took place in Bristol and was mishandled from start to finish. By an amazing coincidence, Lord

Hill's ADC, Major Sir Digby Mackworth, happened to be in Bristol as a private citizen at the time of the riots and got himself embroiled. After the event, some people felt he had taken too much on himself, when it was a matter with which he was not officially involved, but he escaped an official enquiry. Colonel Brereton who commanded the 3rd Dragoons garrisoned not far from the city, was reluctant to use either live ammunition or bayonets without the express instruction to do so from the city magistrates. His behaviour grew more and more inexplicable as events unfolded. The jail had been set on fire and all the occupants released and the Guildhall was destroyed together with the Mansion House, before a message was sent to Keynsham to demand the attendance of the 14th Dragoons[380] under Major Beckwith. A few months later a military commission was set up to enquire into Colonel Brereton's actions. On the fifth day of the trial, he was found shot in bed by his own hand. The eleven charges against him described 'conduct disgraceful to his character as an officer, and prejudicial to good order and military discipline, and tending to destroy the confidence of the troops in their officers, and to reflect dishonour on His Majesty's service.' This case served to underline Robert Peel's long-held belief that a civil police 'for the more effective protection of the public peace against the occurrence of similar commotions' was required and this was included in the King's speech in December.

The year 1831 also saw the eruption of slave riots in the West Indies. In December, a fire broke out on the Kensington estate in Jamaica triggering an uprising of 20,000 slaves led by Samuel Sharpe. This was the largest uprising in any British territory; it ruined at least 20 estates and resulted in 2,000 slaves being killed on plantations in the north-west of the island. It took the British Army and the local militia a month to put down the revolt.[381] One of the outcomes, however, was that it did help to push the Act of Abolition through the English Parliament in 1833 with little opposition. This Act freed at least 800,000 slaves. A great number of both merchant class and members of the aristocracy had interests in the Caribbean and even the famous society and political hostess,[382] Lady Holland, had a share in the Vassall estate, although her husband, Lord Holland, had been a long-time and vocal opponent of slavery. The Act passed into law in 1833 and led to final abolition in 1834. The £20 million paid in recompense to the owners of the plantations for the loss of their labour was probably reasonable in such an unusual situation.

Elizabeth, the widow of John, was faced with a dilemma in 1828. She came from the family Cornish from Exeter, Devon, and they owned plantations in Jamaica from which she derived some income. In August 1828, in anticipation of coming legislation and its subsequent enforcement, a Mr Smith, who was presumably the family's Cumberland estates manager in Jamaica, wrote to Elizabeth from Spanish Town, proposing that she settle her share in the remaining 34 slaves on the plantation on her sister Mary and suggesting the sum of £500 as being a fair price.[383] Elizabeth Hill was a pious lady of profound religious conviction. Her long letters to family and friends read almost like sermons but she had not, so it would appear, done anything to emancipate the slaves on the family plantations and had indeed derived an income from them. Perhaps this was not such an unusual situation at the time.

Hill's first opposite number as Secretary at War in the early 1830s was Sir Henry Hardinge, who agreed with Lord Hill in objecting to the calling out of the military in any part of the kingdom, without the authority and presence of a magistrate to sanction the proceedings, as it would put the officer in command in an impossible situation.[384] No wonder that true soldiers did not care for 'police' duty at home. It had become increasingly difficult to obtain recruits for the yeomanry[385] and the militias now that the glories of Waterloo were becoming a faint memory. Lord Hill did his best with the limited means he had. Indeed, his competent and decisive actions in coping with civil unrest encouraged Lord Melbourne, who served as Home Secretary 1830–1834, and the Whig government, not to oust him as the head of the Army. Hawkstone had its own troop of Yeoman Cavalry commanded first by Sir Robert and then his son, Colonel George Stavely Hill. Both the yeomanry and militias came under the control of the Home Office, except for the inspections which were carried out by general officers appointed by Horse Guards. Even the disposition of regular troops on home duty, including the issue of arms, was controlled by the Home Office. All this, coupled with serious cuts in military numbers and armament, often left Horse Guards with its hands tied. The Commander in Chief did not have much more latitude in the colonies, where the Colonial Secretary had to give his sanction for the disposition of troops.

Rowland retained Lord Fitzroy Somerset as his Military Secretary. 'Fitz' was a good man, if not a brilliant soldier, who had served on Wellington's personal staff in the Peninsula and had lost his right arm at Waterloo. He had swiftly taught himself to write left-handed. He was the youngest of the Duke of Beaufort's numerous sons. In an 1828 memorandum Sir George Napier wrote, 'He [Somerset] has done more good to the Army than all his Predecessors put together [and] carries his popularity with him in every situation.'[386] A charming and gentle person, he made an ideal number two. He was eventually to be made the scapegoat for the charge of the Light Brigade at Balaclava and the appalling sufferings of the Army in the Crimea in the winter of 1854–55[387] where he sadly demonstrated his lack of field experience. He had become more of a politician/administrator during his long years at Horse Guards. Putting most of the blame on him was made all the easier for Lucan and Cardigan since Fitzroy died only ten days after the failed attack on Sevastopol in 1855. Fitz did, however, gave sterling support to Hill at Horse Guards and his very large archive of papers covering this period is extremely interesting. These, the Raglan papers, are held in the Gwent Records Office. You only have to read his letters to and from Lord Hill to realise that this was the ideal Military Secretary; always *au fait* with the current problems or ideas. He almost always knew the soldiers who were pushing for promotion or some honour and could advise Lord Hill accordingly; not to say that Rowland did not have his own knowledge and opinions of many of the supplicants. Hill took Colonel Egerton and Major Digby Mackworth as half pay ADCs and his nephews Captain R. Frederick Hill of the 53rd Regiment, younger son of his late brother John, and Lieutenant George Stavely Hill [388] of the Royal Horse Guards as the other two, the latter the son of brother Sir Robert.

Colonel George Brown, who had had a successful military career in the Peninsula and in America, had just gone to Bermuda with his men when Hill appointed him to HQ Staff in 1831,[389] creating him Deputy Adjutant General. George Brown was known to be a strict disciplinarian and something of a 'flogging' CO. There is a quantity of correspondence between Brown, Willoughby Gordon, Quartermaster General, and Somerset. Gordon and Brown were friends and their letters contain both official matters concerning their work under Lord Hill at Horse Guards, and general chatter.[390] Brown served in various capacities at Horse Guards for more than 20 years, only leaving when Sir Henry Hardinge became Commander in Chief.

It was tough at the top and Fitzroy Somerset could be considered as one of those unsung heroes of the British Army at this point in the second quarter of the nineteenth century, even if he was a 'mere' administrator. Wellington said of him, 'he cannot tell a lie.' Hill was also fortunate in having Sir Henry Hardinge at the War Department during the short Wellington ministry. Hardinge later served as Secretary for Ireland. Ireland was, as always, an intractable problem for London and required a large number of troops. Hardinge had served pretty much throughout the campaigns in the Peninsula and had been the British liaison officer with Marshal Blücher's Army in the Netherlands in 1815[391] and was thus well known to Hill. Together they tried to reorganise and improve the Army's administration. Rowland was responsible for introducing several new measures designed to improve the lot of the private soldiers. These innovations included the establishment of recreational facilities, such as libraries in barracks, sports facilities for games such as cricket and fives, savings banks and generally improving the lot of the rank and file. He also saw that bibles and prayer books were supplied free: cost £800 per annum. When the Whigs were back in power, the Secretary of War tried to get this subsidy discontinued, one of their often rather petty efforts to cut back on the Army's expenditure.

Hill was also, with Wellington's support since their views on the subject were identical after many years of active service, deeply concerned with military discipline and the revision of the system of courts martial. In October 1829 Lieutenant Colonel Bailey was accused of acting with extreme cruelty when ordering punishment by having the 'cat' soaked in brine prior to a flogging, a practice which rendered the punishment much more agonising.

The Court found that Colonel Bailey had no knowledge that this practice was being used although there appears to have been evidence that he did but the Court's decision was that a Commanding officer of a depot standing in a square of four companies witnessing a punishment, the fair military presumption is, and ought to be, that he had a knowledge of this cruel irregularity and that he and he alone is responsible for it ... he must have seen what was going forward ... Whatever may be the sentence of a general court martial, Lord Hill may say that he must hold commanding officers of regiments responsible for what passes in the regiments and battalions under their command ... either they know of such irregularities and knowing them have not prevented them, or the irregularity existing, as has been found in this case, and the officer in command being ignorant of it and not preventing it, he is totally unfit for the performance of the duty required from an officer commanding a body of troops.[392]

Lord Hill also had the King to deal with. A tricky, self-important and vain man, George IV had to be squared up to by the new Commander in Chief and in fact, the King must have soon gained a healthy respect for Lord Hill, who refused to back down on several occasions when his preference for a candidate to fill a particular job did not coincide with that of his monarch. He had only been in office for a matter of days before his determination to do what he felt was correct was tested by the King. His Majesty had wished to gratify the demands of Lord Glenlyon, second son of the Duke of Atholl, in making an appointment to a fine Scottish regiment 'a tip top one, one of those beautiful highland regiments.'[393] Rowland had determined to put Major General Ferguson in command. The King was opposed to Ferguson, who had, it is true, been in various scrapes, but Rowland patently felt he was the man for the job and stuck his neck out on his behalf, threatening to resign if he was overruled. As Creevy wrote, 'and yet little Hill has carried him thro.' Many people were astonished at Hill's success and decisive manner over this affair. The stand off between Horse Guards and the King lasted for ten days.

In many of these affairs, Rowland discussed his feelings and views with Wellington. It would have been hard for him to ignore the fact that he had been Wellington's junior for so long in the Peninsula and that he owed his appointment to the Duke. Hill was politically naïve. Wellington would frequently give his opinion although he said that 'It was his rule to only give his opinion when asked.' Unfortunately, the great Duke's opinion on political matters was not always astute as the years rolled by.

There were some people who still thought that the Duke should be the Head of the Army. General Sir James Steuart even went so far as to write to Wellington saying that he did not consider Lord Hill as Commander in Chief and applied to the Duke, who was then Prime Minister, for the governorship of Dumbarton.

The sharp reply he received from Wellington certainly brought Steuart up very short and he wrote again begging the Duke's pardon for the blunder has made regarding Lord Hill.[394] He had well and truly cooked his own goose as regards Dumbarton! Hill was gratified to be able to give this governorship to his old friend, Thomas Graham, Lord Lynedoch.

> May 22, 1829.
>
> My dear Lord Lynedoch
>
> I cannot forward the official notification of your appointment to the gov-
> ernment of Dumbarton Castle, without, at the same time, assuring you that
> I have never in my life had the opportunity of conferring a favour which has
> afforded me more sincere satisfaction; and I am sensible you will feel grati-
> fied by learning that my nomination has met with the cordial approbation of
> His Majesty.

His Lordship also made his feelings very clear with regard to officers who did not wish to serve in certain postings overseas. The Earl of Westmoreland's son, Major Henry Sutton Fane of the 34th Regiment of Foot, did not wish to go to Nova Scotia and asked his father to try and get him excused from this duty. The request directed to Lord Hill came first into the hands of his Secretary at Horse Guards, Fitroy Somerset. Somerset told Fane that, 'he, who from his rank in society, should be an example to others of zeal for the service and of anxiety to undertake whatever he may be called upon to do, will be cited as having through the influence obtained of his connections been released from an obligation which others have been called upon without exception to fulfil.' Hill had found that it was increasingly difficult to persuade officers to go to such places as Nova Scotia and had therefore made it apparent that there would be no promotion for those who did not accept such postings. Somerset warned Lord Westmoreland that his son could expect no further advancement if Westmoreland should insist that he pass the letter on to Lord Hill.

The autumn of the year 1828 found Ireland in its almost permanent state of unrest and the Marquis of Anglesey, Lord Lieutenant, telling Lord Hill that he needed three more battalions and a cavalry regiment. Anglesey supported Catholic emancipation and was recalled shortly after this. He served in Grey's first administration and then, again, as Lord Lieutenant of Ireland until 1833.

There was more unrest, but of quite a different sort, in Plymouth where there were several thousand[395] Portuguese soldiers. The men themselves seem to have been of a peaceful enough disposition but were under a set of 'ruffians', according to Wellington. These included the Marquis de Palmessa, M de Rezende, M de Barbacena and the Comte de Itabayana. There was some concern that they could obtain arms. Hill was forced to arrange the mounting of a guard every night and the Mayor and police of Plymouth were to assist in watching the men. The suggestion was made that the men be separated from their officers and moved inland where living quarters would be less expensive.[396] On 30 October 1828, the Duke of Wellington wrote to Lord Hill:

> … it is unfortunately impossible to prevent the infamous gang of Portuguese and Brazilian ministers residing in London from arming and equipping their troops stationed at Plymouth in secret and without our having a limit of it. That when so armed they may do with them what they please equally without our knowledge. That is to say they might attack our garrison at Plymouth or they may send to Terceira or Portugal or where they please. This ought not to be … I beg you to recollect that we sent our troops to Portugal in 1827 because Portuguese deserters invaded Portugal from Spain. The difficulty of such an operation from England is tenfold what it would be, or what it was, from Spain … the law enables us to do but little in such a case as this. I believe the alien act may enable us to disperse this assemblage of Portuguese and to fix upon the places at which aliens must reside. If it does not, we can do nothing. I have written to Peel upon that subject.

He advised Hill to be on his guard and to protect the arsenal at Plymouth.

Portugal was a thorny issue; for a second time in the century, the country had called on Britain for help. Brazil had separated itself from Portugal and become an 'empire' in its own right, in 1822, under Emperor Pedro, or Peter I. When King Joao VI[397] (Pedro's father), still ruler of Portugal, died in 1826, great trouble arose over the succession. Pedro would have been the obvious heir but Portugal did not want to be reunited with Brazil and he renounced his rights in favour of his daughter Maria Gloria, aged only eight. She was to marry her uncle, Miguel, Pedro's brother, as soon as she came of age. However, Don Miguel, a Macchiavellian plotter who had schemed against his late father and had been exiled in Austria, immediately threw out the new liberal constitution in favour of his own reactionary policies and backed by the Holy Alliance, a coalition of Russia, Austria and Prussia, formed in September 1815, pressed his claim to be absolute monarch. Britain, bound by ancient alliances with Portugal, sent about 5000 troops under Lieutenant General Sir William Henry Clinton to fight what was to be known as the First Miguelist War. The British troops remained until April 1828, which was just after Hill's appointment as Commander in Chief. Canning said that this small force was 'to defend and preserve the independence of our ally'. The rebellion against the absolutist supporters of Miguel started in Porto and spread to other cities. Many thousands of liberals were either arrested or fled to Britain, Spain or Terceira, one of the islands of the Azores, which became a rallyng point for Portuguese liberals. The Spanish had agreed to permit some of these soldiers to stay in their country for one month but they then sailed to England or Terceira.

It was some of these men who had come to Plymouth and were causing such anxiety to Wellington and Lord Hill. Pedro I of Brazil abdicated in favour of his son in 1831 and went to support the legitimate Queen Maria Gloria in exile in the Azores. The Queen of Spain, followed by France and Britain, all recognised the legitimate sovereignty of Maria Gloria. Knowing how anxious the British were to get rid of the unwelcome presence of the Portuguese soldiers in Plymouth, the Marquis de Palmela demanded an escort from the British Navy to 'officially' transport these men to Brazil. It appears that the British were on the point of recognising Dom Miguel since he was the *de facto* King of Portugal, however unwelcome his reactionary policies might be, and an escort for the liberals was initially refused. Eventually the men did leave and although the ships' papers were 'for Brazil,' most people were aware that they would be heading for Terceira to help the Regency. Count Saldanha, leader of the liberals who had been in Britain, was in one of these ships together with 600 Portuguese troops when they were confronted off the Azores by the Royal Navy. Fortunately, only a single shot was fired, which killed an Englishman![398] The Admiralty had given orders to 'burn, sink or destroy' any vessels trying to land at Terceira, which would seem to have been in total contrast to the previous policy of aiding the liberal faction supporting Maria Gloria. Eventually, the ex-Emperor of Brazil, Pedro 1, attacked Miguel from the Regency's base in the Azores – an enterprise in which he was now aided by the Royal Navy – and forced his abdication. Dom Miguel departed having renounced all claims to the throne. Lord Hill and the British Government had seen the departure of the Portuguese from Plymouth with considerable relief.

On 25 June 1830, Rowland wrote to tell Maria that the King was sinking fast:

From what I heard at the Castle [Windsor] yesterday, I did not think he would have survived the night. It is, so far as it relates to myself, a curious circumstance, that he should have lived to fulfil his promise to me, by appointing me to the governorship of Plymouth, and that this act should in all probability, have been one of his last – probably the last. On Wednesday when the subject was brought before him, he recollected all that had passed respecting this government, and expressed much gratification in ordering his signature to be affixed to my appointment ... With respect to the governorship of Plymouth, it is considered the first in point of honour and importance; and if the governor resides there, it is valuable on account of a good house, land etc. As it is I shall not receive more than £1100 a year, being about £500 more than Hull. I am however, quite satisfied not only with the emolument, but more especially with the manner in which my dying sovereign has marked his favourable opinion of my services ... Parliament is at this moment in a very unsettled, disagreeable state; many members absent; and many voting to please their constituents, in expectation of a general election ... I must now go to the House of Lords where we expect an interesting night.

Lord Hill obviously took considerable pleasure in having his services recognised by the dying King and, with no wife, who better to share his pleasure with than his elder sister?

With the death of George IV, the new King was his affable but somewhat erratic sailor brother, William, Duke of Clarence. This character was only to reign for seven years but it was a period that was packed with momentous changes in the country and, although he was known as Silly Billy for the rambling and often error-strewn speeches he was prone to make, he did accept that reform was important, as was Catholic emancipation. In return for Parliament agreeing to settle his enormous debts, William accepted the necessity of marrying in order to produce an heir. His bride was Adelaide of Saxe Meiningen. His marriage required him to abandon his long time mistress, the actress Dorothy Jordan, which he seems to have done without heartfelt regret. Adelaide was unfortunately unable to produce a living heir but the couple were extremely contented together and it gradually became apparent that William would be succeeded by his niece, Victoria, daughter of his younger brother the late Duke of Kent.

Shortly after his accession, William accepted, with considerable relief, the resignation of another brother, the appalling Duke of Cumberland,[399] the fifth son of George III. Wellington had been both Colonel of the Blues and the regiment's first Gold Stick, succeeding the Duke of York. He had also then become Colonel of the 1st Foot Guards (the Grenadiers). He held these roles until he had to resign as Commander in Chief and Gold Stick on becoming Prime Minister at the end of 1827. The King had appointed his brother the Duke of Cumberland[400] to succeed him, which surprised most observers. He was not a very successful Colonel of the Blues but had a firm belief in the powers invested, as he thought, in the Gold Sticks with regard to promotions and appointments within his regiment.[401] The role of Gold Stick in the Household Cavalry had previously been held in rotation by the colonels of the three regiments but now William IV commanded that all authority should be vested in the Commander in Chief and all appointments and promotions should be made through him. When Lord Hill had become Commander in Chief in 1828, Cumberland had resigned in a sulk as Gold Stick. His resignation was based on a point of etiquette. Cumberland wrote to his brother, 'it appears your Majesty means to place the Gold Stick merely on the footing of a Court Office, which changes the whole character of the situation as it ceases to be a pure military one.'[402] He continued that holding the rank of a senior Field Marshal himself, he could not serve under a mere general, Lord Hill. He was evidently rather taken aback by the rapidity with which his brother, the King, accepted his resignation!

In November 1830, the King appointed Lord Hill to the Colonelcy of the Royal Horse Guards, Blue and also as Gold Stick, to the chagrin of many others – including Lord Londonderry – who considered their claims to be superior. Someone gave the opinion that Hill had already been given sufficient honours.[403] The 'gold stick' was an ebony cane with a gold head embossed with His Majesty's cipher and crown. The role dated from the days of Charles II when his illegitimate son, the Duke of Monmouth, had been the first incumbent. In reality, the Gold Stick's duties were often carried out by his senior subordinate, who thus became known as Silver Stick. The principal duties of Gold Stick were to protect the Sovereign and required attendance on all ceremonial occasions. The Sovereign, at that date, would convey his orders to Gold Stick for transmission to the Household regiments. Gold Stick was always Colonel of one of the Household regiments.

It is possible that the regiment itself had put pressure on the King to appoint Hill as Colonel of the Royal Horse Guards, for two reasons; firstly because he was almost a member of the 'family' with three brothers having served or still serving,[404] and secondly because 'the Waterloo generation was concerned that military eminence was being lost at the expense of fashionable repute.' The appointment of distinguished former operational commanders as opposed to political appointees as Colonel would redress this. Queen Victoria, when she was crowned in 1837, strongly supported this policy regarding the Household Cavalry colonelcies, considering them as fitting rewards for her most senior officers.[405] Brother Clement, now Lieutenant Colonel commanding the Blues,[406] was created Silver Stick. The bachelor brothers were frequent and popular visitors to Windsor. It was probably fortunate that Clement was not married as service in one of the household regiments was extremely expensive! There were many *levees* to be attended and as Gold Stick, Lord Hill's attendance on these occasions, which were probably very boring, was more or less mandatory although he sometimes asked Lord Combermere to stand in for him and vice versa. The plus side of these *levees* was that it gave people of standing, such as Hill, the opportunity to bring younger men to the King's notice.

By this time, Hill was renting Westbourne House just outside of London. This stood in what is today a short unprepossessing road called Lord Hill Street just behind Paddington Station and not where you would expect to find a nobleman's house. In the 1830s it was a leafy, more or less rural area. Here he entertained his old army friends including the Duke, Lord Combermere, Sir Robert Peel, Sir George Murray and Lord Lynedoch, together with the King and Queen. William invited himself saying that he did not dine with people in town but as Lord Hill lived 'in the country' he would come and dine with him. On the King's instructions, his private secretary, Sir Herbert Taylor, had written to Hill confirming his role as Head of the Army under the new monarch and giving his assurance that it was a non-political role. This latter promise was of considerable importance to Rowland as the growing shadow of reform hung over the country. Together with many others, Hill was in fear of revolution spreading across the Channel from France where Charles X had been deposed. In common with many of his fellow Tories, he did not understand the depth of feeling amongst the people of Britain, especially in the larger cities where modern industry was developing fast.

Wellington's failings as a politician, as opposed to his singular qualities as as a soldier, are well known and his short-lived government fell in November 1830. The immediate reasons for this were various but the most obvious was his unshakeable view that the present state of representation was satisfactory and the majority of his Tory Cabinet was in agreement.[407] This was hardly surprising since they came from the great landowning families and had the most to lose through any radical change. When he dissolved Parliament, he put his head on the block by opening the way for the Whigs to win a general election. Failing to understand the mood in the country, he thought that he would obtain support from the limited electorate; but it was hard to take an eighteenth-century Prime Minister and Cabinet into the nineteenth century and the King asked Charles, Earl Grey to form a government. Grey had been in politics for many years and had even petitioned for some sort of reform as far back as 1792. His new ministry was totally committed to reform and also to the final abolition of slavery in the British colonies.

The year 1830 saw the death of the unfortunate William Huskisson, MP for Liverpool and President of the Board of Trade in Wellington's Cabinet. Train travel was just beginning and railways were under construction all over the country. The Duke of Wellington had agreed to open the Liverpool to Manchester line on 15 September 1830; Rowland was amongst the distinguished guests. Unlike the Duke, he was much in favour of this new form of travel although its shortcomings seem to have been similar to those of current times; in the later 1830s, he wrote to nephew Rowland complaining that his journey from Birmingham to London had taken twelve hours. On this September day, the train left Liverpool and halted at Parkside to take on water. The track here was double with the southern track reserved for the engine and three carriages; one for the Duke and his guests, one for the directors of the railway and the third for that essential of all grand openings, the band.[408] Huskisson, together with several other guests got out of one of the carriages on the north-bound track in order to speak to the Duke. Another train, in fact Stephenson's famous Rocket, was moving on the adjacent line and a carriage door swung open throwing Huskisson either against or under this second engine. The others had all scrambled to safety but Huskisson was not very nimble; one of his legs was crushed and the injury was too serious for his life to be saved despite the presence of a doctor on one of the trains. His death was described as the first train accident. Wellington was subsequently not very fond of train travel whereas Hill frequently took the train from Birmingham to London (which was, under normal circumstances, a journey of about nine hours).

The King had determined that the new barracks for the Household troops was to be constructed in 'the birdcage walk' despite those who opposed the idea. There had been aviaries here since the time of King James I who had kept all manner of wild animals in St James Park, even elephants and crocodiles. A more recent version of Wellington Barracks still stands in Birdcage Walk. The original, and very different, barracks were built in 1831 with the work being supervised by Lieutenant General Sir James Kempt. From 1814, by order of the Prince Regent, the two regiments of the Life Guards and the Blues rotated between London and Windsor, which was known as 'Country Quarters'.

An example of Rowland's continuing humanitarian concern for the ordinary soldiers is his anger over the treatment of the 1st Foot Guards (the Grenadier Guards) in Ireland with regard to feeding the men on guard duty in Dublin. The men were expected to cook for themselves rather than receive rations as previously. Lord Hill instructed Major General Sir John Macdonald, Adjutant General at Horse Guards, to convey his displeasure to Lieutenant General Sir Hussey Vivian, Commander in Chief in Ireland, together with Sir Edward Blakeney, over the mess arrangements. It was a long letter but the essence was that

> Lord Hill thinks it unnecessary to suggest to your good sense and military experience that it is at all times less or more hazardous to overthrow suddenly any arrangements bearing immediately upon the soldiers' personal comfort, and which usage may have all but identified with his very nature. These arrangements now under discussion are one of those which Lord Hill has accustomed himself to regard almost in that light, and so impressed is he with the wisdom and expediency of continuing to the soldier the enjoyment of every personal comfort to which he may have been accustomed (except, of course, when the circumstances attendant upon active service call for general privation) that his Lordship would no more have sanctioned this measure than he would have sanctioned a diminution of the soldier's pay.
>
> … Lord Hill considers it unfortunate that Colonel d'Oyley was not particularly directed to report his opinion of the proposed change before it was carried into effect, as his Lordship is satisfied that had the officer commanding the battalion given a decided opinion against it upon the ground of it being likely to engender dissatisfaction in his ranks, Sir Edward Blakeney and you would at once have abandoned it. Now, however, it remains for Lord Hill to meet the case in its present shape, and his lordship has no hesitation in admitting that he approaches it with a feeling not wholly divested of embarrassment. You will readily anticipate that this feeling is produced solely by his Lordship's earnest wish to support you to the very utmost in the discharge of the trust reposed in you as the officer placed in the immediate command of a very large portion of the army. Lord Hill is perfectly convinced that both the non-commissioned officers and soldiers of the battalion of Guards now under your command think themselves unnecessarily deprived of a most essential comfort and that as long as that privation lasts their discontent cannot be eradicated.
>
> When Lord Hill distinctly declares to you that the above is his settled conviction, you cannot but feel that you incur a heavy responsibility by persevering in the new arrangements.[409]

The letter continues by comparing the differences between arrangements for cooking for the men on guard at home in barracks and those in Dublin where the Guards are housed quite differently and that it seems to Lord Hill very obvious that in letting a 'fully accoutred soldier perform all the culinary offices of a cook, whereby his ammunition is in danger of exploding and his appointments are in constant danger of being soiled' is unsatisfactory. Although new cook houses were in the process of being built, Hill had the strongest doubts 'as to the practicability of making such arrangements and is certain that great mischief may arise at any moment from the new system ... His Lordship accordingly urges you to reconsider the whole subject very deliberately.'

This vexed battalion the 1st Foot Guards was being inspected when several men had stepped forward to complain of the new arrangements. All of these soldiers had conducted themselves with perfect respect towards their superiors and Lord Hill hoped that they were not subject to censure.

The letter continues with criticism of the punishments meted out to defaulters involving long marches in the countryside, which Lord Hill feels are degrading to the Army in the sight of the public, at a time when the affairs of Ireland are in a most delicate state.

The letter rounds off with a reminder that alterations to long-established customs should not be put in place without reference to the Commander in Chief. It is a stiff letter. You could certainly not accuse Hill of failing to be 'hands on' when it came to the wellbeing of his men. It was also, of course, a question of common sense; well fed, contented soldiers had no reason to show their displeasure with acts of violence, indiscipline or mutiny.

When Wellington's ministry left office, many people felt that he would return to being Commander in Chief but this would not happen until after Hill's death in 1842. The gossip in Brighton in 1832, as described in a letter from Lord Lyndhurst to Wellington,[410] was that Lord Grey would 'put all his bastards into positions of power: Sir James Kempt to succeed Lord Hill and Napier to replace Fitzroy Somerset, with Digby Mackworth to be made the subject of complaint.' The mooted 'complaint' probably concerned his actions in Bristol when not officially on duty. Wellington indulged in some phrase-making in connection with the Court of Enquiry concerning events at Bristol and preparations for defence in the light of the disturbances both there and in Birmingham: 'Bristol is an example of an Army of Stags with a Lion at the Head of it, better than an army of Lions with a Stag at the Head.'[411]

With regard to the comments that Kempt was to have Horse Guards, the gossip was soon proved wrong; on the contrary it turned out that Lord Grey was quite content to let Lord Hill continue in this role – in fact, he was probably pleased to have a possibly more compliant Commander in Chief than Wellington. Grey had a very large family, both legitimate and otherwise. As a young man when he had first come to London, he had rapidly entered the political scene; what followed was a major scandal. He met Georgiana, the young Duchess of Devonshire who was married to William Cavendish, the 5th Duke. They fell in love and when she became pregnant, she went abroad to Aix en Provence where she gave birth to the child who was to be known as Eliza Courteney. The Duke refused to permit Georgiana to keep the child, despite his own 'natural' children who lived at Devonshire House, and she was taken to be brought up by Grey's parents. In due course, Eliza married Lieutenant Colonel Robert Ellice. Once in power, Grey, as mentioned above, began placing his family in positions of influence and advantage. One son-in-law, now General Ellice, was pushed forward to Lord Hill for a post in command of the garrison at Portsmouth. There exists considerable correspondence on the subject. Initially, it would seem that Hill was not totally dismissive of Ellice's suitability for the Portsmouth command[412] but after several adverse articles in the newspapers had appeared, Grey wrote to Lord Hill asking why he had not told him that he was against the appointment. Hill replied

> I will frankly confess to your Lordship that that if you had not mentioned your wishes, it is probable that the situation becoming vacant, it would not have occurred to me to have offered it to Major General Ellice and that my choice would have fallen upon an officer of more general services but having no doubt of General Ellice's fitness to be employed on the Staff, and seeing by Your Lordship's letter of 25 December that you attached considerable importance to the result of your application and that you were deeply interested in its success, I felt it to be due to your Lordship at once to state that on the removal of Sir Colin Campbell to the Government of Halifax, I should have great satisfaction in proposing General Ellice as his successor at Portsmouth.[413]

Just how 'frank' this is, is up for debate. Grey then demanded to know if Lord Hill had 'any well founded objections' to Ellice's capabilities. Hill wrote to Lord Fitzroy Somerset saying that he hoped Lord Grey would not 'press [Ellice] upon me particularly … but the command in Portsmouth besides being professional is worth four or five times the money.'[414] He had now got himself into a little trouble with the Prime Minister who wrote a chastising letter to him on 22 November 1833, saying that after this 'insinuation … I cannot hesitate to withdraw the application which I before made to you; having no wish to force an extension of favour to Major General Ellice.'[415] Patronage at Horse Guards was often a tricky business.

The word according to Wellington was that Ellice, in any event, was meant to be going to Dublin with the Duke's brother, Wellesley, but the governorship of Portsmouth was worth more money per annum. This led to a prolonged stand-off between the Commander in Chief and the First Secretary regarding 'Lord Grey's desire to heap places upon his family.[416] To all military jobs Lord Hill opposes a firm resistance. He has defeated altogether the plan of giving a red ribbon to

General Ellice who has not seen active service since he was a major and ADC.' Grey pressed this matter with the King who asked Hill why he would not give the honour to General Ellice. Rowland told His Majesty that if such was his wish, then it would be done but that it would cause disatisfaction and he asked the King to consider the likely consequences. Once again William gave way to his Commander in Chief. In spite of his benign exterior, Rowland had shown that he was no pushover! The 'red ribbon' was the Military Order of the Bath, an order of chivalry founded by George I. There were, at this date, three degrees of membership: Companion of the Bath, CB; the Knight Commander or KCB, which was the Order Grey wished for Ellice, and then the top class, the Knight Grand Cross or GCB. When Hill had been invested with the order in 1812, there was only one category, the KB and the numbers awarded were very limited. More recently, they have been handed out fairly liberally. In each class, the Order was suspended on a red ribbon. This decoraton was known colloquially as the 'red ribbon'; the Garter, the highest Order of Chivalry in the gift of the Sovereign, was known as the 'blue' ribbon. By this point in his career, Hill had risen from the original KB to being a GCB.

The Grey papers reveal the extraordinary number of demands he made on Hill, who was by this time left with almost no places available to fill because the Whigs had cut the size of the Army so drastically. Not only did Grey constantly badger his Commander in Chief but almost all his requests were for members of his extended family.

Major General Sir Colin Campbell had been commandant of the garrison at Portsmouth but was now tipped to go to Halifax as Governor of Nova Scotia to replace Sir Peregrine Maitland.[417] He had been in Portsmouth when the French royal family arrived off Spithead, fleeing from the Revolution. On 9 August 1830, when Louis Philippe had been declared King, Charles X abdicated and requested asylum in Britain but was said to know that it might not be possible. The family was permitted to land as private citizens and was housed for a short time at Lulworth Castle. The former King went by the name of Comte de Ponthieu. He was then moved to Holyrood Palace in Edinburgh and in 1832 the Government was delighted to see him leave for Prague at the invitation of the Emperor Franz I. Charles X's minister, the most troublesome Prince Jules Auguste-Armand-Marie de Polignac[418] had been arrested and imprisoned at the time of the July Revolution. He was freed in 1836 with the proviso that he lived abroad and he came to England. England was often the safe haven for well connected refugees. Even Napoleon had begged to be permitted to come there and had promised to live quietly and in peace. John Hobhouse, then Secretary at War, tells the story that the Duke of Sussex called on Polignac together with Lord Hill one day in 1841 and found him spread out on a cross on the floor. Hill immediately said, 'I wish some fellow had come in and nailed him to it.' This seems rather out of character for Hill but everyone present including Lord John Russell found it most amusing.[419]

Another revolution took place in the Netherlands. The artificial union bro-
kered at the Congress of Vienna between Holland and Belgium collapsed, the fnal
stimulus being the revolution in France and the overthrow of the inept Charles
X. The Belgians, almost all Walloons and Roman Catholic were unsuited tor a
'marriage' with the Protestant, sea-going Dutch of' 'low-German' origin. The
English were concerned that too fierce a reaction to Belgium's independence
would merely serve to drive them towards the French. For some time it looked
as if Britain was going to send an army and Lord Hill discussed the possible composition and size of this projected force, which would require taking 1500 troops
from Ireland and calling up of some militia regiments. He received a message
from Lord Melbourne: 'The Dutch disclaim all idea of having intended to move
on Belgium so there is an end to the supposed want of troops for a foreign expedition'.[420] The five most interested parties (England, France, Russia, Austria and
Prussia) met at the London Conference in 1830. On 18 December, the British
Foreign Secretary, Lord Palmerston, moved that Belgium should be acknowledged as an independent state; the former United Kingdom of the Netherlands
was dissolved. At least France had been prevented from gobbling up the Belgians
and Hill had not had to part with any of the troops he was anxious to keep at
home in case of more civil unrest.

On 2 January 1832, Sir Thomas Noel Hill fell ill at Maidstone where he was
commandant of the cavalry depot and died a few days later, He had apparently
suffered from a fever 'caused by a disorder of the stomach and alimentary canal'.
The Shore[421] family rushed to his bedside as did his brother, Clement, but he died
on 8 January. Whatever struck him down initially – 'smart fever', whatever that
might be, according to one of the doctors – he almost certainly died from pneu-
monia. According to a letter from Colonel Richard Egerton, Rowland's private
secretary, to Lord Fitzroy Somerset, 'there never was a more worthy kind hearted
creature than poor Noel.' Although to a great extent prepared for the worst, Tom's
death came as a great blow to Rowland and the whole of the close-knit family.
The fact that at least four brothers had served in the same theatre of war, the
Peninsula, had helped to keep them united.

In 1832, there was mutiny in the 7th Regiment and Somerset wrote to Hill
saying he must see Lord Grey.[422] Hill had a meeting with the Prime Minister
and impressed on him the necessity of commanding officers retaining the powers
of 'instantaneous punishment', without which the Army would in a short time
become an armed rabble. A General Order was issued from Horse Guards in which
the punishment of flogging was restricted without exception to certain offences
therein specified. It was further suggested to officers that they should restrain the
practice as much as possible. Hill proposed solitary confinement as an alternative.
The Whigs were opposed to such an idea, which would be expensive to implement. In 1833, an Enquiry took place into military discipline and the General
Order of the preceding year was formalised.[423] Corporal punishment should only

take place in specific cases: 1) for mutiny, insubordination, and violence or using or offering violence to superior officers; 2) Drunkeness on duty; 3) sale of or making away with, arms, ammunition, accoutrements, or necessaries, stealing from comrades; or other disgraceful conduct. Sir John Macdonald, Adjutant General:

> It will doubtless occur to you that the object of these instructions is not to render the infliction of corporal punishment for the future, more frequent or more certain than it is at present given in the causes to which it is now to be restricted, but, on the contrary, that the intention is to restrain it as much as it may be possible to do so with safety to the discipline of the Army.

The lower classes regarded service in the Army as a sign of failure and in most cases up to this date, it had been exactly that for private soldiers. The standing army in Britain was now very small. Reformers were poised to prise what were seen as aristocratic preserves from those who had, historically, held the reins of power. Great debates took place in Parliament. Joseph Hume the radical reformer led the opposition to flogging. He introduced a bill into Parliament in April 1833[424] but although many spoke in support, others – even Rufane Donkin – were opposed to removing flogging as the final threat short of hanging. Donkin, a staunch Whig, had seen military service in the Peninsula and this had led him to conlcude that sometimes men needed the deterrent of flogging. It was, of course, a 'detestable practice' but the reason given for retaining it was 'that the class of private soldiers were so bad a set of men that they could not be kept in order without it.' The converse, it could be argued, was that the existence of flogging as a punishment deterred 'a better class of man' from entering the Army. By early 1834, there could be seen a marked fall in the number of floggings.

It was in January 1834 that Edward Ellice, brother to General Robert Ellice who had married Lord Grey's illegitimate daughter, Eliza, became Secretary at War. Grey family nepotism, again. Ellice was a clever man who had made a lot of money but when it came to the British Army, his one idea was to cut costs as drastically as he possibly could. He wrote to Lord Hill on 2 January 1834, 'in very strong and solemn terms' according to Somerset, outlining the earnest desire of His Majesty's Government to see that 'every practicable retrenchment consistent with efficiency should be effected.'[425] It all sounds familiar.

Egerton and Somerset evidently were kindred spirits, which was fortunate since they both worked for Rowland. They communicated frequently when either was out of town, mostly on subjects concerning their OC Lord Hill but they also exchanged poetry and jokes. In one rather charming letter from Somerset to Egerton in October 1832 he wishes Egerton a happy birthday with 'Providence did a good turn to the world when you were born.'[426] Somerset hopes that through the kind and affectionate care of Mrs Egerton, he will be preserved to his friends for many, many years.

In 1835, Fitzroy Somerset asked Lord Hill if he could use his influence with William Noel Hill, his cousin, to permit the Somersets to remain in his house in Hampshire that they had been renting and which Lady Somerset liked very much. This was Berwick House (name of the Noel Hill's family title) in Red Rice. The reply was that Noel Hill was probably going to dispose of the house as he had just inherited the title of 3rd Lord Berwick and the estates of Attingham in Shropshire on the death of his childless elder brother, Thomas. The Somersets were most disappointed. Not long after this, Fitz wrote to Lord Hill concerning a Mr Vaughan who had been serving as British Minister in America.[427] Lord Palmerston had suggested that he should receive the same amount as a pension that was paid to ex-ambassadors and that since funds available are tight, he thinks that William Noel Hill,[428] retired Ambassador to the Kingdom of the Two Sicilies, who had just succeeded to a 'large estate,' might have his pension taken away from him and given to Mr Vaughan. A most extraordinary suggestion! It was all the more bizarre because the new Lord Berwick had inherited virtually nothing more than the title and a heavily mortgaged estate.

XVI

REFORM – AND A MOST UNSTABLE EARL

Revolutions on the continent and civil unrest at home naturally led to increased speculation over reform, especially now that Britain had a 'reforming' First Minister in Charles, 2nd Earl Grey. Wellington's government had fallen in 1830 following a politically suicidal speech made by the Duke in the Lords, in the course of which he declared that he saw no reason for reform. In 1831 the first Reform Bill was introduced and thrown out at the second reading in the House of Lords. Hill did not vote; his reasoning was that his role as Commander in Chief of the Army was not a political one, although everyone knew that his politics were staunchly Tory. The second and main reason was simply that he did not agree with it. Prior to the bill being reintroduced to the House of Lords, Lord Hill was summoned to the Palace by the King. His Majesty alluded to the fact that the bill was about to be brought forward again and that he wished it to go into committee which would show the country that the Lords were not averse to some reform and might make alterations. Rowland told William that he still held the same objections to the bill and the King, although displeased, did not show real anger. He was undoubtedly upset by Hill's entrenched attitude, but he appeared to bear no grudge and shortly thereafter presented him with a new sword as a mark of his personal appreciation.

When William spoke with Lord Grey about reintroducing the bill, the Prime Minister, although anxious for some measure of reform and realising that the desire in the country was now driven by the increasing power of the middle classes as well as the factory workers, said he would not do so unless the King was prepared to make as many peers as might be necessary to ensure that the bill got through the Lords. This threat, which might have meant the creation of as many as 150 new peers, was enough to make the Duke of Wellington, leader of the Tories in the House of Lords, tell his party either to vote with the Government or to abstain; most did the latter. The Act of 1832 did not go as far as some of the more liberal members of the Government would have wished but it shocked and amazed many people by the number of 'rotten boroughs' that were eliminated at the stroke of a pen. More change was to follow. Lord Hill joined with his fellow Tory peers and abstained again.

Today, it is hard to imagine that great cities such as Manchester, Sheffield and Birmingham, which were now the power houses of the new industries, still had no proper representation. A Royal Commission was set up in 1833 to look at the question of urban organisation. This recommended that all ratepayers should have a vote in council elections, the council would elect a Mayor, that the council would take responsibility for such matters as the police force and cleaning of the city. The Act only applied to the largest towns, but it gave all ratepayers the right to vote for the new municipalities. The towns were to be divided into 'wards' and this was to be brought into effect before the next election. The Municipal Corporations Act was passed in 1835. It was a direct result of the Reform Act.

Lord Hill had many things to concern him during his fourteen years at Horse Guards but it is true to say that no other subject vexed him as acutely, for so long or so frequently, as the affairs of James Brudenell, 7th Earl of Cardigan. These affairs were often so bizarre that I have chosen to describe some of their exchanges, the reasons and the results in some detail; it was an extraordinary business. It is incredible that Brudenell's behaviour should have occupied so much of the time of the head of the Army.

Brudenell was born in 1797, the only boy in a family of seven girls. Spoiled from birth and almost shockingly handsome, he was headstrong and arrogant. When he was fourteen, his father succeeded as the 6th Earl and the family moved into the Cardigan seat of Deene Park in Northamptonshire. The boy became more and more domineering in his teens and was subject to the fits of uncontrollable rage, which were to erupt at the slightest provocation throughout his life. As a peer of the realm, he was almost above the law and this, coupled with a very large income, gave the young Lord Brudenell a great opinion of himself. His one regret as a very young man was that, as an only son, his father forbade him to enter the Army, which was the only profession in which he was interested. There are differences of opinion as to his intelligence; various sources describe him as 'undistinguished',[429] 'Unusually stupid'[430] and, when at Harrow, as having made 'excellent academic progress'.[431] Wherever the truth lay, he was overbearing, impetuous and reckless. This recklessness was to reach its nadir two decades later.

Probably the best known of his early follies was his elopement with Elizabeth (Tollemache) Johnstone, wife of Captain Frederick Johnstone, whom Brudenell had known all his life. This caused a great scandal and ended in the Johnstones obtaining a divorce once the necessary Act of Parliament had been passed. As a demonstration of how His Lordship's mind worked, he sent a message to Captain

Johnstone's house after the Court had awarded the Captain damages of £1,000 and offered to fight a duel with him: 'Tell Lord Brudenell', Johnstone told the messenger, 'that he has already given me the satisfaction of having removed the most damn bad-tempered and extravagant bitch in the kingdom.'[432] Lord Brudenell was to find this out for himself for himself in the course of the next few years. One thing that came out of the affair was that Brudenell's parents decided that their golden boy might, after all, be better off in the Army. Thanks to purchase and the patronage of the then Commander in Chief, HRH Frederick Duke of York, the young nobleman rose rapidly through the ranks until just two years after his first appointment as a Cornet in the 8th Hussars he had risen to the rank of Captain. In December 1830, Brudenell became a Lieutenant Colonel and in 1831 he purchased command of the 15th King's Hussars. This was a fine regiment which had distinguished itself in the Peninsula and at Waterloo. Brudenell replaced Colonel Thackwell who bequeathed to him a happy, well-ordered, efficient regiment, or so most people thought. Not so it's new Commanding Officer. Brudenell had a sort of mania for making *his* regiment the smartest, the most efficient, the most admired in the British Army. Although there were two or three officers who 'toadied' to their new Commander, most of his brother-officers disliked him intensely. His efforts to bring the regiment to the peak of condition led to constant field days and reviews resulting in many if not most of the horses having sore backs, a fact that he blamed on poor stable management. This together with the constant manoeuvres in hot weather even led to horses collapsing; everything that went wrong was considered to be the officer's or the trooper's fault and they were screamed at as if their Colonel was a sergeant major.

The 15th was stationed in Cork when the first significant row broke out and caught the public's attention. Brudenell's eye had fallen with the utmost distaste on a Captain Augustus Wathen, one of his troop captains and a soldier of long service. He could do nothing right. It did not take long before Brudenell placed Wathen under arrest; the charge was refusal to obey orders. The papers concerning the subsequent court martial were sent to Lord Hill. Lord Hill considered the charges sent to him and ordered the release of the wretched Captain. He also told Brudenell that his officers should learn to live together. The next problem that arose was that Wathen discovered that everything he said in his 'discussions' with his commanding officer was being taken down by the adjutant. By now more than half the regimental officers considered that their Colonel's conduct was unbecoming the character of an officer and a gentleman; the other half thought he was insane. The Commander in Chief, being the sort of man he was, must have been both mystified and shocked by Brudenell's behaviour. The facts were clear, in that Wathen had committed most of the acts with which he was charged, but the nub of the question was whether his behaviour constitute a breach of the Articles of War? After deliberation, the result of the court martial was that Captain Wathen was acquitted and not just acquitted but 'honourably' acquitted. Brudenell found himself accused of conduct 'revolting to every proper and honourable feeling of a gentleman.'[433]. He was both devastated and furious and made the more so by the King's decision that he was to be dismissed from the regiment. Brudenell had convinced himself that the loathed Captain would be the one to be dismissed the service and so the decision was a hammer blow. The newspapers had a field day and none more so than Drakard's *Stamford News*. John Drakard had founded his newspaper with Octavius Gilchrist in 1809. The paper was pro-republican and anti-government and Drakard had complained that 'his difficulties were due to a district where a corrupt and aristocratical influence was almost unbounded'. Brudenell took this to be aimed at himself and as some of the pieces included in the paper gave him personal offence, he, so it is said, gave Mr Drakard a horse whipping on the racecourse in full public view. It was time for Drakard to get his revenge! He was not alone. The moment that Brudenell had received the results of the court martial, he had gone to London as fast as he could. Here he implored Lord Hill to reinstate him, have him court martialled or what ever it might take to prove he had been badly treated. Lord Hill — and also Wellington, to whom he also appealed — told him to go away and try and keep quiet — 'be temperate' as Lord Hill put it — for at least a year.

In October 1835, Fitzroy Somerset wrote to Hill, who was away, that he had been 'favoured with another of his [Brudenell's] disagreeable visits' and had told him that Lord Hill could not recommend him for the appointment to the 11th Light Dragoons, which was vacant. Brudenell had pushed to know why and Somerset, demonstrating a certain degree of desperation, wrote, 'What shall I say to him? He has written for an answer today and it is very desirable that I should be able to give him one.'[434] Fitzroy Somerset wrote that he had scarcely been able to get a word in but had told Lord B that Hill had every disposition to meet with his wishes when it might be practicable. You get the feeling that Lord Hill hoped Brudenell might just go away! No such luck. Brudenell had somehow learned that it was Lord Howick, Secretary at War and son of Lord Grey, who was the block to his being brought back on full pay. This affair occupied Howick, Melbourne and Lord Hill for some time with Rowland feeling that there should be complete understanding between the Commander in Chief and the Government; in this Lord Melbourne was in agreement. Nothing should be done until Howick concurred and was prepared to fight any possible battle in the House of Commons.

Lord Brudenell now made use of his Court connections. His favourite sister, Harriet, was in waiting on Queen Adelaide and persuaded the Queen to help plead her brother's case before the King. William, however, initially stood firm: 'If he had to squabble with them, [Lords Melbourne and Hill] it would not be over so unpromising a case as Lieutenant Colonel Lord Brudenell.' The pressure on William was great; the soft hearted Queen Adelaide and Brudenell wheeled in his father, the old 6th Earl of Cardigan, who fell on his knees sobbing before the King and eventually, having previously refused to interfere with what he called 'Lord Hill's righteous judgement', William finally went so far as to say that 'if Lord Hill advised with him' he would give his 'favourable consideration' to the case. Hill allowed himself to be pressed into agreeing, most reluctantly and entirely against his better judgement, that he would approve Brudenell in another command if he could obtain one.[435] Poor Lord Hill, how he was going to live to regret his statement, 'I have consented to this step because I am unable to endure the distress of this noble family … and because I hope that the author of this distress is now sensible that he cannot be permitted to follow the dictates of his ungovernable temper. I trust this lesson has not been thrown away.'[436] This decision forced by the hand of his Sovereign was to prove a thorn in his side.

Rich and determined, Lord Brudenell immediately purchased the Lieutenant Colonelcy of the 11th Light Dragoons at a price thought to be more than £40,000, which was of course, against the law. There was great uproar following this announcement and there were cries demanding the resignation of the Commander in Chief. To resign over such a matter would surely have been considered a sign of weakness and the option was not taken. The affair gives some weight to one comment of Wellington's about Hill: 'I am not sure that he does not shrink from responsibility.' He was a far nicer character than Wellington and not as tough in his dealings with his fellow men. In all other respects he was in every way responsible. Certainly, he had never 'shrunk from responsibility' when in the field – but the battles with Lord Brudenell were of a very different type. He, together with his Military Secretary, Lord Fitzroy Somerset, dreaded the appearance of Brudenell at Horse Guards or even the arrival of a letter from him.

Brudenell had unfortunately made an unexpectedly good showing before the House and his appointment had been confirmed; many people seemed to be of the opinion that the young officer had been punished sufficiently. It happened that the 11th Light Dragoons had been on service in India since 1819. Brudenell who so despised those 'Indian Officers' was going to have to serve for a while in India himself. It was not to be for long and he ensured that did not have to share the hardships of his troops by taking a very long and circuitous journey to reach India and then spending most of his time either shooting or being royally entertained. He had barely arrived, when news arrived that the Regiment was to return home; it was 1837. How Lord Hill must have wished that the Regiment could stay in India for ever! He had endured a great deal of critical comment and abuse when he had finally acceded to the pleas that Lord B be given another command. The newspapers were full of the case and the *Chronicle* opined 'It is quite clear that Ministers would never have given a regiment to Lord Brudenell.' Pro Tory papers had described Brudenell's meekness under censure, how in his modesty 'he impugns no man's motives; he courts no man's favour.' What derisive laughter this must have evoked at Horse Guards: Brudenell being described as 'meek' was absurd!

Shortly before he left India, Brudenell received the news that his father had died and thus he had become the 7th Earl Cardigan. Several officers of the regiment had chosen to exchange into other regiments[437] rather than to serve under their new Commanding Officer and after the Regiment had been back in England for a few months, it is certain that several more wished that they had done the same.

Back in England on 1 June 1838, there began a long list of upsets principally brought about by Cardigan's ungovernable temper and most of which were to occupy Lord Hill's attention. First of all, he treated some of his 'Indian' officers so roughly that he forced their resignations. His one idea was to make his regiment the smartest and most efficient at whatever cost, financially or physically. He even went so far as to station some of his men along Piccadilly so that they might salute him as he passed!

Next came the 'black bottle' affair. Cardigan was entertaining the Inspector General of Cavalry, Major General Sleigh, an officer who was generally disliked, for a review to be followed by a dinner at regimental HQ in Canterbury. What followed at the grand dinner was of such triviality that it seems almost impossible that it escalated into such a major row. The dinner was sumptuous, the best wines, the choicest food were served. Suddenly a young Captain, J.W. Reynolds, summoned one of the mess waiters and requested a bottle of Moselle for guests who did not care for champagne. Normally, this should have been decanted but in this instance, the waiter put a large black bottle of the Moselle on the table. When Cardigan's eagle eye lit on this dreadful sight, he became apoplectic. A long wrangle ensured the following morning when he sent a message to Reynolds asking for an explanation. The message was carried by a Captain Jones, one of Cardigan's 'toadies'. 'The Colonel has desired me, as president of the mess committee, to tell you that you were very wrong in having a black bottle placed on the table at a great dinner like last night, as the mess should be conducted like a gentleman's table and not like a tavern or pothouse.' Reynolds went to speak to Cardigan and the upshot was that he was arrested. Everyone's honour had, so it seems, been impugned – by a black bottle! Reynolds refused to shake hands with Captain Jenkins and Cardigan rushed off to report his Captain's conduct to the Commander in Chief. Lord Hill was aghast. The squabble had all the makings of another Wathen scandal. Correspondence flew from Cardigan to Horse Guards. Finally, Lord Hill sent word refusing the court martial that Reynolds had requested and administering a stern reprimand to him; he resumed his duties. Horse Guards had had little choice in this affair than to support the Colonel, especially since they had so recently reinstated him in the Army. The affair was soon public knowledge and led to all sorts of fights, jokes and newspaper cartoons; Cardigan reprimanded one of his troopers who had hit a guardsman, the trooper was taken aback. 'My Lord,' he said indignantly 'he called me a "black bottle".'[438] This was but one instance of the 'insult'. The jokes seemed endless.

Cardigan also fell out with his regimental surgeon who had left church by a side door having had trouble fastening his cap. Both parties wrote to Horse Guards; such trivialities infuriated Lord Hill:[439] 'Lord Hill regrets to find that his recommendation to the Earl of Cardigan on a previous occasion has not had the effect of preventing applications to the Horse Guards by way of complaint of the Earl's conduct.'

Once again, the *Morning Chronicle*[440] somehow got wind of the story and this reprimand and proclaimed that it would be best for everyone, including above all his Regiment, if Cardigan left the Army. Nobody agreed more with the views expressed by the newspaper than Lord Hill; he had little hope of such a happy outcome.

When Reynolds applied for some long overdue leave, it was roughly refused. When he asked to be permitted to go on a two-year course at the Senior Military College, now better known as Staff College, he was refused. He resigned his commission. Hill told Somerset to have a meeting with Reynolds' guardian who had been prosecuting his ward's affairs. He then summoned Reynolds to Horse Guards and an agreement was reached that he would withdraw his resignation, have six months' leave of absence, attend the Military College – and there was the express understanding that he should never again be required to serve for a single day under the Earl of Cardigan.[441] The powers that be were very anxious to avoid another scandal involving the 11th Hussars and its tantrum-prone commanding officer. You might say that Reynolds came out of this in the long run quite satisfactorily. Naturally, Cardigan was enraged. None of this prevented articles on 'Black Bottle Reynolds' and the 'buzzing of Bluebottle Cardigan' in what was coming to be labelled as the 'Battle of the Moselle'.[442] Nothing daunted, Cardigan continued to harangue his officers in front of the men.

Cardigan's next victims were another Reynolds – a cousin, Captain Richard Reynolds – followed by Lieutenant Forrest, plus a duel with Captain Tuckett in which the latter was wounded. To take these in reverse order (and so in order of importance) Forrest's crime was that he had locked his room in barracks when leaving for a week's ceremonial duty at the Pavilion in Brighton; since Forrest was known as a mild mannered and efficient officer, Lord Hill wrote him merely a reprimand. Forrest had himself written to Lord Hill saying that 'it was the Lt Col.'s offensive and irritating manner which were in a great degree the cause of the fault I committed in omitting immediate compliance with the order, [to give up the key to his barracks room] should I have received the slightest courtesy I should not now have found myself in the painful position of being reported to the General Commander in Chief.' The affair of the duel Cardigan fought with Captain Tuckett was another matter. As a peer of the realm, Cardigan's trial had to take place in the House of Lords. Needless to say, for once, he proved a polite and calm witness on his own behalf and got off scot free. On 4 November 1840, the traditional Guy in cloak and high boots was carried in procession through the streets to the scene of the bonfire. On 5 November the traditional Guy was nowhere to be seen. In its place was a dummy dressed in the uniform of the 11th (Prince Albert's Own) Hussars. The dummy carried a black bottle, marked 'Moselle' and much to the amusement of the crowd, a brace of pistols labelled, 'Not hair-triggers'. This referred to the type of pistols that had been used in the duel with Captain Tuckett. This naturally caused enormous amusement to the residents of Brighton!

There was plenty of room in all this for more jokes at Cardigan's expense; some of it was directed at the opulent, flashy uniform of the 11th: 'In the new uniform of Lord Cardigan's regiment, are there many frogs?' ... 'I don't know but there are plenty of toads under the coats,' was one. There were indeed several officer 'toads'.

When Richard Reynolds' court martial opened, Wellington was anxious, not about the arrogance of Cardigan, but that the military discipline of the Army should be maintained. In a letter to Lord Hill, he wrote: 'The perusal of Captain Reynolds's letter of 28th August can leave no doubt but that is was intended to act as a provocation to Lord Cardigan to take steps which would have terminated in a duel.' Reynolds had written to Cardigan referring to Cardigan's remark to a Miss Cunynghame concerning the fact that neither Richard Reynolds nor his cousin had been invited to a ball given by the Earl: 'As long as I live they [the Captains Reynolds] shall never enter my house.' Reynolds said that he found this highly objectionable, 'as it is calculated to convey an impression prejudicial to my character and I trust that your Lordship will be good enough to authorise me to contradict it'. It was one of Cardigan's most glaring personality faults that when, as he frequently did, he reached 'flashpoint', he never stopped to consider his actions or words. As the Duke wrote to Hill, 'The disputes were lamentable.' They certainly were and postively dangerous in a man who was put at the head of a regiment of men for whom he was responsible and who were trained to go to war, although it must be said that up until this date, Cardigan had seen no live action.

Following the judgement of the court martial of Captain Richard Reynolds which sentenced him to be cashiered,[443] Hill sent the Adjutant General, Sir John Macdonald, a highly experienced soldier, down to the regimental HQ. All the officers were assembled and the doors were even locked while Sir John read out an 'admonition' from Lord Hill. Despite the room having been locked, the contents of Lord Hill's message were published in full in *The Times* two days later. Lord Hill had written that it was useless for any one else to make any further complaints against the Earl of Cardigan since he had determined not to listen to any further complaints – on this point Lord Hill was peremptory but 'that any future conduct of the Lieutenant Colonel of the Regiment should be promptly enquired into and redressed.'[444] Turning to the Earl, Sir John told him 'with great distinctness' that Lord Hill trusted that in the command of the regiment the noble Earl would in future exercise moderation and forbearance. It was Lord

Hill's opinion that 'the numerous complaints which had been made to him as Commander in Chief would never have occurred if the Lieutenant Colonel of the 11th Hussars had evinced the proper degree of temper and discretion in the exercise of his command.'[445] Lord Hill had already told Cardigan that he should interfere as little as possible in personal matters and to conduct them through the official regimental channels, which would give him the time to consider every act.

This came as a totally unexpected censure and Cardigan 'writhed' as he was criticised in front of all the men whom he had himself so frequently harangued with arrogance, oppression and insult. Cardigan was rapidly acquiring notoriety and was booed and hissed at whenever he appeared in public. The difficulty for Lord Hill was that the Earl did not care a hoot for all of this. His arrogance now led him to ignore letters from the Commander in Chief and there was really not very much that Hill could do about it without being made to appear foolish himself. One can better understand the Earl's reckless behaviour later in the Crimea when you have heard of his earlier escapades; following the battles of the Crimea, he was to be accused of 'indifference, neglect of his brigade, callous lack of responsibility for his men', none of which could be erased by his acts of extraordinary bravery. His was surely a warped personality.

There were many more instances of his bad behaviour towards those of his officers to whom he felt superior but he was not in general known as a 'flogger.' However, he did make a considerable error of judgement in April 1841 when he ordered a flogging on Easter Sunday. Private William Rogers was ordered to receive the maximum of 100 lashes. This punishment was carried out in the Riding School following morning service. Once again, Lord Hill was furious with Cardigan and issued a General Order in which the final paragraph reads '... it may be clearly understood that the sentences of military courts are not to be carried into execution on the Lord's Day, excepting in cases of evident necessity, the nature of which it cannot be requisite for him to define.' *The Times* was outraged:

> ... we can imagine no exigency short of mutiny itself, by which it could possibly be justified.
>
> What then is to be done with this inveterate offender, this plague spot of the British Army who seems to exist for the single purpose of setting public opinion at defiance and bringing discredit upon the unwise clemency which restored him, after one well-merited disgrace, to employments for which he is by temper and character thoroughly disqualified.

Hill and Melbourne had many discussions about whether or not Cardigan should be removed from his command. Melbourne wished to do it before the House of Commons made it impossible not to do it but Hill, seeing events from the point of view of the Army, which was to be quite separate from the control of politicians, was annoyed with Melbourne and his Cabinet for putting a pistol to his head. Horse Guards held again to its determination not to be pushed about by politicians. Hill had probably been buying a bit of time in order to discuss all of this with Wellington, The Duke was against sacking Cardigan saying that the deed had been improper and incorrect but not a military offence. Cardigan actually went so far this time as to write a 'very proper letter' to Fitzroy Somerset expressing his regret for having punished the man on a Sunday. As he now realised, it had shown a lack of judgement.

Lord Hill may have taken some solace from the fact that the United Services Club was not to be browbeaten either. In the summer of 1841, Cardigan's name was proposed for membership. The noble Earl received 28 black balls, which sounds like a record. Most people had been surprised at the sheer effrontery which had led to his name being proposed in the first place. Having been blackballed (18 blacks) a second time, he started his own club but this soon foundered. When the Duke of Wellington became Commander in Chief once again following Hill's death in December 1842, he was so infuriated by the requests for honours, deserved or otherwise, and the antics of men such as Cardigan and Lord Londonderry, that he said caustically that they needed a department dedicated to their affairs alone.

When the Earl went to the Crimea, he had still never been on a field of battle and once again, displayed a complete lack of control; Lord Hill would have been horrified – but then he would probably never have sent Cardigan in the first place.

XVII

TO FLOG OR NOT TO FLOG?

In 1836, another Royal Commission[446] was established to enquire into the matter of punishment in the Army. Lord Hill was to give evidence on 12 February 1836. He was questioned in detail as to his career in the Army and the commands and staff positions he had held.

Q: In the early part of your service, the frequency of corporal punishment was much greater than it is now?
A: Certainly.
Q: Can your Lordship inform the commissioners at what period there began to be a feeling against that frequency of corporal punishment and a reduction of it in the Army?
A: It appears to have attracted the attention of the Commander in Chief sometime about 1811 or 1812.
Q: Were there at that time any orders given out from HQ recommending greater caution in passing sentence of corporal punishment?
A: Yes, a confidential circular letter of which I beg to hand in a copy, was issued by order of HRH the Duke of York, Commander in Chief.

This circular letter was handed round – included in it was a proposal by Lord Hill, item 8, of a defaulters' book. There were numerous further questions including one as to whether it might be a good idea to copy the Prussian Army in having two classes of soldier, only the second of which received corporal punishment. .Lord Hill was opposed to this. He did not think it was a good idea to have two levels of punishment for two classes of men.

Q: Do the well behaved do better in Battle?
A: No, the ones who get into scrapes as often distinguish themselves as the former.

Lord Hill agreed that more facilities in the barracks would be a good thing. It was something he had already taken steps to implement. One thing that he was opposed to, however, was the creation of small rooms within the barracks, whatever their purpose; he felt that such spaces gave groups of malcontents the chance to meet together and to foment trouble.

When asked if he thought the provision of chaplains and religious instruction were adequate, he replied 'I think they are too small.'

On the question of the quality of new recruits, he was asked whether he thought that they were now of better 'description' after a long period of peace? He answered: 'I think they are, we are more particular as to the character of recruits now than we were in time of war.'

He handed in a copy of the list[447] of crimes for which corporal punishment could still be used and was asked if he was still of the opinion that it remained necessary to maintain the power of inflicting corporal punishment. He answered that

> when we come to consider the greater operations of war, that in such, one must be the example of obedience, good order and discipline to our allies, and the terror of our enemies, on account of our possessing these same qualities – I cannot conceive that there is a man with information upon the subject who will think otherwise than that if the state is to have an army, we must maintain in it the use of corporal punishment.

Many other senior and serving officers including Sir Henry Hardinge gave their evidence during the enquiry which had also covered the question of the length of service a man was required to give in order to be eligible for a full pension. Howick had written to Lord Hill on 14 April 1836. Howick had evidently misunderstood Hill's proposal of a shorter period of 25 years for infantry and 28 for cavalry; previously the length had been 28 and 30 years respectively. Lord Hill felt, with good cause, that the amount of half pay/pension of 6d a day was too small. The confusion had arisen between retirement with a disability and discharge at the soldier's own request. Howick wanted the points clarified.

Hill made the point that with the infantry employed throughout 'vast' colonial possessions, very few men could be capable of performing all the duties of a soldier carrying weight upon a march after a period of 21 years service. The Paymaster General proposed 25 and 28 years and 'hopes this will satisfy Lord Hill'. Hill preferred 21 years but acceded to the Paymaster General and Secretary of War; it was obviously a case of a tug of war, as was not uncommon, between the holder of the purse strings and the Commander in Chief. Hill was still concerned with treatment in the regiments and in 1839 he issued a circular to all General officers and Commanding Officers of Regiments and Depots asking what benefit 'good conduct' medals had conferred upon the Army. Could any suggestions be made? The Company Defaulters' book should be reinstated and Hill said he would be proposing this to the Secretary at War for immediate adoption. Lord Hill required all the commanding officers to examine every record of offences and insisted that the commanders must take the utmost care in doing this, especially with regard to trivial offences, which might blight the soldier's service and which might have been better dealt with by a simple admonishment.[448] The question of going on half pay was often difficult. Some soldiers went on half pay owing to their health, sometimes for as long as a year. Hill decreed that such men should appear before a medical board.

By the second half of the 1830s, Canada was proving a problem to the Mother Country. It is certain that Britain underestimated the amount of disaffection in Canada. The only thing that Upper Canada and Lower Canada had in common was the certainty that neither wished to be incorporated into America. The rebellion in 1837 arose from the French majority in Lower Canada, who wanted all power under a central 'elected' assembly, which, by dint of their vastly superior numbers, they would control. Although still in the minority, the number of British immigrants was increasing rapidly and it was aided and supported by Lieutenant General Sir John Colborne who had been Lieutenant Governor of Upper Canada since 1828.

Colborne had made himself unpopular with the French by probably giving the newcomers[449] too much help and encouragement. In 1836 he was put in command of the British Army and led his troops to suppress the 1837 rebellion. In London Lord Hill was occupied in finding sufficient forces to send to serve under Sir John, who had, of course, been in his Corps in Adam's 3rd brigade of the 2nd Division at Waterloo at the head of the famous 52nd Regiment. Colborne had also served under Lord Hill in the 52nd for many years in the Peninsula.

Lord Hill often penned a few lines to his nephew, Rowland, at Hawkstone, after a busy day. One such letter was sent on the day that the news arrived of a revolt breaking out in Montreal: 'I fear we shall have a troublesome winter. Sir J Colborne asks for more troops.' The British Government was somewhat dismissive of Sir John's qualities because he kept it very short of detailed news but Hill trusted him, perhaps too much. Colborne was recalled in 1836 as Lieutenant Governor but was immediately made Commander in Chief of the armed forces in North America and acting Governor General of British North America. A true Tory, he was a strong supporter of the Church of England and an opponent of 'responsible government'. His views could be said to have contributed to the revolt in 1837, which had also been fuelled by the reactionary measures adopted by the then Lieutenant Governor of Upper Canada, Sir Francis Bond Head, who was to leave Canada in 1838 following a very short stay in the country. Head was to take great exception to the criticism which was made of him in

Durham's report. Lord Durham had been sent out as High Commissioner. He returned to London in high dudgeon after only six months in November 1838 and settled down to write his report and recommendations, published in 1839. Many of his views were highly unpopular at the time but were ultimately to be largely adopted – the idea of a unified nation and 'responsible' government. He was a clever, energetic and imaginative man, a liberal with a great ability to grasp the essentials. For example, he attributed many of the problems in Lower Canada to racism, recommending that Lower Canada with its majority of French should have self-government but not Home Rule. Hill, who must also be considered reactionary in his views by this late stage of his life, did not approve of Durham's proposals and wanted Colborne to be appointed as Governor General; this did happen after Durham's unexpectedly rapid return home. Hill obtained a peerage for Colborne.[450]

One of Durham's actions during his short stay as High Commissioner was to parade the King's Dragoon Guards and the 43rd Foot on the edge of the Niagara Falls in full view of the Americans on the opposite side. He doubtless thought that this show of force would demonstrate to the Americans that Britain valued her Empire and was prepared to defend it. Britain retained Major General Sir John Harvey in command in New Brunswick with Sir Colin Campbell still in Nova Scotia.

With a young Queen now on the throne things were very different at Court – there was scarcely a Tory to be seen. Lord Hill seems to have got on quite well with Victoria who probably regarded him as a sort of benign uncle. Lord Melbourne described Lord Hill as 'dull' and it is likely that there was little in common between the old soldier and the smooth courtier although they had many dealings together.

One of the last civil problems that required the use of the Army during Lord Hill's life would be the actions of the Chartists. They demanded that every man over 21 should have the right to vote by secret ballot; that any man might be eligible to stand for Parliament regardless of property; that Members of Parliament should receive a wage to enable the working class to serve and that all constituencies should be the same size. The best known of the leaders were John Frost and Feargus O'Connor, men who were prepared to use force to obtain their demands. Once again, England had civil disorder and had to use her soldiers despite the growing police force. Hill disliked, in common with most senior officers, using his men for this purpose; he felt it was not fair on them to send them against an armed rabble when they were very tightly regulated as to the circumstances in which they could fight back. One of the first and most important of the Chartist uprisings was at Newport, Gwent, not far from Hawkstone. At the time of the disturbance Lord Hill was staying at Powis Castle nearby and he stopped in Shrewsbury on his way to London in order to find out more details. He was informed that the small military force stationed near Newport, the 45th,[451] deserved great credit. This force consisted of only one captain, one lieutenant, one ensign, three sergeants and 56 private soldiers. It had only been the day before the attack was made that rumours began to circulate that the Chartists were secretly assembling several thousand – some say four thousand – supporters; they had kept the secret so well that the magistrates and authorities were in complete ignorance. Lieutenant Grey was especially singled out for his excellent conduct. At daybreak he, together with 28 of the men and two sergeants, were deployed in a strategically placed house and kept the mob at bay. Lord Normanby told Hill that the Lieutenant had saved the town. One of the objects of the Chartist's rising in Newport was to proceed from there the short distance to Monmouth and release one or more of their leaders, such as Henry Vincent, who were prisoners in the gaol. Several leading members of the movement were arrested and 21 were charged with high treason, including John Frost. Ben Wilson, a Chartist from Yorkshire, wrote that a successful rising at Newport would have been the match that ignited a countrywide uprising. As it was, the movement gradually slipped into infighting and division. Frost, together with several of the others, was transported 'for life' but he was pardoned several years later and allowed to return home. There is a John Frost Square in the centre of Newport.

XVIII

DECLINE AND DEATH

In 1837 England had a new ruler: the young Victoria, daughter of the late
Duke of Kent, the only legitimate heir of all the sons of George III. Lord Hill
had an amicable relationship with the young Queen and she was prompt to
congratulate him on his nephew's wife having produced a healthy heir. In the
last years of the 1830s, he gave up his lease on Westbourne House and moved to
Belgrave Square where he shared a house with the Egertons. However, the long
years in the field, the bouts of fever that recurred quite frequently, together with
an 'alimentary' or bowel complaint that often troubled him, all meant his health
was less than robust. He failed to attend several grand dinners in the summer of
1842 as a result of his health. His brother, Francis, who was much younger, died in
April and Rowland was too weak to to attend the funeral.

It is doubtful that he attended the Waterloo Banquet of 1842, held on 20 June. It
was attended by Prince Albert and '80 covers were laid' using the famous Potsdam
dessert service given to the Duke by the King of Prussia. One of the toasts was
'Lord Hill and the British Army'. His brother Clement was certainly there, just
before he left to take up command of an army in India as a Major General. The
jungles of India were a far cry from commanding one of the Household regiments
with all its ceremonial duties. Clement was rather the unsung hero of the brothers. He was evidently very popular, as shown by the heartfelt letter written by his
ADC announcing his death. Poor Clement, he died in the middle of the jungle
far from his native land. There is a memorial to him in Trinity Church, Bangalore,
put up by his officers. Until recently, there was also a large equestrian statue of him
in the centre of Bangalore but India decided to rid itself of such colonial relics a
few years ago.

In August 1842, Hill resigned. He probably should have tendered his resignation earlier than he did; all old warhorses stay in harness too long! There have
been few great soldiers who have proved themselves as good in government.

Perhaps one of the greatest compliments paid to Lord Hill had been in the House of Commons some years earlier, on 22 May 1835. Sir Rufane Donkin, a vocal and frequent critic of Lord Hill, the Army and the Tories in general, said he

> … felt bound as a soldier to bear his testimony to the honest and impar-
> tial manner in which Lord Hill had distributed the patronage of the
> Army. He believed that never for one moment since that Noble Lord
> has taken office had he given way to private feeling or political bias in
> his distribution of the Army patronage at his disposal. Although opposed
> in politics to Lord Hill, he felt it his duty to bear his testimony to the
> impartiality always manifested by the Noble Lord.

During his time as Commander in Chief, Rowland had had eleven different sec-
retaries of war to deal with[452] but even those most politically opposed to him paid
him the compliment of saying that he had never used his position, when in the
role of Commander in Chief, to abuse the gift of patronage within his control.

Did Hill succeed as Commander in Chief? He certainly implemented many
'civilising' changes that contributed to the wellbeing of the troops but he, like
Wellington and several of the other senior Peninsular generals who still held high
office, was of another age. When the British Army went to the Crimea, its leaders
were all over 60 years old and the last great battle campaigns of the British Army,
those of the Peninsula and Waterloo, had been fought nearly 40 years previously
with the training and much of the equipment of the Army still being of the
Napoleonic age. It was, in Woodham Smith's words, 'creaking and inefficient'. It
has also been referred to as 'the Peninsular Army brought out of the cupboard and
dusted down.'[453] The Whig Government detested the whole military establishment and kept Horse Guards grotesquely short of funds and must bear its share
of the blame. Matters were as, Mallinson writes, 'not helped by the Army's being
presided over by old heroes with an aversion to anything new'. [454]

One of Lord Hill's last official acts was to write to Sir Robert Peel on the well-
worn subject of reforming military punishment. He received a gratifying letter
from Sir Robert, whom it must be admitted was relieved that Hill was finally
retiring. Most of the letter did not refer to punishment:

Whitehall, Aug 24, 1842

My dear Lord Hill
I have received the commands of the Queen to acquaint you that in consideration of your high character, your eminent military services in the field, and
the ability, integrity and zeal with which you have discharged for many years
the important duties of the office of Commander of the Forces, her Majesty
proposes to raise you to the rank of Viscount; and in order that there may be a

permanent record of your public services, to confer the title with remainder to your nephew, Sir R. Hill.

It is very gratifying to me personally, who have so long had the satisfaction of being acquainted with you, and have had so many opportunities of judging of your merits as a servant of the Crown, to be the channel of a communication which will, I trust be acceptable to you …

On his retirement being gazetted, several people wrote to Peel asking that Hill be raised to a higher rank of the peerage. He was duly created Viscount. His nephew and heir, young Sir Rowland, contended that it should have been an Earldom! Sir Rowland was already the 4th baronet and succeeded his uncle as the second Viscount.

Lord Hill was undoubtedly delighted that, finally, his efforts with regard to punishment were put into effect by the Whig Government. He had pushed for the punishment cells and plans had finally been drawn up in 1838. It was not how-ever until 1842 that the Secretary at War, Lord Howick, later to succeed his father as 3rd Earl Grey, managed to see that 'the difficulties which hitherto occurred in carrying into effect an efficient system of military imprisonment as a substitute for corporal punishment' were overcome. Hill had pressed this matter very hard and it was one of his last victories in the summer before he died.

There is a rather sad letter in the Raglan papers. It is dated 15 November 1842, from Fitzroy Somerset to his daughter Katherine Somerset saying that he has heard from Richard Egerton that Lord Hill is 'shrunk to nothing' and dozes away half his time and that the day before he had had a very nasty shivering fit. Somerset fears the worst.[455]

Hill spent the last months of his life at Hardwicke. Here his doctor was Doctor Darwin, father of Charles Darwin, who lived in Shrewsbury. He became very weak rather rapidly and could soon not leave his room. He took comfort from the presence of his two clergymen nephews, the Reverend John Hill, who had married Charlotte Kenyon and who lived and farmed the Citadel and was perpetual curate of the little church of Weston under Redcastle, at the gates of Hawkstone. The second nephew was the Reverend Francis Hill, son of diplomat brother Sir Francis. Rowland took great solace from his religious faith and died on December 10, saying,

I have a great deal to be thankful for; I believe also that I have not an enemy in the world. With regard to my religious feelings, I have not power to express much and never had; but I do trust I am sincere; and I hope for mercy.

Shrewsbury had wished to give the local hero a splendid funeral but his wishes were predictably simple; he chose to be buried in the church of St Mary Magdalene, Hadnall, where he had worshipped in the last years of his life. He had recently paid for the restoration of the church tower and is buried in a crypt beneath it; sisters Maria and Emma are also buried here. There is a large monument to Lord Hill in the church with the figures of a shepherd and a soldier flanking a couched lion with his Lordship's coat of arms behind. His coffin was escorted to the church by soldiers of the 53rd Regiment (Kings Own Shropshire Light Infantry) who had marched from Shrewsbury of their own volition to pay their last respects to their former Colonel. There is also a monument to the General in the garrison church in Portsmouth.

He died as he had lived, a Christian believer and a true servant of the Crown, beloved of all whose lives he had touched. Sir Charles Oman wrote at the end of his mammoth *History of the Peninsular War,* 'I have never seen a hard word of 'Daddy Hill' in any of the hundred Peninsular diaries that I have read.'[456] A fitting tribute.

Here is the letter from His Grace the Duke of Wellington to Sir Rowland Hill, Baronet.[457] dated 12 December 1842:

My dear Sir Rowland,

Your letter of the 10th giving me the melancholy account of the death on that morning of your uncle, my old companion and friend, Lord Hill, reached me yesterday.

You may conceive better than I can express how much I have felt his loss. More than thirty-five years have elapsed since I had the satisfaction of being first connected with and assisted by him in the public service; and I must say that from that moment up to the latest period of his valuable and honourable life, nothing ever occurred to interrupt for one moment the friendly and intimate relations which subsisted between us …

APPENDIX ONE

THE DUCHESS OF RICHMOND'S BALL

Although the famous ball on the eve of Waterloo has been mentioned previously, it could be of interest to some readers to have the guest list. The Duchess, who was a strong character, must have been extremely annoyed when her carefully orchestrated evening was abruptly broken up. We do not know precisely who attended but the list is interesting simply for the number of the upper class English who had managed to cross the Channel to play in Brussels that summer.

Of course, by no means all of those on the list were in a position to attend; after all, it was held on the very eve of war. There were four Hill brothers on the list but Lord Hill was certainly not in attendance. The Duke had to admit that he had been 'humbugged' by Napoleon on this occasion, when the news was brought to him during the evening that led to the rapid departure of all the dashing young soldiers in attendance. For the full story of the extraordinary event, see *The Duchess of Richmond's Ball* by David Miller.

Their Royal Highnesses the Prince of Orange and his brother Prince Frederic
The Duke of Brunswick, who was one of the first senior officers to be killed
Captain de Lubeck ADC to the Duke of Brunswick
The Duc d'Arenberg, father of:
Prince Pierre d'Arenberg who had been held prisoner in Whitchurch, Shropshire
Prince Auguste d'Arenberg, his brother
The Duke and Duchess of Beaufort and one of their daughters
The Duc et Duchesse d'Ursel
Le Marquis et La Marquise d'Assche
Le Comte et la Comtesse d'Oultremont
The Dowager Comtesse d'Oultremont and daughters
Comte et Comtesse Liedekeerke and her daughter
Comte et Comtesse Latour Lupin
Comte et Comtesse Marcy d'Argenteau
Comte et Comtesse de Grasiac
Comtesse de Luiny
Comtesse de Ruilly
Baron and Baronne d'Hooghvoorst
Mademoiselle d'Hooghvoorst and Monsieur C.DF. d'Hooghvoorst
Monsieur et Madame Vander Capellan

Baron de Herelt

Baron de Tuybe

General Baron Vincent (wounded in the battle)

Baron Brockhausen

General Pozzo de Borgo

General Alava, Spanish General who served with the Allies

Comte de Belgade

Comte de la Rochefoucauld

General D'Ooudenarde

Colonel Knif, an ADC

Colonel Decayler

Major Ronnchenberg, an ADC

The Earl and Countess Conyngham and the Lady Elizabeth Conyngham

The Viscount Mount Charles and his brother the Hon. Mr Conyngham, later to succeed as
     second Earl

The Countess Mount Norris and Lady Julianna Annesley

The Dowager Countess of Waldegrave

The Duke of Wellington, he did attend

Lord and Lady Fitzroy Somerset – neither were present

Lord and Lady John Somerset, brother to above

Mr and the Lady Frances Webster

Mr and the Lady Caroline Capel and Miss Capel

Lord and Lady George Seymour and their daughter Miss Seymour

Colonel Felton Hervey, ADC

Colonel Fremantle, ADC to the Duke

Lord George Lennox, son of Duke of Richmond and ADC to Wellington

Lord Arthur Hill (the fattest man in the army!) no relation to Rowland Hill

Colonel Tripp

The Honorable Major Percy, an ADC who brought back three Eagles

The Honorable Cathcart, ADC

The Honorable Sir Alexander Gordon ADC to Wellington, killed in the battle

Sir John Byng, commanded 2nd brigade of Guards

Sir Colin Campbell

Lieutenant General Sir John Elley, Deputy Adjutant of the Cavalry

Sir George Scovell, Staff Corps of Cavalry

Lord Hill, Commanding 2nd Corps, not present

The Honorable Orlando Bridgeman, ADC to Lord Hill

Captain Digby Mackworth, ADC to Lord Hill

Major H. Churchill, QMG and ADC to Lord Hill

Lieutenant Colonel Sir Robert Chambré Hill, brother to above, Commanding 'the Blues',
     slightly wounded

Sir Thomas Noel Hill, Assistant Adjutant General and brother to above

Colonel Clement Hill, brother to above, slightly wounded

Sir William Ponsonby, Commanded Union Brigade of Cavalry, killed

Lieutenant Colonel Sir Andrew Barnard, Commander 1st Battalion 95th foot

Major General Sir Denis Packe, 9th brigade

Major General Sir James Kempt, 8th brigade

Sir Pulteney Malcolm, Royal Navy

Lieutenant General Sir Thomas Picton, 5th Division, killed

Major General Sir Edward Barnes, Adjutant General, wounded

Sir James Gambier

The Honorable General Dundas

Lieutenant General Cooke, Commander 1st Division

Major General Peregrine Maitland, 1st Brigade of Guards, later eloped with Sarah, daughter of the Duke of Richmond

Major General Frederick Adam, Commanded 3rd Infantry brigade, not present

Colonel Washington

Colonel Woodford

Colonel Rowan, 52nd Regiment, later Commissioner of Police

Colonel Wyndham

Colonel Cumming

Colonel Bowater

Colonel Torrens, at Horse Guards during Peninsula War

Colonel Fuller

Colonel Dick, 42 regiment

Colonel John Cameron of the 92nd, killed

Colonel Barclay, ADC to HRH Frederick Duke of York

Mr and the Lady Charlotte Greville

The Viscountess Hawarden

Sir Henry and Lady Susan Clinton, in command of 2nd Division

Lady Alvanley and the Miss Ardens

Sir James and Lady Craufurd and Miss Craufurd

Sir George and Lady Berkeley

Lady Sutton and Miss Sutton

Sir Sidney and Lady Smith and the Miss Rumbolds

Sir William and Lady Delancey

The Honorable Mrs. Pole

Mr and Mrs Lance, Miss Lance and Mr Lance

Mr Creevey and the Miss Ords

Mr and Mrs Greathed

Mr and Mrs Lloyd

The Honorable Sir Charles Stuart, Minister at Brussels

The Earl of Uxbridge, commander of the cavalry, lost his leg at the end of the battle

The Earl of Portarlington

The Earl of March, son of the Duke of Richmond and ADC to HRH the Prince of Orange Nassau

General the Lord Edward Somerset, in command of Household Brigade of Cavalry, wounded

Lord Charles Fitzroy

Lord Robert Manners, son of the Duke of Rutland

Lord Rendlesham

Lord Hay, ADC killed in action

Lord Saltoun

The Viscount Apsley, son of Earl Bathurst

The Honorable Colonel Stanhope

The Honorable Colonel Abercromby, wounded

The Honorable Colonel Frederick Ponsonby, wounded

The Honorable Colonel Acheson

The Honorable Colonel Stewart

The Honorable Percival

The Honorable Stopford

The Honorable John Gordon

The Honorable Edgecombe
The Honorable Seymour Bathurst, ADC to General Peregrine Maitland
The Honorable Forbes
The Honorable Hastings Forbes
The Honorable Major Dawson
Major General Sir Hussey Vivian, Commander 6th Cavalry Brigade
Mr Horace Seymour, ADC
Major Gunthorpe, ADC to General Peregrine Maitland
Major Hamilton, ADC to Gen Sir E. Barnes
Major Harris, Brigade Major to Gen. Sir Hussey Vivian
Major Hunter Blair, wounded in the battle
Captain Kean, ADC to Sir Hussey Vivian
Captain Fitzroy
Captain Widman, ADC to Lord Uxbridge
Captain James Franceer
Captain Verner
Captain Elphinstone, taken prisoner on June 17th
Captain Webster
Captain Somerset, ADC to General Lord Edward Somerset
Captain Charles Yorke, not present
Captain Gore, ADC to General Sir James Kempt
Captain Packenham
Captain Dumaresq ADC to Sir John Byng, wounded
Captain Dawkins ADC
Captain Disbrowe ADC to Gen Sir George Cook
Captain George Bowles
Captain Hesketh
Captain Gurwood (editor of Wellington's dispatches)
Captain Allix
Mr Russell, ADC
Mr Brooke
Mr Huntley
Mr Lionel Hervey, a diplomat
Mr Leigh
Mr Shakespear
Mr O'Grady
Mr Smith, Brigade Major to Sir Denis Packe, killed
Mr Fludyer
Mr John Montagu
Mr Henry Montagu
Mr Augustus Greville
Mr Baird
Mr Robinson
Mr James
Mr Chad
Mr Dawkins
Dr Hyde
Mr Hume
The Reverend Samuel Briscall

LORD HILL'S II CORPS AT WATERLOO

II Corps

Lt General Sir Rowland Hill, GCB (27,321)
Aides de Camp   Lt Colonel C. Hill, Royal Horse Guards*
                                 Major R. Egerton, 34 Foot
                                 Major C.H. Churchill, Military Secretary, 1 Foot Guards
                                 Captain D. Mackworth, 7 Foot
Extra Aide de Camp   Captain the Hon. O. Bridgeman, 1 Foot Guards

2nd Division

Lt. General Sir Henry Clinton (6,833)
Aides de Camp   Captain F. Dawkins, 1 Foot Guards
                                 Captain J. Gurwood, 10 Hussars

3rd British Brigade

Major General Frederick Adam
Aide de Camp   Lt. R.P. Campbell, 7 Foot
Extra Aide de camp   Captain C. Yorke, 52 Foot
Major of Brigade   Major Thomas Hunter-Blair, 91 Foot
1 Battalion/52 (Oxfordshire Light Infantry)   Lt Col. Sir John Colborne (1,038)
1 Battalion 71 (Glasgow Highland) Light Infantry   Lt Col. Thomas Reynell (810)
6 companies of the 2 Battalion/95 Rifles Regiment   Major John Ross (585)
2 companies of the 3 Battalion/95 Rifles   Major Amos G. Norcott (188)

1st King's German Legion Brigade

Colonel G.C.A. du Plat
1st Line Battalion KGL   Major W. Robertson (411)
2nd Line Battalion KGL   Major G. Muller (437)
3rd Line Battalion KGL   Lt Col. F. de Wissell (494)
4th Line Battalion KGL   Major F. Reb (416)

3rd Hanoverian Brigade
Colonel Hew Halkett
Bremervorde Landwehr Battalion	Lt Col. Schulenberg (632)
Osnabruck Landwehr Battalion	Major Count Munster (612)
Quackenbruck Landwehr Battalion	Major Baron C.W. von dem Hunefeld (588)
Salzgitter Landwehr Battalion	Major von Hammerstein (622)

Artillery
Lt Colonel Gold (442)
Captain Samuel Bolton's Battery, RFA, 217 (5) 9lb guns (1) 5.5 inch howitzer
Major Augustus Sympher's Battery, KGLH, 225 (5) 9lb guns (1) 5.5 inch howitzer

4th Division
Lt General Sir Charles Colville (7,212)
Aides de Camp	Captain J. Jackson, 37th Foot
	Lt. F.W. Frankland, 2nd (Coldstream) Guards
Extra Aide de Camp	Captain Lord James Hay, 1st Foot Guards

4th British Brigade
Colonel Mitchell
3 Battalion/14 (Buckinghamshire) Regiment	Major Francis S. Tidy (571)
1 Battalion/23 (Royal Welsh) Fusiliers	Lt Col. Sir Henry W. Ellis (647)
51 (2 Yorkshire West Riding) Light Infantry	Lt Col. Hugh Henry Mitchell (549)

6th British Brigade
Major General G. Johnstone
Aide de Camp	Captain C.G. Gray, 95 Rifles
Major of Brigade	Captain S. Holmes, 78 Foot
2 Battalion/35 (Sussex) Regiment	Major C. McAlister (570)
1 Battalion/54 (West Norfolok) Regiment	Lt Col. J. Earl Waldegrave (541)
2 Battalion/59 (South Lincolnshire) Regiment	Lt Col. H. Austin (461)
1 Battalion/91 (Argyllshire) Regiment	Lt Col. Sir W Douglas (824)

6th Hanoverian Brigade
Major General Sir James Lyon
Aide de Camp	Lt James McGlashan, 2 Light Battalion KGL
Major of Brigade	Captain Ritchie, 1 Ceylon Regiment
Lauenberg Field Battalion	Lt Col. Benort (533)
Calenburg Field Battalion	Major Schnehen (634)
Nieuburg Landwehr Battalion	Major Hollender (625)
Hoya Landwehr Battalion	Lt Col. Grote (629)
Bentheim Landwehr Battalion	Major Croupp (608)

Artillery

Lieutenant Colonel Hawker (507)

Major Brome's battery, RFA, 269 (5) 9lb guns (1) 5.5 inch howitzer

Captain Karl von Rettburg's Battery, Hanoverian Foot Artillery, 238 (5) 9lb guns (1) 5.5 inch
    howitzer

Cavalry

Lieutenant General Lord Henry William Paget, 2nd Earl of Uxbridge (14,482)

1st British (Household Cavalry) Brigade	Major GeneraL Lord Edward Somserset (1,349)
2 Squadrons of the 1st Life Guards	Lt Colonel Samuel Ferrior (228)
2 Squadrons of the 2nd Life Guards	Lt Colonel the Hon. Edward P Lygon (231)
2 Squadrons of the Royal Horse Guards (the Blues)	Lt Colonel Sir Robert Hill (237)
4 Squadrons of the 1st Kings Dragoon Guards	Lt Colonel William Fuller (530)

Attached to General Hill was the Corps of Prince Frederick of the Netherlands with the 1st
Netherlands Division, Lt General J.A. Stedmann (6,389), and the Netherlands Indian Brigade
under Lt General C.H.W. Anthing (3,583). At the head of the so-called Reserve Corps was
Field Marshal the Duke of Wellington with 25,597 men.

*Lieutenant Colonel Clement Hill had in fact returned to his regiment for this Campaign.

DIVISION AND BRIGADE ORGANISATION AND CHANGES, 1808–1814

This was compiled by C.T. Atkinson, Fellow and Tutor of Exeter College, Oxford, 1912. At first glance, it may appear as an endless list of the same names being switched around in the Peninsular Army but there are patterns that emerge such as the scattering of companies of riflemen, ie the 5/60[1], amongst many of the divisions. These were the 'sharp shooters', the riflemen of the Army, who used the Baker rifle and did not carry a bayonet but a 22 sword-bayonet. Initially, they were brigaded with the 95th (the Rifle Brigade) carried the Baker rifle. They all wore green tunics instead of the traditional red of the British Army.

Another point is the formation of the 'Provisional Battalions' as the war wound its way on, the result of regiments being decimated in battle or by disease leading to the remnants being cobbled together.

1809

On 22 April when Wellesley arrived the troops were brigaded as follows:

Cavalry: GOC Cotton (Stapleton Cotton). 14 Light Dragoons, 16 Light Dragoons, 2 squadrons 20 Light Dragoons, detachment 3 Hussars KGL (Kings Own German Legion)[2] : Fane's brigade (not at the Douro – Porto), 3 Dragoon Guards, 4 Dragoons.
Guards' Brigade (H Campbell). 1 Coldstream, 1/3 Guards (Scots), 1 company 5/60.
1st Brigade (Hill). 1/3, 2/48, 2/66, 1 company 5/60
2nd Brigade (Mackenzie). 2/24 (attached), 3/27, 2/31, 1/45
3rd Brigade (Tilson). HQ and 5 companies, 5/60,2/87,1/88.
4th Brigade. (Sontag). 97, 2nd detachments,1 company 5/60.
5th Brigade (A. Campbell). 2/7, 2/53, 1 company 5/60
6th Brigade (R. Stewart). 29, 1st detachments
7th Brigade (Cameron). 2/9, 2/83, 1 company 5/60
KGL (Murray, Langwerth and Drieberg). 1, 2, 5, 7 Line KGL, detachment Light Battalion KGL
The 3rd, 4th, 5th, 6th, 7th brigades each included a Portuguese battalion
(nb: The 'Battalions of Detachments' were composed of convalescents and stragglers left behind

---

1   The Royal American Rifles
2   The Kings Own German Legion was originally composed of volunteers from Hanover of which King George III was the Elector. They were excellent troops. Their light companies included riflemen.

from the regiments which had marched from Portugal under Sir John Moore in the preceding autumn.)

The organisation in divisions dates from June 18. It was originally as follows:

Cavalry: GOC, Payne. A (Fane) 3 dragoon guards, 4 dragoons; B (Cotton), 14 and 16 Light Dragoons. Unattached 2 squadrons 20 Light Dragoons, 23 Light Dragoons, 1 Hussars KGL, detachment 3 Hussars. KGL

1st Division: GOC Sherbrooke. A (H. Campbell), 1 Coldstream, 1 Scots; B (Cameron), 2/9, 2/83; C (Langwerth), 1 and 2 Line KGL detachment, light battalions KGL; D (Low), 5 and 7 line KGL

2nd Division. GOC Hill. A (Hill), 1/3, 2/48, 3/66; B (R. Stewart), 29, 1st detachments

3rd Division. GOC Mackenzie. A (Mackenzie), 3/27, 2/31, 1/45; B (Tilson), 5 companies of 5/60, 2/87, 1/88

4th Division, GOC, A Campbell. A (A. Campbell). 2/7, 2/53; B (Sontag), 97 2nd detachments.

Subsequent changes were as follows:

Cavalry: 20 Light dragoons and detachment 3 Hussars KGL, left the Peninsula before the end of July.

By June 21 a new brigade, C was added, under G. Anson, composed of 23 Light Dragoons and 1 Hussars KGL.

On November 24, Granby Calcroft was commanding for A for Fane, absent.

By November 24, 1 Dragoons (who arrived at Lisbon in October) replaced the 16 Light dragoons in B, now under Slade, as Cotton was assisting Payne in command of the division; 16 Light Dragoons were transferred to C *vice* 23 Light Dragoons, ordered home after their losses at Talavera.

1st Division: 1/40 from Seville, replaced 2/9 going to Gibraltar and relieving 1/61, who joined before Talavera, on which 1/40 transferred to IV B

After Talavera, 2/24 and 2/42 were added to I B, 2/83 being sent down to Lisbon.

At Talavera, H. Campbell was wounded, Stopford replacing him in command of the division and brigade, but from November 8 to December 15, Hulse had the brigade, Langwerth having been killed at Talavera, Beck of 1 Line KGL succeeded to his brigade, but the two KGL brigades were amalgamated under Low from November 1.

2nd Division: By June 21 Tilson (from IIIB) had taken over Hill's own Brigade. Before Talavera 1/48 (arrived at Lisbon June 22 on being relieved at Gibraltar by 2/30) had been added to IIB.

In September, a new brigade, C under Caitlin Craufurd, was added, composed of 2/28. 2/34, 2/39 and at about the same time, 2/31 (from IIIA) was added to IIA. By November 1, 1/57 (from Gibraltar) replaced 1st detachment in IIB, the battalion of Detachments having been broken up.

From December 15 on, IIA was under the command of Duckworth of 2/48.

3rd Division: Tilson moving to IIA, was replaced by Donkin (June 31).

Before Talavera 2/24 replaced 3/27 (sent down to Lisbon) in IIIA.

Mackenzie was killed at Talavera, and the division passed under the command of R. Crauford (Robert), whose brigade, 1/43, 1/52 and 1/95, arrived just too late for the battle, and waa apparently added to the division in place of Mackenzie's brigade, which was amalgamated with Donkin's. On September 15, 2/87 was ordered down to Lisbon for garrison duty, 2/24 being transferred to IIB and 2/31 to IIA about the same time.

In October, Donkin gave up his brigade, Mackinnon obtaining command.

4th Division: Myers of 2/7 seems to have commanded IVB, of which Kemmis had taken command *vice* Sontag.

At Talavera A Campbell was wounded, and had to go home, the division being without a definite GOC till the arrival of Lowry Cole in October.

In September 1/11 (arrived at Lisbon from Madeira in August) was added to IVA. On the

Battalions of detachments being sent home (October), 3/27, in garrison at Lisbon since after the Douro, replaced the 2 Battalion in IVB.

1810

On January 1, the composition of the Army was as follows:

Cavalry: GOC, Payne; Cotton second in command, A Fane, 3 Dragoon Guards, 4 Dragoon Guards; B Slade, 1 dragoons 14 light dragoons; C (G. Anson), 16 light Dragoons, 1 Hussars, KGL

1st Division: GOC Sherbrooke. A (Stopford), 1 Coldstreams, 1 Scots; B (A. Cameron), 2/24, 2/42, 1/61; C (Low), 1, 3 5 and 7 Line, KGL, detachment Light Battalion, KGL

2nd Division: GOC, Hill. A (Duckworth, temporarily), 1/3, 2/31. 2/48, 2/66; B (R. Stewart), 29, 1/48. 1/57' C (C. Craufurd). 2/28, 2/34. 2/39

3rd Division: GOC R. Craufurd. A R. Craufurd, 2/7, 1/11, 2/53; B (Mackinnon), 1/45, 5/60, 1/88

4th Division: GOC Cole. A (Myers acting for Cole), 2/7, 1/11. 2/53; B (Kemmis) 3/27, 1/40,97; C (Lightburne), 2/5, 2/58. This brigade was added to IV on Janaury 2.

Subsequent changes were:

Cavalry. Payne went home before June 1st, Cole obtaining sole command from June 3.

On April 1, the 13 Light Dragoons arrived at Lisbon joining the army in May, and being attached to Hill's division, along with four regiments of Portuguese cavalry, the whole under Fane who gave over his brigade to de Grey from May 13. Two troops of the regiment went Cadiz but rejoined the regiment in September.

Before the end of the year, Fane appears to have gone home ill.

1st Division: On April 26 Cotton was posted to the command of the division, *vice* Sherbrooke, home ill, but gave place to Spencer, June 3, on getting the Cavalry Division.

In the 'States' of March 8 to August 1, no brigadier is given for I B. On August 4 Lord Blantyre (of 2/42) was appointed to command IB 'during the absence of Brigadier General Cameron'. Cameron was back in command from October 1, but on November 26 he was invalided home, Blantyre probably commanding again.

By the orders of September 12, 1/79 (just arrived from Cadiz), was posted to IB *vice* 1/61, to be transferred to a new brigade to form part of the 1st Division. These orders were suspended from September 14, and at Bussaco, 1/7 (arrived from Halifax before end of July) and 1/79 formed a brigade (I D) under Pakenham.

On October 6, orders were given for the transfer of Pakenham's brigade to the 4th Division, the exchange between the 1/61 and 1/70 having been carried out previously, and a new brigade was added under Erskine, comprising 1/50 (arrived September 24), 1/71 (arrived September 26), 1/92 (arrived in October, before the 6th), and I company 3/95.

2nd Division: On June 20 Leith was appointed to command 'Tilson's brigade,' ands to command the division 'under Hill,' but in the 'State' of July 8 his name appears as commanding the brigade composed of 3/1, 1/9 and 2/38. On August 8 orders were issued to W. Stewart to take command of Tilson's brigade and of the divison under Hill. In November Hill went on sick leave.

Leith's name ceases to appear in the returns as commanding IIA from July 8, and W. Stewart's name appears in his place from July 27. When Stewart commanded the division, Colborne of 2/66 had the brigade. C. Craufurd died in September, and at Bussaco Wilson of 2/39 commanded IIC. On September 30 Lumley was posted to command it.

Before September 1 R. Stewart had gone home ill, and at Bussaco Inglius (of 1.57) commanded IIB. On October 8 Hoghton was posted to it.

3rd Division: From January 8 on 5/60 no longer appear in the Returns as belonging to the division and their place in the brigade was taken by 74, who arrived at Lisbon February 8, and are mentioned in orders on February 22 as in IIIB.

On February 22 the division was reorganised, R. Craufurd's brigade becoming, with two
battalions of Cacadores, the Light Division. Mackinnon's brigade now became IIIA and
Lightburne's brigade was transferred from the 4th division and became IIIB. The headquarters
and three companies 5/60 were posted to Lightburne's brigade, the remaining companies
having been posted to IA, IB, IIA, IIB, IIC, IVA, IVB. At the same time a Portuguese brigade
composed of the 9 and 21 regiments (under Harvey) was added to the division.

At Bussaco Champlemond was in command of the Portuguese brigade, by October 29 Sutton
had it, Champlemond being wounded at Bussaco.

On September 12 2/83 was posted to IIIB, 2/88 having arrived from Cadiz to relieve them
September 4. However, they had not joined their brigade by Bussaco. When they did join,
2/58 was detached from IIIB for garrison duty at Lisbon. 94 (arrived from Cadiz September
20), were added to IIIB on October 6, and on October 10 Colville was posted to command
the brigade *vice* Lightburne who went home.

4th Division: On the transfer of Lightburne's brigade to the 3rd Division the other two brigades
changed places, Kemmis' becoming IVA, and being Cole's brigade, but under the immediate
command of Kemmis. A. Campbell who had rejoined, took command of his old brigade.

The 3 and 15 Portuguese were added to the division, as a brigade under Collins.

At Bussaco the Portuguese consisted of the 11 and 23, the 3 and 15 having been removed to the
5th Division.

On October 6 A Campbell's brigade was removed from the Division to become the nucleus of
the newly-formed 6th Division, its place being taken by Pakenham's from the 1st Division, ie
1/7, 1/61, to which the Brunswick Oels[3] Light Infantry (arrived Lisbon September 17) were
added.

On November 12 the Brunswick Oels were removed to the Light Division, but one company
was posted to IVB, two more being detached to provide the newly-formed 5th Division with
extra light troops. Their place in IVB was taken by the newly arrived 1/23 from Halifax, Nova
Scotia.

On November 17 2/7 and 1/61 were ordered to exchange, IVB thus becoming the Fusilier
Brigade.

Light Division: Formed on February 22 by the removal of R. Craufurd's brigade from the 3rd
Division, the 1 and 3 Portuguese Cacadores being added to it. On August 4 it was broken
up into two brigades, as follows: A (Beckwith of 1/95), 1/43. 4 companies 1/95, 1 Cacadores;
B (Barclay of 1/52) 1/52, 4 companies 1/95, 3 Cacadores. Barclay having been wounded at
Bussaco, Wynch of 1/4 got the brigade (in Orders of November 14).

A company of 2/95 (from Cadiz) was added to A before October 1. On November 12 nine
companies Brunswick Oels joined B.

5th Division: Officially this division first appears in the 'State' of August 8, when the 3/1, 1/9 and
2/38[4], are first called the 'Fifth Division,' a Portuguese brigade, Spry's (ie 3 and 15 Line), being
added, and Leith being GOC.

On August 4 J.S. Barns of 3/1 was appointed to command the British brigade, being superseded
by Hay September 30.

On October 6 orders were issued that Leith should command the 5th Division, and that it should
be composed of Brigadier-General Hay's brigade, a brigade made up of 1/4 (from England,
they first appear in the 'State' of November 15), 2/30 (from Cadiz) and 2/44 (from Cadiz), and
Spry's Portuguese.

On November 5 Dunlop was posted to VB, hitherto under its senior battalion commander.

---

3   The Brunswick troops were both hussars and infantry. Their light companies included sharp
shooters. Often known as 'the death or glory boys' or more prosaically, by the British troops, as the
'Brunswick Owls'.

4   These regiments had arrived at Lisbon in April but having been at Walcheren were not sent into
the field till July, since the 8th of which month they had been shown as a brigade under Leith.

On November 12 a company of the Brunswick Oels was posted to each of the British brigades.

6th Division: Ordered to be formed October 6, by taking A. Campbell's brigade out of the 4th Division and adding Eben's Portuguese (ie 8 Line and Lusitanian Legion) to it: A. Campbell being GOC.

On November 14, Hulse was posted to A. Campbell's brigade.

On November 17, 1/61 from IVB exchanged with 2/7.

In addition to the Portuguese brigades attached to the 3rd, 4th, 5th, and 6th divisions, there were at leave five others, two of which, the 4th under Archibald Campbell (=4 and 10 Line), and 2nd under Fonseca (=2nd and 14 Line) formed a divison under Hamilton, which acted throughout under Hill. Wellington says that he intended to organize this division like the rest, but the heavy losses at Albuera and the consequent necessity of reforming the 2nd Division made it impossible for him to carry out his resolve. (see *Wellington Dispatches*, viii, III).

The remaining brigades were the 1st (Pack's), consisting of the 1 and 16 Line and 4 Cacadores; the 6 (Colleman's), 7 and 19 Line and 2 Cacadores. On the formation of the 7th Division in March 1811, Coleman's brigade was posted to it, the other two remaining unattached.

The 12 and 13 Line and 5 Cacadores seem to have formed yet another brigade under Bradford, but in October the 13 Line was in garrison at Abrantes.

Spry's brigade ranked at the 3rd, Eben's as the 7th, Sutton's as the 8th and Collins' as the 9th.

1811

On January 1 the Army was organised as follows:

Cavalry. GOC Cotton. A (de Grey), 3 Dragoon Guards, 4 Dragoons; B (Slade), 1 Dragoons, 14 Light Dragoons; C (G. Anson), 16 Light Dragoons, 1 Hussars, KGL; unbrigaded, 13 Light Dragoons.

1st Division. GOC Spencer. A (Stopford), 1 Coldstream, 1 Scots, 1 company 5/60; B (?Blantyre, acting), 2/24,2/42, 1/79, 1 company 5/60; C (Low), 1, 2, 5 and 7 Line, KGL, detachment Light Battalions, KGL; D (Erskine), 1/50, 1/71, 1/92, 1 company 3/95.

2nd Division. GOC W. Stewart. A (Colborne), 1/3, 2/31.2/48. 2/66, 1 company 5/60; B (Hoghton), 29, 1/48,1/57, 1 company 5/60; C (Lumley), 2.28,2/34.2/39, one company 5/60.

3rd Division. GOC Picton. A (Mackinnon), 1/45. 1/74,1/88; B (Colville), 2/5 3 companies 5/60, 2/83, 94; also Sutton's Portuguese.

4th Division. GOC Cole. A (Kemmis), 3/27.1/40, 97, 1 company 5/60; B (Pakenham), 1/7, 2/7, 1/23, one company Brunswick Oels; also Collins' Portuguese.

5th Division. GOC Leith. A (Hay), 3/1, 1/9, 2/38, 1 company Brunswick Oels; B (Dunlop) ¼,, 2/30, 2/44. one company Brunswick Oels; also Spry's Portuguese.

6th Division. GOC A Campbell. A (Hulse), 1/11. 2/53, 1/61, 1 company 5/60; also Eben's Portuguese.

Light division. GOC, R. Craufurd. A (Beckwith), 1/43. 4 companies 1/95, 1 company 2/95, 1 Cacadores; B (Wynch), 1/52. 4 companies 1/95, Brunswick Oels, 3 Cacadores.

Portuguese. Hamilton's division, brigades under Fonseca (2nd) and Archibald Campbell (4). Unattached brigades under Pack (1), Ashworth, late A. Campbell (5), Coleman (6), and Bradford (10).

Subsequent changes were:

Cavalry. Cotton went home January 15, returning April 22; in his absence Slade commanded the division until March 7 when Erskine seems to have been placed in command of both the Cavalry and the Light division. While Slade had the division, his brigade was apparently under Hawker of 14 Light Dragoons., and from March 1 to May 15, G. Anson being absent, Arentschildt of 1 KGL Hussars commanded C.

On March 19 Long was posted to command the cavalry of the force usually under Hill, but commanded by Beresford during Hill's absence. At Albuera Lumley (of IIC) was in commad of Beresford's cavalry, Long's conduct not having given satisfaction to the Marshal. On May 11 Erskine was appointed to command 'the cavalry south of the Tagus.'

On June 13 a new brigade, D, was formed under Long composed of 13 Light Dragoons and 2 Hussars KGL, two squadrons of which had landed April 8. On June 18 the 11 Light Dragoons (arrived June 1) replaced the 13 transferred to Slade's brigade.

On June 19 a reorganisation of the cavalry in two divisions was ordered, as follows:-

1st Cavalry Division. GOC Cotton. B (Slade), 1 Dragoons, 13 and 14 Light Dragoons; C (G. Anson),16 Light Dragoons, 1 Hussars, KGL; also Madden's Portuguese.

2nd Cavalry Division. GOC Erskine. A (de Grey), 3 Dragoon Guards, 4 Dragoons; D (Long), 11 Light Dragoons, 2 Hussars, KGL.

On July 19 another reorganisation took place, the final result being as follows:-

1st Cavalry Division. GOC, Cotton. B (Slade), 1 Dragoons, 12 Light Dragoons (arrived July 1), *vice* 13 (to C) and 14 (to D); C (G. Anson), 13 and 16 Light Dragoons; E (V. Alten, a new brigade), 11 Light Dragoons (from D), and 1 Hussars, KGL (from C); Madden's Portuguese

2nd Cavalry Division. A (de Grey), 3 Dragoon Giuards, 4 Dragoons; D (Long) 14 Light Dragoons, 2 Hussards, KGL

On August 1, 9 Light Dragoons (newly arrived) were posted to Long's brigade, together with 13 Light Dragoons, which exchanged from C with 14th.

On August 30, a new brigade, F, was added, comprising 4 Dragoon Guards, arrived August 15, and 3 Dragoons, arrived before August 20, its commander being Le Marchant. By October 1, 5 Dragoon Guards had been added to this brigade.

On October 5 de Grey's brigade was transferred to the 1 Cavalry Division to which Le Marchant's was attached by Orders of November 8, the Portuguese brigade being struck off that Division.

From December 8 on the States do not give any GOC for the 2nd Cavalry Division.

1st Division. On January 23 Nightingale was posted to IB; on February 6 Howard obtained ID when Erskine was transferred to the command of the 5th Divison. On June 8 H. Campbell's name is given in the 'State' as in command of IA , Stopford being transferred to IVB (in orders for this June 18). Nightingale departing to Bengal before June 25 his brigade had no permanent commander till July 28, when Stopford got it.

Owing to the heavy losses of the 2nd Division at Albuera and its consequent reconstruction, Howard's brigade was transferred to it on June 6 and at the same time the detachment of the Light Battalions of the KGL, hitherto in IC, rejoined those battalions which had been posted to VIIA.

On June 26 orders were issued for the 7 Line KGL, to go home, its rank and file being drafted into the other three battalions. On July 21 1/26 were added to IB, having recently arrived from England.

On August 9, Graham was appointed to command the Division, Spencer having gone home in July, he received leave July 25. From December 1 onward IB appears in the 'States' as having no GOC.

2nd Division. The heavy losses at Albuera led to the reorganisation of the division, detailed in Orders June 6. Howard's brigade of the 1st Division was transferred to the 2nd Division, becoming IIA. The remainder of the brigades of Colborne and Hoghton (who was killed) were formed into a Provisional Battalion, less 1/48 and 2/48; 1/48, to which the rank and file of 2/48 were drafted (the cadre of 2/48 going home), was transferred to IVB.

This provisional Battalion was placed in Lumley's Brigade, of which Abercromby (of 2/28) had had temporary command at Albuera, while Lumley was in charge of the cavalry. At the same time, Ashworth's Portuguese brigade was definitely attached to it; this was the 5th Brigade, which had been under A. Campbell in October, 1810, but had come under Ashworth by March 11; it comprised the 6 and 18 Line and 6 Cacadores.

Before the end of May Hill returned and took over command of the division, as well as of the whole force commanded by Beresford at Albuera.

On July 22 1/28 newly arrived from Gibraltar, was posted to Lumley's brigade.

On August 7 orders were issued for 1/3 and 1/57 to resume their separate formations, large drafts having arrived from their second battalions in England. The division was again formed in three brigades, Howard's being IIA, and 1/23, 1/57, and the Provisional Battalion, (ie 29 [3 companies], 2/31 [4 companies] and 2/66 (3 companies) forming IIB apparently under Inglis of 1/57, while 1/28, 2/28, 2/34, and 2/39 under Lumley formed IIC.

On August 21 2/28 was drafted into 1/28, and sent home and the company 3/95, hitherto in Howard's brigade, were transferred to Beckwith's brigade of the Light division, being replaced in IIA by a company of 5/60, there being three with the Division.

On September 21 Byng was posted to command IIB, and on October 9 Wilson was appointed to command IIC Lumley having gone home sick early in August.

On October 3 orders were issued for 29th to go home to recruit; on October 20 1/39, just arrived from Sicily, was added to IIC, 2/39 being drafted into it and sent home by Orders issued December 17.

3rd Division. Orders of March 5 direct the transfer of the headquarters companies 5/60 to IIIA, 2/88, on garrison duty at Lisbon since September 4, 1810, being added to IIIB. On July 10, 2/88 was ordered to be drafted into 1/88, and the cadre sent home.

On July 22 the 77 were added to IIIB.

From July 1 to October 31 Mackinnon was absent from his brigade, ill. Wallace of 1/88 commanding it in his place.

On December 22 Colville was transferred to the command of the 4th Division, in Cole's absence on leave, J. Campbell of the 94 getting IIIB.

The Portuguese brigade of this division was under Power at Fuentes d'Onoro; in September Palmeirim commanded it.

4th Division. By February 1 the headquarters and 9 companies Brunswick Oels had been added to IVA , having been removed from the Light Division, but on the formation of the 7th Division (March 5) they were removed to it.

On January 23 Houston was appointed to IVB *vice* Packenham but left the brigade again March 5, on being appointed to command the 7th Division: Myers would seem to have commanded IVB till Albuera, where he was killed. On June 18 Stopford was appointed to command IVB, but was transaferred to IB on July 28, Packenham again getting IVB. From November 15 onwards the 'States' do not give any brigadier for IVB, but it continued to be described as 'Packenham's'.

After Albuera 2.7 was drafted into 1/7, the remnants being sent home June 26; 1/48 from the 2nd Division was added to IVB June 6. On October 3, the 97, a single battalion regiment, was ordered home in consequence of its severe losses.

On December 22 Colville was appointed to command the Division, Cole having gone home ill.

At Albuera Harvey was in command of the Portuguese brigade of the division, to which 1 battalion Loyal Lusitanian Legion had been added on March 14: by September this unit was renamed 7 Cacadores, the brigade was then again under Collins, who at Albuera, had led a provisional brigade from the Elvas garrison (5 Line, 5 Cacadores).

5th Division. From February 1 to February 6 the division was without a GOC, Leith being absent: on February 6, Erskine was appointed to command it, but was transferred to the command of the advanced guard (the Light Division and cavalry) from March 7 to April 22. During this period Dunlop seems to have commanded the Division, Egerton of 2/44 commanding VB.

On May 11 Erskine was appointed to the 2nd Cavalry Division, and Dunlop again had temporary command of the division until October 2, when G.T. Walker was appointed to command his brigade, By December 1 Leith was again in command of the division.

On March 14 the 2nd Battalion, Loyal Lusitanian Legion had been added to Spry's Portuguese brigade. By September it had been renamed 8 Cacadores.

6th Division. Orders of March 5 directed the addition to the divisions of a new brigade under Burne (of 1/36), comprising 2 and 1/36.

It seems to have been intended to put the Brunswick Oels into the 6th Division, but on the formation of the 7th Division (March 5) they were put in C. Alten's brigade.

On July 21 1/32, arrived at Lisbon before July 8, was posted to VIB.

A Campbell leaving for India in November, the division was without a definite GOC till the end of the year, Burne commanding it temporarily.

On March 14 the Loyal Lusitanian Legion was removed from the Portuguese brigade of the division, and distributed as Cacador battalions to the 4th and 5th divisions, being replaced by the 12 Kline, formerly in Bradford's brigade. At Fuentes, Madden commanded the Brigade.

Light Division. Wynch dying January 6, the 2nd Brigade was without a commander till February 7, when Drummond (of 1/52) was appointed to it. Craufurd having gone home on leave before February 8, the division had no GOC, but was under Erskine from March 7 on, together with the Cavalry who also were in the advancned guard.

On March 5 2/52, newly arrived at Lisbon was added to Drummond's brigade.

R. Craufurd returned April 22 and took over the division from Erskine.

By August 1 Beckwith had been invalided home, Andrew Barnard of the 95 commanding the brigade in his place.

On August 21 the headquarters and four companies of the 3/95, which had gone out to Cadiz in 1810, arrived at Lisbon and were added to the 1st brigade, the company 3/95, hitherto with IIA , being also added to the same brigade.

Drummond dying before September 8, Vandeleur was appointed to the vacant brigade on September 30. By October 1 another company 2/95 had been added to the 1st Brigade.

7th Division. Orders were issued on March 5 for the formation of this division, to be composed of two British brigades under C. Alten and Long, and Coleman's Portuguese, ie 7 and 10 Line and 2 Cacadores The composition of the British brigades is not given, but General Orders say that the Brunswick Oels should be in Alten's brigade and the Chassseurs Britanniques (arrived at Lisbon from Cadiz, January 28) in Long's. The other regiments in the division were 51 (arrived during February), 85 (arrived March 4), which were in Long's brigade and the 1 and 2 Light Battalions, KGL, in Alten's. These last only landed on March 21 and did not join the division till it came down with Wellington from Almeida to the Guadiana Valley for the second siege of Badajoz. Till then they had been attached to the force under Beresford: Schwertfeger[5] says these Battalions formed part of the 2nd Division but this does seem quite accurate. As they had no casualties at the siege of Badajos, in which the 7th Division suffered severely, one may presume that they finally joined the division after the siege was raised.

Thus the British brigade (at first there was only one) was 51, 85, Chasseurs Britanniques[6], Brunswick Oels. On March 31 Sontag was posted to it *vice* Long, removed to command Beresford's cavalry, March 19.

On July 19 68 (just arrived) was posted to VIIB.

Houston was invalided home before August 1, Sontag commanding the division. By October he too was invalided (his ADC received orders to rejoin his regiment on October 29). Alten was in temporary command, C. Halkett, commanding his brigade. VIIB was without a GOC from October 15 till de Bernewitz got it on December 23.

On October 3 85 (a single battalion regiment) was ordered to go home to recruit.

The Portuguese brigade was under Doyle at Fuentes; by September Coleman was back in command.

---

5   Geschichte der, KGL, i. 317
6   this regiment was formed in 1801 from French *émigrés*. Subsequently other nationals joined, many of them either prisoners of war or deserters.

Portuguese. No changes seem to have taken place in Hamilton's Division, or in Pack's brigade, but the other unattached brigade was under McMahon in September, and included the 13 and 22 Line and 5 Cacadores, the 12 Line having been transferred to the 6th Division.

1812

On January 1 the organisation of the Army was as follows:

Cavalry. 1st Division. GOC Cotton. B (Slade), 1 dragoons, 12 Light dragoons; C (no GOC, G Anson, absent), 14 and 16 Light Dragoons; E (Cuming of 11 Light Dragoons in absence of V. Alten), 11th Light Dragoons, 1 Hussars, KGL; A (no GOC, de Grey absent), 3 Dragoon Guards, 4 Dragoons; F (Le Marchant), 4 and 5 Dragoon Guards, 3 Dragoons.

Cavalry. 2nd Division, No GOC; D (Long), 9 and 13 Light Dragoons, 2 Hussars, KGL.

1st Division. GOC Graham. A (H. Campbell), 1 Coldstreams, 1 Scots, I company 5/60; B (?Blantyre) for Stopford), 2/24, 1/26, 2/42.1/79, 1 company 5/60; C (Low), 1, 2, 5 Line, KGL

2nd Division. GOC Hill. A (Howard), 1/50, 1/71, 1/92. I company 5/60; B (Byng), 1/3, 1/57, 1st Provisional Battalion) ie 2/31 and 2/66), 1 company 5/60; C (Wilson), 1/28, 2/34, 1/39, 1 company 5/60; also Ashworth's Portuguese.

3rd Division. GOC Picton. A (Mackinnon), 1/45, Headquarters 5/60, 74, 1/88; B (J. Campbell for Colville), 2/5. 77, 2/83, 94; also Palmeirim's Portuguese.

4th Division. GOC Colville (for Cole). A (Kemmis), 3/27, 1/40, I company 5/60; B (?Pakenham), 1/7, 1/23, 1/48, I company Brunswick Oels; also Collins' Portuguese.

5th Division. GOC Leith. A (Hay), 3/1, 1/9, 2/38, I company Brunwick Oels; B (Walker), 1/4, 2/30, 2/44. I company Brunswick Oels; also Spry's Portuguese

6th Division. No GOC, Burne in temporary charge. A (Hulse), 1/11, 2/53, 1/61, 1 company 5/60; B (Burne), 2, 1/32, 1/36; also Madden's Portuguese.

7th Division. No GOC, Alten in temporary charge. (C. Halkett for Alten), 1 and 2 Light Battalions, KGL, Brunswick Oels; B (de Bernewitz), 51, 68, Chasseurs Britanniques: also Coleman's Portuguese.

Light Division. GOC, R. Crauford. A (? Barnard), 1/43, 4 companies 1/95, 3 companies 3/95, 1 Cacadores; B (Vandeleur), 1/52, 2/52, 4 companies 1/95, 3 Cacadores.

Portuguese. Hamilton's division, with brigades under Fonseca and Arch.Campbell. Unattached brigades under Pack and McMahon.

Subsequent changes were:

Cavalry. On January 1 the 1 and 2 Dragoons, KGL, under Bock arrived at Lisbon: they remained near there till March 12, joining the army at Estremoz March 23, and being reckoned as the 2nd Brigade (= G) of the 2nd Cavalry Division.

By January 8 V. Alten was again in command of his brigade.

Several changes took place under orders issued January 29; the 3 and 4 Dragoon Guards were posted to Slade's brigade, from which the 12 Light Dragoons were removed to G. Anson's, the 4 Dragoons replaced the 4 Dragoon Guards in Le Marchant's, and de Grey's brigade disappeared. F. Ponsonby of the 12 Light Dragoons took command of C in Anson's absence.

By April 8 Erskine had resumed command of the 2nd Cavalry Division, to which Slade's brigade was transferred April 14, Bock's joining the 1st Division.

On July 1, an exchange was ordered between the 11 and 14 Light Dragoons: G. Anson who had resumed command of his brigade, having 11, 12, 16 Light Dragoons, V. Alten 14 Light Dragoons and 1 Hussars, KGL.

At Salamanca Cotton was wounded, and Le Marchant killed. While Cotton was disabled, Bock commanded the Cavalry, de Jonqueres having his brigade. W. Ponsonby, 5 Dragoon Guards, succeeded to Le Marchant's brigade (by orders of July 23). Cotton rejoined before October 15, but had to go home again in December invalided. From August 1, V. Alten was absent but rejoined by the middle of September.

By orders of October 17th, 2 Hussars, KGL, were transferred to V. Alten's brigade.

1st Division. Stopford resumed command of IB before February 1, but was gone again by April 8. On May 7 Wheatley was appointed to command the brigade until Stopford's return.

1/26, being too sickly for field service, was out of IB before March 8, being sent down to Lisbon, and thence to Gibraltar to relieve 1/82. Their place in IB was taken by 1/42, just arrived from England, and posted to IB, April 23. On May 19 1/42 was ordered home drafting its rank and file into 1/42, 2/58 was posted to IB by orders of April 2: on June 1 its transfer to VB was ordered, but 'orders will hereafter be given as to the regiment joining the brigade.' It seems to have remained with IB till after the retreat from Burgos.

Graham going home ill July 6, H. Campbell was appointed to command the division, Fermor getting IA.

Wheatley died September 1, Stirling (of 1/42) being appointed to IB September 11.

On October 11 E. Paget was posted to command the division, but he was taken prisoner November 17, his place being taken by W. Stewart, who had just returned to the Peninsula.

After the retreat from Burgos the division was reorganised. A new brigade of Guards was added, composed of 1/1 (Grenadier)[7] Guards who arrived at Corunna from England, October 1 and joined the army on the Carrion October 24, and 3/1 Guards, who had been at Cadiz, and came up to Madrid with Skerrett's column. This was ordered October 17, but cannot have been carried out till later. On November 10 Howard was transferred from IIA to command this brigade. On November 11 Stirling's brigade was ordered to be removed to the 6th Division, the company of 5/60 attached to it remaining in the 1st Division. On December 6 the 1 and 2 Light Battalions, KGL, were removed from VIIA to the KGL brigade of the 1st Division.

2nd Division. In orders of April 14, Tilson-Chowne (formerly Tilson) was appointed to command the Division 'under Hill', but though present at Almaraz in May does not seem to have been present to the end of the year. Howard being transferred to the 1st Division, November 10, Cadogan (of 1/71) took command of IIA.

3rd Division. At Ciudad Rodrigo Mackinnon was killed (January 19) his brigade going to Kempt – in orders February 8.

At Badajoz Picton and Kempt were wounded (April 6), Wallace taking over Kempt's brigade, and also having temporary command of the division when Picton was disabled: Forbes (of 1/45) then commanded IIIA.

After the fall of Badajoz 77 (a single battalion regiment) was sent down to Lisbon, being much reduced.

On June 28 Packenham was appointed to command 'Colville's brigade in the 3rd Division', ie IIIB. At Salamanca he commanded the division, Picton having gone sick again, Wallace and J. Campbell having the brigades.

1/5 that arrived in May was posted to IIIB June 1, both battalions were at Salamanca, but on July 27 2/5 was drafted into 1/5, the skeleton going home in October.

By Orders of October 17 2/87, which had come up from Cadiz with Skerrett, was posted to IIIB, , then still called 'Colville's'.

Wallace was invalided home after the retreat from Burgos.

Packenham was to retain command of the division till the return of 'Colville or some other' (Wellington dispatches, v, 399), his name does not appear in the 'States' as commanding IIIB after November 1; Colville apparently came back before the end of the year.[8]

On April 8 Power took over the Portuguese brigade, Champlemond, who had it *vice* Palmeirim by March 17, having been wounded at Badajoz: 12 Cacadores were added to it on April 8.

4th Division. On February 9, Bowes was appointed to command 'the brigade late under Packenham', ie IVB. In April Colville was wounded at Badajoz, and the division was without a

7   they would not be designated 'Grenadiers' until after Waterloo
8   quoted as October in the Dictionary of National Biography

GOC till Cole returned – before July 8.

At Salamanca (July 22) Cole was wounded, and was absent in consequence until October 15. In Cole's absence W. Anson, who was appointed to IVA April 9, would have commanded the division. The vacancy in IVA was caused by the departure of Kemmis – before April 1: at Badajoz Harcourt (of 1/40) commanded IVA.

Bowes was transferred to the 6th Division May 2, and it would appear that Ellis (of 1/23) commanded IVB temporarily. He certainly was in charge of it at Salamanca, and apparently kept it till Skerrett was appointed to it on October 17, but his force from Cadiz only joined Hill on October 26, and the arrangements ordered on October 17 can hardly have been carried out at once.

Skerrett's brigade (3/1 Guards, 2/47, 2/87 and 2 companies 2/95) seems to have acted with IV after joining Hill's force, but was broken up when operations ceased.

Orders of October 17 directed 1/82, which had come up from Gibraltar in June, and was with the 4th Division at Madrid, to join IVB, but the battalion was transferred to VIIA by orders of November 28, the 20 which arrived in December being posted to IVB instead. On 1/82 joining, 1/48 was transferred to IVA.

On December 6 the 2nd Provisional Battalion (ie 2nd and 1/53) was posted to IVA.

By Salamanca Stubbs had taken over command of the Portuguese Brigade, which had been under Harvey by March 17, and at the siege of Badajoz.

5th Division. At Badajoz Walker was wounded (April 6): his brigade had no regular GOC till Pringle was appointed to it June 28.

On May 10 2/4 arrived at Lisbon during April, was posted to VB. In June 1/38 came out and was present at Salamanca apparently with VA, but it only appears as part of that brigade in the 'States' of August 8 and afterwards.

Orders of June 1 directed 2/58 to join VB, but the battalion seems to have been with IB till reorganised as part of the 3rd Provisional Battalion in December.

Hay was absent from June 8, Greville of 1/38 commanding the brigade till July 31, when Hulse was transferred to it. Hulse must have also commanded the division, as Leith was wounded at Salamanca and invalided home. Hulse dying (September 6), Pringle commanded the division, until Oswald was appointed to it (October 25), when Pringle reverted to his brigade, of which Brooke (of 4th) had been in command.

Orders of June 18 directed 1/9 to exchange with 2/30 and 2/44, but these were cancelled June 28. E. Barnes was in Orders to command VA October 28, but seems to have been with the brigade at Villa Muriel three days earlier. On December 6 he was transferred to VIIA. Hay appears to have returned before December 31.

On December 6 Orders directed the drafting 2/4 into 1/4 and 2/38 into 1/38, the skeletons being sent home, also for forming 2/30 and 2/44 into a Provisional Battalion, the 4th. By orders of October 127, 2/47 of Skerrett's column had been posted to VB which then was described as Walker's Brigade.

6th Division. On February 9 H. Clinton was appointed to command the division.

By April 1, VIB was without a brigadier: Bowes was appointed to it May 2, but he was killed in the attack on the Salamanca forts (June 24). .On this, Hinde, of 32, commanded the brigade, being appointed definitely to it September 30, but ante-dated to June.

On Hulse being transferred to VA, July 31, VIA was without a brigadier, Bingham of 2/53 being actually in command, until the amalgamation of the two brigades by Orders of November 11. At the same time Stirling's brigade was transferred from the 1st Division to the 6th. 1/91, which arrived at Corunna October 8, being added to it by Orders of November 28 – it actually joined December 14.

On December 6 orders were issued for the formation of 2nd and 2/53 as the 2nd Provisional Battalion, and of 2/24, and 2/58 as the 3rd Provisional Battalion, and for their transfer to IVA and VIIA respectively.

The Portuguese Brigade was under Eben until April 30, when the Conde de Rezende took command. It was joined by 9 Cacadores on April 10. Rezende was invalided in November, and succeeded by Madden.

7th Division. On May 2 Alten was transferred to command the Light division: John Hope being given command of the 7th. Halkett of 2 Light Battalion, KGL, seems to have commanded VIIA though in the 'States' no brigadier is named from May 2 till December 6, when E. Barnes was appointed to it.

Hope having quit the Army on account of his health September 23, the division had no GOC till October 25, when Lord Dalhousie was appointed to it, having been put on the Staff of the Army September 12.

On November 28, 1/6, newly arrived from England, was added to VIIA, then called 'Colonel Halkett's', and 1/82, from IVB, was added to VIIB.

Orders of December 6 directed the transfer of the Light Battalions, KGL, to the 1st Division, the 3rd Provisional Battalion (ie 2/24 and 2/58) being added to VIIA. The Portuguese Brigade was under Palmeirim in March; later it seems to have been under Doyle of the 19 Line.

Light Division. At Ciudad Rodrigo (January 10), Craufurd was killed, and Vandeleur wounded; Barnard then took command of the division, and Gibbs of 1/52 of the 2nd Brigade. By April 15 Vandeleur had resumed command, 1/52 was drafted to 1/52 by Orders of February 23, the skeleton beng sent home.

On May 2 C. Alten received command of the division.

By May 8 1/95 had been united in the 2nd Brigade but Orders of August 24 again divided it, 3 companies in each brigade; before the end of the year it was again united and placed in the 1st Brigade.

Two more companies 2/95 came out from England in May, and joined those already out, the four being in the 2nd Brigade. Two more came up from Cadiz with Skerrett, and joined the brigade.

3/95 seems to have been transferred temporarily to the 2nd Brigade, but was back in the 1st by the end of the year.

The 20th Portuguese, which had come up with Skerrett, were posted to 'Beckwith's brigade', October 17.

Portuguese. In April, 1812, Power had replaced Arch. Campbell in command of the 4th Brigade, while Bradford had the 11th *vice* McMahon: this now included the 5 Cacadores, 13 and 24 Line.

By July Power had exchanged the 4th Brigade for the 8th, which was in the 3rd Division. A. Campbell would seem to have again commanded the 4th to which on April 8, the 10 Cacadores were added.

1813

On January 1 the Army was organised as follows:

Cavalry. 1st Division. No GOC., Cotton absent. F (W. Ponsonby), 5 Dragoon Guards, 3 and 4 Dragoons; C (G. Anson), 11, 12, and 16 Light Dragoons; E (V. Alten), 14 Light Dragoons, 1 and 2 KGL Hussars; G (Bock), 1 and 2 KGL Dragoons.

Cavalry. 2nd Division. No GOC., B (Slade), 3 and 4 Dragoon Guards, 1 Dragoons; D (Long), 9 and 13 Light Dragoons.

1st Divison. GOC, W. Stewart. A (Howard), 1/1 Guards, 3/1 Guards, 1 company 5/60; B (Fermor), 1 Coldstreams, 1 Scots, 1 company 5/60; C (Low), 1, 2 and 5 Line, KGL., 1 and 2 Light Battalions, KGL although some accounts have them under Halkett.

2nd Division. GOC, Hill. A (Cadogan), 1/50, 1/71, 1/92, 1 company 5/60; B (Byng), 1/3, 1/57, 1st Provisional Battalion (= 2/31, 2/34. 1/39, 1 company 5/60; also Ashworth's Portuguese

3rd Division. GOC, ?Packenham. A (no brigadier), 1/45. headquarters 5/60, 74, 1/88, 94; also Power's Portuguese.

4th Division. GOC, Cole. A (W. Anson), 3/27, 1/40, 1/48, 2nd Provisional Battalion (= 2nd and 2/53), 1 company 5/60; B Skerrett, 1/7, 20th, 1/23. 1 company Brunswick Oels; also Stubbs' Portuguese.

5th Division. GOC ?Hay. A (Hay), 3/1.1/9,1/38, 1 company Brunswick Oels; B (Pringle), 1/4, 2/47, 4th Provisional Battalion (= 2/30 and 2/44), 1 company Brunswick Oels; also Spry's Portuguese.

6th Divison. GOC H. Clinton. A (Stirling), 1/42. 1/79, 1/91, 1 company 5/60; B (Hinde), 1/11, 1/32. 1/36, 1/61; also Madden's Portuguese.

7th Divison. GOC Dalhousie. A (Barnes), 1.6, 3rd Provisional Battalion (= 2/24 and 2/58), Headquarters and 9 companies Brunswick Oels; B (de Bernewitz), 51, 68,1/82; Chasseurs Britanniques; also Doyle's Portuguese.

Light Division. GOC, C. Alten. A (no brigadier present; still called Beckwith's), 1/43. 1/95, 3/95, 1 Cacadores; B (Vandeleur), 1/52, 2/95, 3 Cacadores, ? 20th Portuguese.

Portuguese. Hamilton's division, brigades under ? Fonseca and Campbell. Unattached brigades, Pack's and Bradford's.

Subsequent changens were:

Cavalry. By January 25 a new brigade (H) was added, composed of two squadrons each of 1 and 2 Life Guards and Royal Horse Guards, O'Loghlin had apparently been appointed to command it, but by Orders of November 28, 1812, F.S. Rebow was appointed to command it in his place. It ranked as 3 Brigade, 2nd Division, but was transferred to the 1st on February 5. In March it was under Sir Robert Hill[9], Rebow having gone home.

Orders of March 3 directed the distribution among the regiments remaining in the Peninsula of the horses of 4th Dragoon Guards, 9 and 11 Light Dragoons, and 2 KGL Hussars, these regiments going home. Their place was taken by a new brigade (I), under Colquhoun Grant, of 15 Hussars, composed of the 10, 15 and 18 Hussars: this first appears in the 'States' on April 15.

Orders were issued April 21 for the amalgamation of the two divisions, 'under the command of Sir S. Cotton': Cotton did not, however, rejoin till June 25, and in his absence Bock seems to have commanded the cavalry, his brigade being under Bulow.

On May 20 Fane, appointed a Major General on the Staff April 24, was given B *vice* Slade who had been ordered home April 23.

On July 2 orders were issued to transfer the 18 Hussars to V. Alten's brigade, *vice* the 4 Light Dragoons moved to Long's which had been reduced to one regiment by the departure of the 9 Light Dragoons (out of the 'States' by April 4). Lord E. Somerset at the same time was given command of the Hussar brigade *vice* Grant and Vandeleur, that of C *vice* G. Anson, removed to the Home Staff.

On September 6 Grant was appointed to take over Long's brigade, Long having apparently gone home before the Battle of the Pyrenees, as his name was not among the commanders of Cavalry brigades thanked by Parliament on November 8 for those operations. On November 24 Hussey Vivian was appointed to take Grant's place.

7 Hussars arrived in Spain in September, and were added to the Hussar brigade. They would seem to have been with the brigade by October 21 but were not in orders till November 24.

In October O'Loghlin seems to have taken over the Household Brigade, he had been placed on the Staff June 17.

1st Division. In March Howard replaced W. Stewart in command but on May 19 Graham was Appointed to command the division. Howard acting as his assistant while Graham commanded the left wing of the army. On October 8, Graham resigned command and went

---

9   Brother to General Sir Rowland Hill who commanded the 2nd Division.

home ill.Sir John Hope[10] took his place; he was placed on the Staff October 10, as from September 25.

While Howard commanded the division, his brigade was under Lambert; It missed Vittoria, (June) being too sickly to take the field with the army and only joined in August.

On July 2 Lambert was transferred to VIB, and Maitland got the brigade.

Low went home May 6, the KGL being certainly one brigade only at Vittoria, where Halkett commanded them.

Lord Aylmer's brigade (76, 2/84 and 85) which is first mentioned in Orders on July 23, and joined the army during August, may be reckoned as part of the 1st Division with which it always acted. By Orders of October 17, 2/62 was added to it *vice* 2/84 transferred to VB. On November 24 the 77 (from Lisbon) was added to it.

On October 20 Hinuber was appointed to command the KGL Infantry.

2nd Division. On March 25 W. Stewart was appointed to command the division 'under Hill's direction'. At the same time G.T. Walker got Howard's brigade, on the latter taking over the 1st Division from Stewart.

Wilson died in January and O'Callaghan of 39th commanded the brigade till July 23, when Pringle was appointed to it. On May 1, Wellington had written that he was keeping it vacant for Oswald should Leith come out and take over the 5th Division.

At Vittoria Cadogan was killed and J. Cameron of 92 took over IIA; he was wounded at Maya (July 25) and Fitzgerald of 5/60 commanded, till Walker actually joined in August. On November 18 Walker was transferred to command the 7th Division, Barnes being appointed to IIA November 20.

3rd Division. Pakenham was transferred to the 6th Division January 26, the Division being under Colville who had returned before that date. Picton rejoined in May, Colville reverting to the command of his brigade. Picton was again absent from September 8, but returned just before the end of the year. Colville was in command at the Nivelle (November), but was transferred to command the 5th Division, when Picton came back in December.

The II Cacadores were posted to Power's brigade before April 26 taking the place of the 12.

Brisbane, appointed to Staff of Army, January 7, was given command of IIIA, *vice* Kempt, March 25.

Colville being given temporary command of the 6th Division on August 8, Keane commanded IIIB, as also when Colville came back to the division.

4th Division. By orders of July 2 Skerrett was transferred to the Light Division, his brigade going to Ross of 20.

By September 1 the Portuguese brigade was under Miller: at the Nivelle (November 10) Vasconellos had it.

5th Division. While Hay commanded the division Greville of 28 had his brigade. In April Oswald took over the division and commanded it till Leith returned – August 30. Leith was wounded at San Sebastian on September 1, and Oswald again took command; but at the Bidassoa, (October 9) Hay was in command, Greville having VA. On March 9, Robinson was appointed to 'Walker's brigade', ie VB.

On April 12, 2/59 from Cadiz was added to VB; on May 10 the 4th Provisional Battalion was ordered to return home. On October 17, 2/84 from Lord Aylmer's brigade was added to VB, 2/477 being transferred to VA. Robinson was wounded before Bayonne December 10, and his successor, Piper of 4th, being wounded next day, the command passed to Tonson of 2/84.

At the passage of the Bidassoa the Portuguese brigade was commanded by de Regoa and until the end of the year.

6th Division. On January 26 Pakenham was appointed to command the Divison in Clinton's absence. On June 25 he was appointed Adjutant General and Clinton returned and resumed command. By July 22 Clinton was again absent, Pack getting the Division. At Sorauren (July

---

10 Not the same John Hope who commanded the 7th Division in 1812.

28) Pack was wounded, and Packenham took over the division temporarily, giving it over to Colville before August 8. Colville seems to have still been in command at the passage of the Bidassoa (October 9), but Clinton then returned, Colville reverting to the 3rd Divison.

Pack had been appointed to command VIA, *vice* Stirling, July 2, Lambert at the same time getting VIB, *vice* Hinde. Stirling commanded VIA when Pack got the division, but went home in October.

The Portuguese brigade was under the command of Madden till the autumn: Douglas of the 8 Line had it at the Nivelle.

7th Division. By April 16 de Bernewitz was no longer in command of his brigade, to which Inglis was appointed May 21, though at Vittoria, Grant of 1/82 commanded it but Inglis took charge before the Pyrenees.

Le Cor received command of the Portuguese brigade on March 9. When he was promoted in November, Doyle had it.

Dalhousie went home after the Bidassoa, October 9, and at the Nivelle (November 9) Le Cor was in command. On November 18, G.T. Walker was given command 'in Dalhousie's absence.' Le Cor would seem to have been transferred to command the Portuguese division

On Barnes returning to the 2nd Division November 20, his brigade seems to have gone to Gardiner.

Light Division. On March 23, Kempt was appointed to A. On July 2 Vandeleur was transferred to a cavalry brigade, Skerrett getting B. At the passage of the Bidassoa, and to the end of the year, Colborne of 52 was in command of B, *vice* Skerrett, who went home in September.

The 20th Portuguese never joined the Division: in place of them on April 26, the 17 Portuguese appear in its 'State'.

Portuguese. Hamilton had had to give up command of his Portuguese division in February, owing to ill-health, upon which it was under Silveira, the brigades being under Da Costa and Campbell during the battles of the Pyrenees. By the passage of the Nivelle (November 9) Hamilton was again in command, Buchan had Da Costa's brigade, but during the fighting on the Nive (December 9–11), Le Cor had the Division and Buchan and Da Costa the brigades. Buchan was ordered to transfer himself to the Portuguese Brigade of the 7th Division on November 9, but this move was countermanded.

When Pack was moved to a British command (July 2) his brigade went to Wilson, who commanded it at the Bidassoa, but had been replaced by A. Campbell by the Nive (December 9), Wilson having been wounded, November 18.

Bradford seems to have retained the other unattached brigade all year.

1814

On January 1 the organisation was as follows:–

Cavalry. GOC Cotton. I (O'Loghlin), 1 and 2 Life Guards, RHG; F (W. Ponsonby), 5 Dragoon Guards, 3 and 4 Dragoons; C (Vandeleur), 12 and 16 Light Dragoons; D (Vivian), 13 and 14 Light Dragoons; E (V. Alten), 18 Hussars, 1 KGL Hussars; G (Bock), 1 and 2 KGL Dragoons; G (Fance), 3 Dragoon Guards, 1 Dragoons; H (Somerset), 7, 10 and 15 Hussars.

1st Division. GOC Hope, with Howard as assistant; A (Maitland for Howard), 1/1 Guards, 1 company 5/60; B (Stopford), 1 Coldstreams, 1 Scots, 1 company 5/60; C (Hinuber), 1, 2 and 5 Line, KGL; 1st and 2nd Light Battalions, KGL; D (Aylmer), 2/62. 76, 77, 85.

2nd Division. GOC W. Stewart[11]. A (Barnes), 1/50, 1/71, 1/92. 1 company 5/60; B (Byng), 1/3, 1/57. I Provisional Battalion (2/31 and 2/66), 1 company 5/60; C (Pringle), 1/28, 2/34. 1/39, 1 company 5/60; also Ashworth's Portuguese.

3rd Division. GOC Picton. A (Brisbane), 1/45, Headquarters 5/60, 74, 1/88; B (Keane), 1/5. 2/83, 2/87, 94; also Power's Portuguese.

---

11 Hill was always there overseeing the Division.

4th Division. GOC Cole. A (W. Anson), 3/27. 1/40, 1/48, 2nd Provisional Battalion (2nd and 2/53), 1 company Brunswick Oels; B (Ross), 1/7, 1/20, 1/23, 1 company 5/60; also Vasconcellos' Portuguese.

5th Divison. GOC Colville. A (Hay), 3/1, 1/9. 1/38, 2/47. 1 company Brunswick Oels; B (Robinson), 1/4, 2/59, 1 company Brunswick Oels; B (Robinson), 1/4, 2/59, 2/84, 1 company Brunswick Oels; also de Regoa's Portuguese.

6th Division. GOC Clinton. A (Pack), 1/42,1/79, 1/01, 1 company 5/60; B (Lambert), 1/11. 1/32, 1/36, 1/61, 1 company 5/60; also Douglas' Portuguese.

7th Division. GOC Walker. A (Gardiner), 1/6, 3 Provisional Battalion (2/24 and 2/58), Headquarters Brunswick Oels; B (Inglis), 51, 68, 1/82, Chasseurs Britanniques; also Doyle's Portuguese.

Light Division. GOC C. Alten. A (Kempt), 1/43, 1/95, 1 Cacadores; B (Colborne), 1/52, 2/95, 3 Cacadores, 17 Portuguese.

Portuguese. Le Cor's Division, with Da Costa and Buchan commanding brigades. Unattached brigades under A. Campbell and Bradford.

Subsequent changes were:

Cavalry. By January 16 several changes had taken place; V. Alten had gone and Vivian had been transferred to his brigade, Fane having transferred from B to D (late Vivian's). Bock also went (he was drowned off the coast of Brittany in February), about the same time.

From January 25 W. Ponsonby was absent, Lord C. Manners of 3 Dragoons commanding his brigade.

By March 25 Arentschildt (of 1 KGL Hussars) had been given Bock's old brigade: on Vivian being wounded (April 8) Arentschildt was transferred to E, and Bulow got the 'German Heavy Brigade'.

Fane's name appears in the 'States' as commanding both B and D. According to the *Regimental History of the 14th Hussars* by Colonel H.B. Hamilton, he commanded both working them practically as a division, the brigades being respectively commanded by Clifton of the Royals (B) and Doherty of the 13 Light Dragoons (D).

1st Division. 1/37 joined Aylmer's brigade before March 25. On April 14, Stopford was wounded at Bayonne and his division went to Guise.

2nd Division. On February 15 Pringle was wounded, and O'Callaghan commanded the brigade.

It was arranged that when Lord Dalhousie rejoined and resumed command of the 7th Division, Walker should revert to IIA and Barnes take over IIIB, but Walker was wounded at Orthez and went home, so the arrangement was never carried out.

By January 16, Harding had replaced Ashworth in command of the 5 Portuguese brigade.

3rd Division. No changes: Brisbane was slightly wounded at Toulouse.

4th Division. Ross was wounded at Orthez (February 27), and the brigade was without a GOC.

5th Division. After February 1 Robinson was absent. Hay was killed before Bayonne April 14.

6th Division. Pack was wounded at Toulouse, as was also Douglas. 1/32 missed Toulouse, being at San Jean de Luz refitting.

7th Division. Walker was wounded at Orthez, and went home; Dalhousie arriving almost immediately after the battle and resuming command.

By January 16, the Portuguese brigade was under Doyle (he may have got it when Le Cor obtained command of the Portuguese division).

Light Division. 1/43 and 1/95 both missed Orthez, being away refitting.

Portuguese. Da Costa was ordered back to Portugal before March 15.

ENDNOTES

1 General Jean Androche, Duc d'Abrantes. For some reason, Napoleon never created him a Marechal.

2 'A soft answer turneth away wrath; but grievous words stir up anger,' Proverbs 15, 1.

3 'Unconventional and uncouth' was one description of Picton. 'A rough mouthed Devil' was Wellington's description.

4 Killed at the storming of Ciudad Rodrigo.

5 These letters are all in the British Library Add. Mss 35059-35-67.

6 The Rev. Rowland was so well known that his death was minuted in Cabinet papers.

7 This omission also occurs in Gurwood, probably for the same reason.

8 Add mss. British Library 3059 – 3067.

9 He happened to be in London with sister Emma and about to go to see a play when the Government called on him to leave for Brussels immediately and to hold the Prince of Orange's hand until Wellington could arrive from Vienna.

10 Add.mss 35063.

11 Her given name was Mary but she was always known as Maria; Teffeteller writes as if there were two different people. Their mother was also Mary and this is probably why she was known as Maria.

12 On an officer requesting leave in Lisbon, Wellington would grant two days as being quite long enough, he said, to spend in bed with a whore.

13 Quoted in the *Shrewsbury Chronicle* dated 30 August 2001.

14 Clement served as his ADC throughout the war, Robert commanded the Royal Horse Guards Blue and Thomas Noel was Colonel of the 1st Portuguese regiment.

15 Spencer was eventually replaced because of the pessimistic letters he wrote, to Wellington's great relief.

16 He was only promoted to this rank in 1811 and climbed up the Army List to become a full general in 1825.

17 Griffiths, Arthur, the *Wellington Memorial*, pp 314, 315.

18 Eighth son of the 4th Duke of Beaufort.

19 This is his full official title.

20 Somerset was to become 1st Baron Raglan.

21 Hill's uncle, Sir Richard Hill, 2nd Bt. created a three-mile-long lake at Hawkstone partially in order to create local employment.

22 Rowland Hill's uncle, the Rev. Rowland Hill, a renowned preacher and a man who could draw 'football' size crowds when he preached.

23 Rowland Hill was created KB in 1811, later he received the more senior creation of GCB.

24 In fact the senior branch of the de la Hylles had settled at Court of (Hulle) Hill near Ludlow earlier.

25 Titles have to pass through the direct line in the first generation.

26 Thomas and Samuel were the sons of Richard Hill's twin sisters, Elizabeth and Margaret. Samuel was childless and so his estates went to Thomas. The Attingham Hills were eventually to acquire the title of Lords Berwick.

27 In 1796, although the sitting member, he was opposed by his cousin, William Hill of Attingham, there was much bad feeling between the two sides of the family and John Hill lost his seat. A commemorative Election Jug was optimistically ordered in advance of the Election, giving a majority to John Hill; in fact on this occasion, he lost. (See colour plates.)

28 'Blue' came from their first Colonel, the Earl of Oxford. They always wore blue coats.

29 At this time it consisted of more than 16,000 acres.

30 His father had been advised that a period of military study would be useful.

31 Later Lt General Sir James Delves Broughton.

32 An account appears in *The Life of Sir Richard Hill* by Edwin Sidney.

33 Sidney, Rev Edwin, *The Life of Sir Richard Hill*.

34 Add.mss British Library 35066 contains Hill's correspondence when in this office.

35 Son of his brother, Sir Robert Chambré Hill.

36 This was just before the Duke of York's reforms of 1797, which stated that three years must be spent in each rank before promotion could be achieved.

37 Hill achieved his rapid promotions just before the Duke of York introduced this rule.

38 Hill's bugbear when at Horse Guards, Lord Cardigan, certainly paid a fortune for his Colonelcy of the 15th Hussars.

39 Following the Battle of Waterloo in 1815, all officers were advanced one rank in the army.

40 More discussion of this will be found later on. See also 'Inside Wellington's Peninsular Army' by Ron McGuigan for an excellent description of rank and the system of promotions.

41 Harris, Benjamin, 95th Rifles, 'Rifleman Benjamin Harris, 1808-1809', *The Road to Corunna*, Constable, 2001.

42 Raglan Papers, D3135/116a-164.

43 *soit dit* a relation but I cannot find the connection.

44 Later Lord Hood.

45 Later to become Lord Lynedoch but referred to in this ms as Thomas Graham.

46 Sometimes called 'Old Pivot' thanks to his love of drill.

47 He next saw him when O'Hara was Governor of Gibralter in 1801.

48 Hill later discovered that he had been kept in the common jail and fed on artichokes and bullock liver.

49 Sidney, *Life of Lord Hill*, p 18

50 *Royal Military Panorama*, January 1814.

51 Sidney, *Life of Lord Hill*, p 18

52 As a Colonel of Artillery.

53 General Jacques Dugommier at siege of Toulon; Sidney, *Life of Lord Hill*.

54 Balgowan being the name of Graham's estate.

55 Lynedoch Papers, National Library of Scotland.

56 Often today ' Ile Dieu'.

57 Delavoye, Alex M., *Life of Thomas Graham, Lord Lynedoch*, Richardson, 1880.

58 At Toulon; see above.

59 It would not be until 1808 that the Army was told to cut its queues, to almost universal approval.

60 The better off would use powder as opposed to flour.

61 *Soldiers at War*, Sergeant Robertson 92nd Foot 'A foot soldier in Egypt.'

62 Sir Robert Wilson's *History of the Egyptian Campaign* describes the conduct of the 90th as being most honourable and praiseworthy.

63 The Foudroyant had previously been captured from the French.

64 Ms 3640, National Library of Scotland.

65 This news came in dispatches via Constantinople.

66 Sergeant Robertson of the 92nd gives a good description of the horrors of the march in his chapter in 'Recollections'.

67 Hill's own notes state that they encamped before Cairo on 16 June. Dispatch published in *The Times* of 5 June describes the surrender of the fortress and garrison of Rosetta to Colonel Spencer and the taking of 700 prisoners.

68 Often referred to as just General Hutchinson, 2nd Earl of Donoughmore.

69 Philip J. Haythornthwaite, *The Armies of Wellington*, p.161.

70 In Hill's words.

71 His conversion so that he could live with (and marry) his Egyptian woman had included the assurance that he would not have to undergo circumcision.

72 'Dossier Bonaparte et l'Orient' from *Napoleon* issue no. 50, Nov.- Dec 2008, Jan 2009.

73 Add. 3059 – 3067.

74 *Royal Military Panorama,* 3, January 1814, p.315.

75 This is the first mention of Currie who was to serve under Hill for many years. He was killed at Waterloo.

76 Letter from Frederick, Duke of York to Lord Cathcart and from Lord Cathcart to Rowland Hill, October, 1805.

77 Sidney, *Life of Lord Hill.*

78 Corunna would surely have counted as a failure despite Moore having claimed victory.

79 The name of Noel was for his godfather, Noel Hill, the first Lord Berwick of Attingham. Later, Wellington often referred to him as 'Sir Noel', although his elder brother always calls him Tom or Thomas.

80 M. Glover, *The Peninsular War,* p. 23

81 Hill's so-called 'Epitome', Add mss 35067, British Library. It gives Hill's personal analysis of events in Spain and Portugal before the British arrived in the Peninsula. It was probably written around 1818 and no doubt echoes the thoughts of many at the time.

82 General Androche Junot, Duc d'Abrantes, one of Napoleon's best generals and the most surprising amongst them not to have been created a Marechal. He committed suicide in 1813.

83 This is not expanded on: it was probably just the army from the Gironde that was moved south.

84 Admiral Siniavin proved a problem to Junot, he belonged to a party in Russia which was opposed to France and as such was not expected to 'show too much zeal in supporting the projects of Napoleon'.

85 General Louis Henri Loison who executed nine Portuguese in cold blood at Caldas da Rainha on 9 February 1808.

86 General Francisco Xavier Castanos, 1st Duke of Bailen, who had achieved a victory against the French at Bailen in 1808 but was then defeated at Tudela.

87 Ironically this was precisely what happened to Napoleon when imprisoned on St Helena.

88 Married to the Emperor's sister, Caroline.

89 Elder brother Joseph, who was proclaimed King on 2 May. Unfortunately for him, he was far from Napoleon's equal.

90 Francisco Xavier, Duke of Bailen.

91 Jose Palafox y Melzni, Duke of Sarragossa, had been with his master, Ferdinand, in Bayonne but managed to escape to Aragon where he raised an army.

92 Hill's orders are in Hill papers, add.mss 35064.

93 Add. Mss British Library.

94 Wellington to RH dated 23rd June, 1808, add mss. 3059 British Library.

95 Oman, vol 1, pp.75-6.; Wellington to Hill dated 23 June 1808, add mss. 3059 British Library.

96 With the fall of Madrid to the French, Cadiz assumed great importance for the Spanish. It was the temporary capital.

97 The mad King of Sweden, Gustav IV, after many stormy interviews with Moore, had forbidden him to land.

98 Said by Wellington to be 'a very good officer but as drunken a dog as ever lived.'

99 Spencer was quite senior on the Army List and a Lt General.

100 De Laborde is how he appears in French texts.

101 Not to be confused with 'Black Bob' Crauford.

102 Senior brigade commander's position of honour.

103 Henry Fane started life in the Peninsular Army as an infantry officer. In 1809 he was serving in the heavy cavalry.

104 Oman, p.259.

105 Letter from Wellington to the Duke of York, 22nd August, 1808.

106 Jacques Garnier, Administrateur de l'Institut Napoleon.

107 They were to be conveniently – for them – landed in La Rochelle.

108 Hill's *Epitome,* written some years later, Add.mss 35067.

109 There are many graphic descriptions of this Spanish General, none flattering: Colborne, 'a perverse, stupid old blockhead'; Costello, 'that deformed-looking lump of pride, ignorance and treachery'.

110 Joachim Blake was a General of Irish extraction; a soldier of fortune. In the later years of the war, he fought with the guerrillas.

111 Oman, vol 1, pp 168-72.

112 Bryant, Arthur, *Years of Victory*, Collins, 1944.

113 He had actually been told they were at Salamanca and sent William Carr Gomm to discover the truth.

114 Ian Fletcher, p. 7.

115 ibid p.166.

116 Austria had now thrown in her lot with the Allies.

117 'Black Bob' Crauford was to take his Light Brigade to Vigo.

118 Lewis, John ed., Ridleman Harris in *Soldiers at War: The Road to Corunna*, Robinson, 2001.

119 Oman, vol 1, p.591.

120 It was principally 2nd battalions that were first sent to the Peninsula.

121 Sidney, *Life of Lord Hill*.

122 Also in add mss. 36066.

123 Foy who was in charge of the French troops in the eastern suburb must be held guilty of negligence.

124 John Waters knew the surroundings of Porto very well having previously worked for Warre, the Port Shippers in the city.

125 He would subsequently have to have the arm amputated; he managed excellently with only one!

126 Developed by British artillery officer Major, later Major General, Henry Shrapnel (1761–1842).

127 Clement sometimes refers to his brother as 'Rowland' and sometimes as the 'General.'

128 Later Sir Digby Mackworth of Glen Usk.

129 After General Lowry Cole.

130 Wellington had had him as his Quartermaster in India from 1801-1805 and had suffered from his 'alternations of torpor and feverish activity'. Murray was put in command of an army on the east coast of Spain at the end of the Peninsular War; he had to be removed.

131 Three majors and General Paget.

132 One account has twenty soldiers of the KGL having drunk 41 bottles at one go.

133 The sole reason that they had not been killed in some horrible fashion was that the peasants had immediately recognised a senior officer and knew they would be paid for bringing him in.

134 Joaquin Blake, Spanish General of Irish descent, not a very successful general.

135 On Wellington having interceded for them, the number was reduced to 40.

136 An excellent vantage point being high above the plain.

137 The clearest description of this night raid is found in Longford, *Wellington – Years of the Sword*.

138 It is irritating but typical of Sidney that he does not say who this was.

139 Sidney, *Life of Lord Hill*, p 111

140 Fortescue, *History of the British Army*, vol vii p.239. A rare occasion when Hill swore – mildly it must be said!

141 Hill estimates the combined forces of the French at 50,000, more than twice the number of the Allies.

142 His Brigade Major.

143 Egyptian Campaign of 1801.

144 The British have always claimed it as a victory but some have described it as another inconclusive bloodletting.

145 Horace Francois Bastien de la Porta, later a Marechal of France, commanded the IV Corps at Talavera.

146 Sidney, *Life of Lord Hill*, p 113.

147 Slade was a disaster as a general, his behaviour at Sahagun, where he let down Paget and only arrived at the very end of the action, was typical.

148 Marquis Pedro Caro y Sureda La Romana, In 1807, he had been forced by Napoleon into leading a corps of Spanish troops, in Northern Europe under Bernadotte, as guarantee of Spain's support for France. He was a member of the Supreme Junta.

149 General Joseph Henry, Comte de La Bispal, Spanish general who was of Irish descent.

150 O'Donnell was another Spanish general with Irish antecedents and no more successful than Blake.

151 Although he sometimes admits, in frustration, to his pen failing him in his attempts to convey his experiences.

152 Sometimes spelled 'Reynier'.

153 General Jean Androche, Duc d'Abrantes.

154 W.H.Fitchett *Battles and Sieges of the Peninsular War*, p.34.

155 Rowland Hill's brother, Thomas Noel Hill.

156 Charles George Moore Smith *The Life of John Colborne, Field Marshal, Lord Seaton*, Elibron Classics, p.140.

157 VII dispatch of 28.1.1811.

158 There is mention of them in a sale catalogue for the farm at the Citadel, Hawkstone, in the 1890s, so they thrived in England!

159 Santarem is, today, the centre of bull fighting in Portugal.

160 General Maximilien Sebastien Foy, badly wounded at Busaco.

161 Gurwood.

162 Glover, Michael, *Wellington's Army in the Peninsular War, 1808-1814*, David and Charles, 1974.

163 Clement received his promotion to Captain in April.

164 There were certainly times when he was exasperated by Romana especially over his commissariat, which was usually wanting.

165 Presumably he had brought out one of his brother John's horses.

166 The foundation of a flock which certainly lasted at the Citadel farm, Hawkstone, until the end of the century.

167 The author's great grandfather.

168 General Jean Baptiste Girard, a brave general who fought all over Europe and was finally mortally wounded at Ligny in 1815.

169 See Uffindell *Great Generals of the Napoleonic Wars and their Battles*, p.136.

170 Blakeney's *A Boy in the Peninsular War*.

171 idem p.226.

172 The nickname for the 28th was 'The Slashers'. In 1764 the regiment was on garrison duty in Montreal. A local magistrate, Mr Thomas Walker, was making life intolerable for the troops. A group of them in disguise decided to teach him a lesson and in the ensuing melee part of the magistrate's ear was cut off. Hence the soubriquet.

173 The Prince was engaged to the niece of Empress Josephine.

174 General Francisco Ballesteros was a rather inept general who had ideas above his station and was enormously jealous of Wellington's appointment as Generalissimo. He made a bid for power in 1812 and was imprisoned in North Africa.

175 General Jean Henri Dombrowski, born in Cracow before moving to France in 1795 and raising a Polish legion. He eventually retired to Poland after the fall of Napoleon in 1814.

176 The 'Forlorn Hope' was the generally suicidal first wave of attackers storming a breach during the attempt at forcing a siege. Usually led by a volunteer junior Lt, most of the men were expected to be killed but enough should survive to make way for a more successful attack by those coming after.

177 Beresford.

178 *Memoires of Lejeune*, vol ii, p.108.

179 This was a pontoon bridge, the old Roman bridge having already been destroyed.

180 Presumably the wife of his brother Robert Chambré Hill.

181 This seems likely to actually have been Blackness Castle, Linlithgow, looking over the Forth. This castle served as a prison for a large number of French during the wars at the end of the 18th and early 19th centuries.

182 Oman *Wellington's Army* vol.V, p.281.

183 He was to command Hill's cavalry in the march to Madrid but was then declared mad and cashiered.

184 Carefully selected.

185 Christopher Tilson added Chowne to his name in 1812 as he evidently thought it more distinguished after inheriting an estate. He was a rather moderate general and incurred Wellington's displeasure.

186 Robert Ballard Long was another controversial character who fell out with many of his superiors, especially Marshall Beresford.

187 Names as given in Gardyne's *History of the 92nd*; another example of the exceptional bravery of the 92nd.

188 The enemy's colours.

189 4 Etrangers. For an eyewitness description of the taking of Fort Napoleon see *Recollections of the Storming of the Castle of Badajos* by Capt. MacArthy, assistant engineer.

190 Erskine eventually committed suicide by jumping from a window in Lisbon.

191 Glover, *The Peninsula War*, page 146.

192 Much has been written about the exact events at Maguilla. Oman, Fortescue, and actual witnesses do not agree, see Oman, vol.V, p 523, Wellington's Dispatches, IX, 242.

193 Fletcher Ian, *Galloping at Everything* p.169.

194 Wellington leter to Hill dated Salamanca, 18 June 1812.

195 Dispatches vol. viii, p.112.

196 Letter from Wellington to Beresford, 30.3.1811 quoted from Gurwood.

197 Fletcher, Ian, *Galloping at Everything,* p. 173.

198 General Bertrand Clausel who fought throughout most of the Peninsular War and took command at Salamanca after Marmont was wounded. He was also wounded himself.

199 Captain Charles Somers Cocks, a brave and charming observing officer and a great favourite of Wellington. He was killed at the siege of Burgos in 1813.

200 *Peninsular War, a New History,* p.405.

201 One of two soldier brothers, the other being the less distinguished Victor, a cavalry officer.

202 Brother to the legitimate King of Spain, Ferdinand, who was in exile in France.

203 This was a rare occasion when Hill's troops disgraced themselves, being dead drunk.

204 Gleig, G., *The Life of the Duke of Welling*ton, p.334.

205 Letter to Maria dated November 25, 1812 written on the march from Ciudad Rodrigo.

206 Later Sir James Willoughby Gordon, KCB, Quartermaster General at Horse Guards in the 1830s.

207 Colonel Torrens to Wellington.

208 Aldington, Richard, *Wellington.*

209 General Barney White-Spunner, *Horse Guards,* Macmillan 2006.

210 William Noel Hill was to succeed his brother as 3rd Lord Berwick.

211 Robert Blakeney of the 28th foot.

212 Nicknamed 'The Cumberland Gentlemen'.

213 Another sister.

214 Letter to Maria dated January 12th at Coria.

215 This is quoted in Add mss. letter of Feb 12, 1813. Picton must have been absent through illness during part of 1812 and early 1813 but returned in time for Vittoria. *Wellington's Army* p.369 – Divisional and Brigade Organisation.

216 Wellington's brother, Henry, who was in Cadiz.

217 RH's own capitals.

218 Hill had not been present, he was at that date returning from sick leave in England.

219 Taken from Sidney's *Life of Lord Hill*, pp. 235, 236.

220 idem p.277

221 Later Marechal, Honoré Charles Michel Joseph.

222   Napoleon 1, issue no. 32, La Bataille de Vitoria.

223 Colonel Henry Cadogan was killed in the battle.

224 Colonel Cadogan was a much loved and admired officer. He fell at the head of the 71st as they stormed the heights above the village of Puebla. His last wish was to be carried to a neighbouring high point from which he could watch the successful charge, which he witnessed before dying.

225 Longford, *Wellington: The Years of the Sword,* p.310.

226 As reported in *The Times,* 3 July 1813.

227 Perhaps the only time when Wellington was grateful for disobedience! Thomas Picton was an unconventional and uncouth Welshman, 'A rough mouthed devil', as described by Wellington but a brave man who died at Waterloo.

228 Oman, vol. VI, p.402.

229 Oman, vol I, p.448 'Hill discharged his part of the scheme to admiration, as he always did anything committed to him.'

230 Graham's failing eyesight had been apparent for some months to those around him.

231 See Esdaile p.449.

232 Many of which contained women.

233 The British private soldiers were always pleased to capture French packs, which were much better designed and lighter than their own.

234 Today the chamber pot is in the proud possession of The King's Own Hussars and is now put to a different use. Champagne is drunk from it on guest nights and the toast is 'the Emperor'.

235 Ammunition wagons.

236 See Mark Urban, *The Man who broke Napoleon's Codes,* p.10.

237 idem p. 274.

238 Moyle Sherer, *Recollections* , p. 246.

239 Bryant, *The Age of Elegance.*

240 He fell out with Beresford who relieved him of his brigade for Albuera.

241 Not to be confused with his far more successful younger brother, Charles von Alten.

242 Oman, *Wellington's Army* p.367.

243 Wellington to Hill, 'Caseda, June 28th, 1813'.

244 Figures vary amongst sources but it seems pretty accurate to say that only about 100,000 men returned from approximately half a million who set out.

245 Aldington Richard, *Wellington* p.186.

246 Theodore Maximime Gazan de la Peyriere was an excellent soldier, probably underappreciated.

247 Howie Muir, *Inside Wellington's Peninsular Army* p.151.

248 Stewart was a strange officer. Wellington: 'It is necessary that Stewart should be under the particular charge of somebody.' After Albuera, that somebody was RH. Left to himself, he frequently showed poor judgement and disobedience to orders.

249 Bell, George, *Rough Notes of an Old Soldier.*

250 Hill was in overall charge despite Stewart being the named Divisional Commander of the 2nd.

251 The different Armies of the North, Centre etc. had been amalgamated.

252 The Royal Military Calendar, 1815, by John Philippart, vol iii, pps 242, 243.

253 Known collectively as 'The Battles of the Pyrenees'.

254 D/MIC/X1.

255 D/MIC/X44, X47 and X49.

256 No further word can be found about her.

257 Actually this must have meant John Colborne.

258 One of Hill's most faithful ADCs.

259 Longford *Wellington, the Years of the Sword,* p.327.

260 The first rockets, invented in 1808 by Sir William Congreve, Bt. of the Royal Laboratory at Woolwich, were notoriously erratic but were eventually employed by Wellington in 1814 in the South of France. For the full story see *British Rockets of the Napoleonic and Colonial Wars* by Carl Franklin.

261 Using Graham's words.

262 Murray's army was intended to divide and divert the French armies. He was eventually court-martialled for quitting Tarragona but in the end was only charged with losing the guns. Michael Glover described him as 'a stupid and irresolute officer'.

263 Later Colonel.

264 Following Beresford's handling of Albuera, Wellington always kept a wary eye on his work.

265 Glover says he left the field, p.307.

266 Bunbury resigned his commission, Oman vol VII, p.271.

267 Bell, *Rough Notes,* pp.126–141, 'War or Peace'.

268 Glover, pp.307–308.

269 Perhaps contemporary copies.

270 National Archives, Scovell Papers WO37/12/5.

271 Oman, *Wellington's Army* p.238.

272 Wellington papers 1/613/21.

273 Wellington papers WP1/613/27.

274 G. Bell, p.308.

275 In common with Beresford, he had failed as a commander of Hill's detached corps at Albuera during Hill's sick leave in England.

276 Sir John Fortescue, *History of the British Army,* v 9.

277 Blakiston, *Twelve Years of Military Adventures in three quarters of the Globe.*

278 Except for French silver.

279 Forgers, surely.

280 Sidney *Life of Lord Hill* p.271.

281 Oman, vol. VII, p.292.

282 Valencay was where Ferdinand had been imprisoned ever since Napoleon had tricked him out of his throne.

283 Don Carlos believed in the Divine Right of Kings to rule absolutely, and was a rigid and pious man whose descendants would found the Carlist family of 'pretenders' in Spain.

284 Oman, vol. VII, pp. 322–323.

285 All these rivers rise high in the Pyrenees and cause serious flooding after heavy storms or falls of snow; they are also excellent fishing rivers!

286 Cole, John William, *Memoirs of British Generals distinguished during the Peninsula War,* vol 2.

287 HQ were now at Sauveterre on a Roman site.

288 Resembling the Pont Valentre, which crosses the Lot at Cahors a little further to the north.

289 Letter from Soult to Minister of War, February 28th.

290 Oman, vol VII p.383.

291 Pensaguel.

292 He had the shame of surrendering his army to the Spanish General Castanos at Baylen in July 1808, which led to his disgrace and a period spent in prison.

293 Oman, vol VII pp. 501–502.

294 The King was extremely fond of oysters!

295 Bragge, William, *Peninsular Portrait, the Letters of Captain W. Bragg,* 1963.

296 The incumbent Lord Mayor.

297 Sir Rowland Hill, Kt. 1492-1561.

298 Quoted from a letter in the Museum of the City of London. The Sir Rowland alluded to was also, at least twice, Master of the Worshipful Company of Mercers, the oldest of the City Livery Companies of London.

299 The Rev Rowland's wife, Mary, was a Tudway.

300 The Monument in London in memory of the great fire.

301 Harrison was to be responsible for the alterations to Hardwicke Grange.

302 The Hill family were Masons at that time.

303 'A Description of The Column in Shrewsbury in Honour of General Lord Hill', Shropshire County Council.

304 Idem.

305 In May 1815, Davies had been appointed as Hill's Orderly Sergeant.

306 His father, King Wilhelm, was of course, 'the Old Frog'.

307 The Waterloo diary of Sir Digby Mackworth from *The Army Quarterly,* vol. XXXV.

308 His 'gaoler' on Elba was Sir Niall Campbell who found it a boring occupation and at the time of Napoleon's escape, had gone off to the Italian mainland to visit his mistress.

309 Part of this would become Belgium.

310 King's Own Shropshire Light Infantry.

311 Digby Mackworth, as above.

312 Since Rowland wrote that Clement had accompanied him on the 31st, this is a little hard to understand, perhaps he had returned to fetch the horses.

313 Blakeney, Robert, *A Boy in the Peninsular War.*

314 In addition to the Prince the party included at least one General officer.

315 Hill was an admirer of Marlborough and the Battle of Oudenarde had been fought just over 100 years before, in 1708.

316 A title must usually descend through the direct line for at least the first generation.

317 Many years ago, I was told by Field Marshal Sir Gerald Templer that an officer then serving in the Blues was said to have been descended from an illegitimate son of the General; it seems unlikely.

318 Lord Hill did not climb up the list to become a full General until 1825! It was a case of dead men's shoes.

319 Sidney, *Life of Lord Hill.*

320 Lady Georgiana became Lady de Ros and her sister, Sarah, was to marry Sir Peregrine Maitland, a much older widower; the match was considered something of *a mesalliance* by her family.

321 See appendix.

322 The General was certainly miles from Brussels at his Corps HQ.

323 The French would claim it as their victory and they probably did have the best of it.

324 I think a special mention should be made of this regiment. Again and again, their ranks were winnowed in battle but they always filled the gaps and returned for more.

325 The Association of Friends of the Waterloo Committee: 'The Waterloo Secret Revealed' by Nigel Sale.

326 Allan Mallinson, *The Light Dragoons,* p.78.

327 The 13th Hussars. An officer of the 13th wrote 'Our last and most brilliant charge, was the moment that Lord Hill, perceiving the movement of the Prussian Army, and finding the French Imperial

Guard on the point of forcing a part of the British position, cried out "drive them back, 13th," such an order from such a man, could not be misconstrued, and it was punctually obeyed.'

328 Sir Colquhoun Grant.

329 Major General Carl von Muffling was serving as liaison officer between Wellington and Blücher.

330 1st Foot Guards, who were subsequently called the Grenadier Guards for having crushed the French grenadiers.

331 Adams brigade including the 52nd, the 71st and the 95th.

332 Some commentators say that this phrase was never used; but it was their rallying cry.

333 Sir Digby's account was lent to the Rev Edwin Sidney for his Life of Lord Hill.

334 History of Lord (Colborne) Seaton's Regiment, the 52nd Light Infantry at the Battle of Waterloo, Chapter VI.

335 He was to recover amazingly well and continued to serve.

336 Later to be General Sir Thomas Brotherton.

337 An officer of the Royal Engineers, John Sperling, 1872, p.133; letter from Brotherton to Captain Siborne of the 52nd.

338 Although Colborne received two decorations, he always felt hard done by.

339 Today the General's decorations are in the Sheesh Mahal Museum in Patiala, India. They were purchased at Sothebys in April 1910 by the Maharajah of Patiala. Unfortunately the museum is now closed and difficult to access.

340 As a Major General, he was sent to Madras in 1841. He died there of a fever. There is a memorial to him in Trinity Church, Bangalore.

341 Joseph Fouche, the much feared Minister of Police who had voted for the execution of Louis XVI.

342 'The Battle of Waterloo, a series of accounts published by authority, British and Foreign', published in 1816, see pp 234–235 for Ney's letter to Otranto.

343 Battle of Ligny on the 15th.

344 'The Battle of Waterloo containing the series of accounts, British and Foreign etc.' pub. John Booth, London and J Fairbairn, Edinburgh, 1816; account sent by Marshal Blücher from Dusseldorf, June 26.

345 *The Times* newspaper, London.

346 These events were reported in *The Times* of 26 July.

347 Perhaps more accurately, the Gate or *'Porte'*.

348 There is some doubt as to whether this was Emma or Jane. The latter was a woman of formidable personality and intellect who lived to the age of 93.

349 Dumb animal.

350 This story was allegedly told by Sir Edward Barnes to Digby Mackworth.

351 It has been suggested that Talleyrand tried to give him a passport to enable him to leave France but that he had refused.

352 Lynedoch mss 3615.

353 SCRO 665/350.

354 SCRO Eyton papers 665/468.

355 Shropshire Records Office, Bygott papers ref. 665–468 gives June, some sources say August.

356 SCRO 665/468 and Rev J.C. Hill papers series 549/.

357 The French considered his appointment as 'insensitive'.

358 SCRO 549/112.

359 Sir Digby Mackworth had been with him for many years. The National Portrait Gallery has an 1818 mezzotint of Sir Digby by William Say, after Henry William Pickersgill RA. Pickersgill was a famed portraitist and his subjects included William Wordsworth, Nelson and Wellington.

360 Creevey papers vol. II, p.278.

361 Killed in Egypt.

362 Her sketchbook is in the SCRO.

363 *Liverpool Courier*.

364 Add.mss 35066, British Library.

365 Add mss. 35064.

366 *The Times*, 4 October, 1822.

367 Wellington Papers, WP1 764/10.

368 He had been permitted to sell his commission.

369 WP1/756/32.

370 As described in *The Times*.

371 From the legal reports of *The Times* of 9 December 1830 and 24 December 1829.

372 Also responsible for the column in Shrewsbury.

373 There were approximately. 81,000 soldiers in the UK in 1828.

374 Manchester was a city of about 200,000 people but with no Parliamentary representation.

375 Babington, Antony, *Military Intervention in Britain*, Routledge, 1990.

376 Wellington Dispatches, New Series , 1.128 Memo from Wellington to Lord Liverpool, June 1820.

377 Another reason may have been the affairs of his brother Sir Robert Chambré Hill.

378 Jac Weller, *Wellington*. The official address for correspondence for Horse Guards was 'Stable Yard'. Hence this chapter title.

379 Frederick Robinson, Viscount Goderich and later Earl of Ripon, known as 'Goody' Goderich.

380 As mentioned previously, nicknamed the Emperor's Chambermaids after they found Joseph's silver chamber pot at Vittoria.

381 Adam Hochschild, *Bury the Chains.*

382 Doyenne of the Holland House Set, a brilliant circle of Whig politicians and intellectuals.

383 SRO records of the Rev J.C. Hill, series 549.

384 Parliamentary Debates, series III, 1832, p.968.

385 Nephew, Sir Rowland Hill, Bt., was the commander of the North Shropshire Yeomanry Cavalry.

386 Raglan Papers D3135/1.100.

387 By then 1st Baron Raglan.

388 George was the son of Sir Robert Chambré Hill.

389 He must have been Assistant Adjutant General since Sir John Macdonald held the senior role.

390 Brown Papers Ms 2841, National Library of Scotland.

391 He lost his hand at the Battle of Ligny and therefore did not serve at Waterloo.

392 Wellington Papers, WP1/1054/13.

393 Creevy Papers, v. 2, p.240.

394 Wellington Papers, WP1/1024/10.

395 Some say 2500 and other sources 4000.

396 WP1/964/33.

397 He had been Acting Regent for Queen Maria of Portugal in 1808 when Junot took Lisbon and the English Fleet rescued the Royal Family.

398 Hansard, House of Lords, February 18th, 1830.

399 Thomas Garth was possibly the illegitimate son of the Duke of Cumberland and his sister, the Princess Sophia, 12th child and 5th daughter of George III, although she had had an affair with General Garth, one of her father's equerries. The boy was brought up by Sir Herbert Taylor, private secretary to George III. On the King's death, Wellington, as one of the King's executors, burned any possibly incriminating letters to avoid scandal or the possibility of the young Captain trying blackmail; he was paid off. Some historians have argued that she never had a child.

400 The Duke of Cumberland was to become King of Hanover.

401 White-Spunner, General Barney, *Horse Guards*, p 356.

402 Arthur, Sir George, *The Story of the Household Cavalry,* p 634.

403 Letter dated February 1 from Wellington to RH, quoted p.335 *Life of Lord Hill.*

404 Sir Robert, Colonel Clement and Lt Edward.

405 White-Spunner, *Horse Guards* p 358.

406 Sir Robert had resigned from the Blues, probably embarrassed by the scandal that had broken in 1823.

407 The exception was Robert Peel, the Home Secretary who was pro at least some sort of reform.

408 The *Liverpool Mercury.*

409 WP1/1201/21.

410 WP1/1213/13.

411 Raglan Papers D3135/1/124.

412 GRE/B32/12 Durham University Library.

413 GRE/B32/12/37/2 Durham University.

414 D3135/1/378 Raglan papers (Fitzroy Somerset Papers) Gwent Records Office.

415 GRE/B32/12/38, Durham University.

416 *Three Nineteenth-Century Diaries*, ed. Aspinall, 1831.

417 Maitland had married Lady Sarah Lennox to the chagrin of her family, the Duke and Duchess of Richmond.

418 It has been suggested that he was the natural son of Charles X.

419 Lord Brougham's *Recollections*, pp 35–36.

420 D3135/1/129, 21 September 1832.

421 Thomas Noel's wife was Anna Maria Shore, daughter of 1st Lord Teignmouth.

422 Raglan papers D3135/1.129 Fitzroy Somerset to Hill.

423 Copy of a Confidential Circular to 'Officers Commanding' from the Adjutant General published in *The Times,* 24 August 1833.

424 Hansard, vol 17, 49–68.

425 Raglan papers D3135/1.135-136 of 2.1.1834.

426 Raglan papers (Somerset) D3135/1/374/93 Gwent Records Office.

427 Raglan Papers, D3135/1.374.156.

428 The new Lord Berwick had briefly been engaged to Lady Hester Stanhope and although he never married, had an Italian mistress and at least two children by her.

429 Thomas, Donald, *Cardigan*, p.10;

430 *The Greville Memoirs*, 1814–1860, Macmillan 1938.

431 David Saul, *The Homicidal Earl*, Abacus, 1997, p.19.

432 *The Reason Why*, p.21.

433 Proceedings of the General Court Martial.

434 D3135/1.374.169.

435 Woodham Smith; Thomas, Donald.

436 Thomas, Donald, *Cardigan*, p 62.

437 154 chose to remain.

438 *Cardigan* p.91.

439 ibid, p.129.

440 7 January 1841.

441 *The Globe*, 16 and 17 September 1840.

442 *Cardigan* p.93.

443 He was later reinstated in the army in April 1842 and served in the 9th Lancers.

444 Woodham Smith, Cecil, *The Reason Why*, p.74.

445 Thomas, Donald, *Cardigan* p 99.

446 Lord Wharncliffe was the Chairman; the following was reported in *The Times* of 28 March and the days following.

447 Circular letter of 1833 to commanding officers.

448 NLS mss 2839, 2840.

449 The population increased by a half in the early 1830s.

450 1st Baron Seaton.

451 Nottinghamshire Regiment of Foot.

452 A quite disproportionate number of them part of Lord Grey's family!

453 Strachan Hew, *Wellington's Legacy: Reform of the British Army 1830-1854.*

454 Mallinson Allan, *Light Dragoons.*

455 Raglan Papers, D3135/1.373./6.

456 Sir Charles Oman, *History of the Peninsular War*, vol vii, p.525.

457 This Rowland is the eldest son of Lord Hill's elder brother, John, who had died young. He was to inherit his grandfather's baronetcy and his uncle's viscountcy and by gross extravagance set the family on the path to bankruptcy.

BIBLIOGRAPHY

Primary Sources

Hill Papers, add. mss British Library 35059 – 35067. Autograph letters containing correspondence to and from Hill and the Duke of Wellington, Sir George Murray, Thomas Graham and Hill's large family, especially his sister Maria. Any quotations of letters, unless stated to the contrary, come from this archive.

Grey Papers, University of Durham. Correspondence between Earl Grey and Hill over appointments for his family and affairs between Horse Guards and the government.

Wellington Papers, University of Southampton Library.

The Michell Papers, Dorset County Records Office. Papers kept by Hill's Military Secretary, Captain Churchill, in the latter stages of the Peninsular War.

Bygott Papers, Shropshire County Records Office, series 731. Bygott solicitors acted for the Hills.

Somerset (Raglan) Papers, Gwent County Records Office. Letters from and to Lord Fitzroy Somerset, Lord Hill, Colonel Egerton and others connected with Horse Guards. There are also personal family letters.

Scovell Papers, National Archives. Papers of Sir George Scovell who 'cracked' many of the French codes.

Rev. J.C. Hill papers, SCRO, collections 549, 592, 811 An eclectic collection of Hill papers with a few relating to the General.

Eyton Papers, SCRO. Papers referring to the bankruptcy of Thomas Eyton.

Dispatches of Field Marshal The Duke of Wellington ed. by Colonel Gurwood in 8 vols 1852.

Lynedoch (Graham) Papers, National Library of Scotland.

Sir George Brown's Papers, the National Library of Scotland.

Some papers of Sir Rowland Hill as Commander in Chief, amongst War Office papers in the National Archives.

'Mackworth's Waterloo Diary', published in the *Army Quarterly*. Mackworth lent his diary to the Rev. Edwin Sidney, Hill family domestic chaplain, who wrote a biography of Lord Hill, published 1845.

Printed Sources

The Battle of Waterloo, a series of accounts of British and Foreign armies, pub. 1816

Aldington, Richard, *Wellington*, William Heinemann, London, 1946

Arthur, Sir George, *History of the Household Cavalry*, Constable, 1909

Aspinall, Oglander, C. *Freshly Remembered: The Story of Thomas Graham, Lord Lynedoch,* 1956

Babington, Anthony, *Military Interventions in Britain*, Routledge 1990

Bell, George, *Rough Notes of an Old Soldier*, 1867

Blakeney, Robert, *A Boy in the Peninsular War*, Naval and Military Press, 2007

Blakiston, *Twelve Years of Military Adventures in three quarters of the Globe*

Bragge, William, *Peninsular Portrait, letters of Captain W. Bragge,* 1963

Broughton, Lord, *'Recollections'*

Bryant, Arthur: *The Great Duke,* Collins, 1971

Chandler, David, *Dictionary of the Napoleonic Wars*, Wordsworth Editions, 1999

Costello, Edward, *Rifleman Costello*, Leonaur 2005 – originally published 1841

Creevey, Thomas, *The Creevey Papers*, in 2 vols

David, Saul, *The Homicidal Earl,* Abacus, 1998

Esdaile, Charles, *The Peninsular War*, Allen Lane 2002

Fitchett, William, *Battles and Sieges of the Peninsular War*, Leonaur, 2007

Fletcher, Ian, *Galloping at Everything, British Cavalry in the Peninsular War and at Waterloo,*
　1808-1815, Spellmount 1999

Fortescue, Sir John, *History of the British Army*, vols 7, 8, 9, 10, 11

Gardyne, *History of the 92nd* (Gordon Highlanders)

Gleig, G., *The Life of the Duke of Wellington*

Glover, Michael, *The Peninsular War; A Concise Military History*, Penguin 1974

Greville, Charles, *The Greville Memoirs*

Griffiths, Major Arthur, *The Wellington Memorial, Comrades and Contemporaries*, George Allen 1897

Harris, Rifleman Benjamin: 'Recollections: The Road to Corunna' in *Soldiers at War*, ed. C. Hibbert

Haythornthwaite, Philip J, *The Armies of Wellington*, Arms and Armour 1994

Hibbert, Christopher, *Wellington, a Personal History*, Harper Collins, 1997

Holmes, Richard, *Redcoat*, Harper Perennial 2001

Holmes, Richard, *The Iron Duke*, Harper Collins, 2002

Lewis. Jon E. (ed) *Soldiers at War*, Constable 2001

Longford, Elizabeth, *The Years of the Sword*, Weidenfeld & Nicolson, 1969

Longford, Elizabeth, *Pillar of State*, Weidenfeld & Nicolson, 1972

Moore Smith, G, *The Life of John Colborne*, John Murray, 1903

Muir Rory; Burnham Robert; Muir Howie; McGuigan Ron, *Inside Wellington's Peninsular*
　Army, Pen and Sword, 2006

Napier, Major General Sir William, *History of the War in the Peninsular,* Constable, 1992

O'Byrne, Robert, *Victories in the Peninsula and the South of France*

Oman, Sir Charles, *Wellington's Army,* Edward Arnold, 1912

Oman, Sir Charles, *A History of the Peninsular War,* vols 1 – 7

Parkinson, Roger, *The Peninsular War*, Hart Davis, 1973

Reid S, *Wellington's Highlanders*, London 1992

Robertson, Ian, *Wellington at War in the Peninsula, 1808-1814*, Pen and Sword, 2000

Robertson, Ian, *A Commanding Presence: Wellington in the Peninsula 1808–1814*, Spellmount, 2008

Robertson, Ian, *Wellington Invades France,* Greenhill Books, 2003

Sherer, Captain Joseph Moyle, *Recollections of the Pensinsula*, Spellmount, originally pub. 1823

Sidney, Edwin, *The Life of Lord Hill*, pub. 1845

Stocqueler, J.H, *A Personal History of the Horse Guards, 1750 – 1872,* Hurst and Blackett, 1873.

Thomas, Donald, *Cardigan*, Cassell & Co., 1974

Teffeteller, Gordon, *The Surpriser*, University of Delaware, 1983

Uffindell, Andrew, *Great Generals of the Napoleonic War and their Battles, 1805-1815,* Spellmount, 2003

Urban, Mark, *The Man Who Broke Napoleon's Codes: The Story of Sir George Scovell*, Faber & Faber, 2002

Weller, Jac, *Wellington in the Peninsula*, London 1962

Weller, Jac, *Wellington at Waterloo*, London 1967

White-Spunner, Major General (now Lt-Gen) Barney, *Horse Guards*, Macmillan, 2006

Wood, Sir Evelyn, *Cavalry in the Waterloo Campaign*, London 1895

Woodham Smith, Cecil, *The Reason Why,* Constable 1953

Periodicals

Army Quarterly　　　　　　　　　　*London Gazette*

Morning Chronicle　　　　　　　　　*Napoleon!: Magazine du Consulat et de l'Empire*

Royal Military Panorama　　　　　　*Shrewsbury Chronicle*

The Times

INDEX